Implementation of Civil Rights Policy

Implementation of Civil Rights Policy

Edited by

Charles S. Bullock III
University of Georgia

Charles M. Lamb
State University of New York at Buffalo

Brooks/Cole Publishing Company
Monterey, California

The Brooks/Cole Series on Public Policy

Charles O. Jones, *University of Virginia*
General Editor

© 1984 by Wadsworth, Inc., Belmont, California 94002.
All rights reserved.
No part of this book may be reproduced, stored in a retrieval system, or transcribed,
in any form or by any means—electronic, mechanical, photocopying, recording,
or otherwise—without the prior written permission of the publisher,
Brooks/Cole Publishing Company, Monterey, California 93940,
a division of Wadsworth, Inc.

Printed in the United States of America

10 9 8 7 6 5 4 3 2

Library of Congress Cataloging in Publication Data

Main entry under title:

Implementation of civil rights policy.

    Bibliography: p.
    Includes index.
    Contents: Search for variables important in
policy implementation / Charles S. Bullock III
and Charles M. Lamb—Voting Rights Act,
implementation and impact / Richard Scher and James
Button—Equal educational opportunity / Charles
S. Bullock III—[etc.]
    1. Civil rights—United States—Addresses,
essays, lectures. 2. United States—Politics
and government—1945-   —Addresses, essays,
lectures. I. Bullock, Charles S., 1942-
II. Lamb, Charles M.
JC599.U5I46   1983   353.0081'1   83-2668
ISBN 0-534-01259-0

Subject Editor: *Marquita Flemming*
Manuscript Editor: *Adrienne Mayor*
Production Editor: *Fiorella Ljunggren*
Interior and Cover Design: *Vernon T. Boes*
Illustrations: *Tim Keenan*
Typesetting: *Graphic Typesetting Service, Los Angeles, California*

To
Charles S. Bullock, Jr.
Elenor D. Bullock
Opal Tune Lamb

Contributors

Q. Whitfield Ayres is Assistant Professor of Government and International Studies at the University of South Carolina. His research emphasis is on education and civil rights policy and the public policy process.

Charles S. Bullock III is Richard B. Russell Professor of Political Science and a Research Fellow of the Institute for Behavioral Research at the University of Georgia. His research on various aspects of legislative politics and policy implementation has appeared in a number of political science, education, and sociology journals, including the *American Political Science Review*, *Journal of Politics*, *American Journal of Political Science*, *American Politics Quarterly*, and *Social Science Quarterly*.

James W. Button is Associate Professor of Political Science at the University of Florida. He is the author of *Black Violence: Political Impact of the 1960s Riots* and has published several articles on black politics and the civil rights movement.

Charles M. Lamb is Associate Professor of Political Science at the State University of New York at Buffalo. He has served on the staff of the University of Alabama, George Washington University, and the U.S. Commission on Civil Rights. He is the author of *Land Use Politics and Law in the 1970s* and the coeditor (with Stephen C. Halpern) of *Supreme Court Activism and Restraint*. His books in progress include *Judicial Conflict and Consensus* (coedited with Sheldon Goldman), *The Federal Government and Fair Housing*, and *Warren E. Burger and Criminal Justice: Judicial Philosophy and Behavior*.

Harrell R. Rodgers, Jr., is Professor of Political Science at the University of Houston. He has previously taught at the University of Georgia and the University of Missouri at St. Louis. He has published a number of books and articles on various aspects of American politics and has done extensive research on civil rights and welfare policy.

Richard K. Scher is Associate Professor of Political Science at the University of Florida. He is coauthor (with David R. Colburn) of *Florida's Gubernatorial Politics in the Twentieth Century* and has also published other works on Southern politics and the civil rights movement.

Foreword

Douglas Rae introduces his important analysis of equality by reflecting on ideas into action.

> Success comes to political ideas not when they are justified in seminar and speech, but at the moment of their application to life and society. The triumph of Bentham's utilitarianism lay not in its (always mixed) hold on the professoriate, but in its application to society by bureaucrats, economists, and prison wardens. The liberal theory of right finds success not in Locke or Mill, but in the promulgation and enforcement of the laws by which liberal societies are distinctively governed. And so it is with equality. Its success and importance lie not in its crystalline beauty among abstract conceptions, not in its wonderful symmetry, not even in its moral power, but in countless attempts to realize equality in polity, economy, and society. [*Equalities*, Cambridge: Harvard University Press, 1981, p. 1]

Charles S. Bullock III and Charles M. Lamb have produced a work that deals directly with the "countless attempts to realize equality in polity, economy, and society." They and their coauthors direct attention to the implementation of the many significant civil rights laws passed during the 1950s and 1960s. Clearly, if the idea of equal opportunity is to have practical meaning for those experiencing generations of discrimination, then laws enacted must be fully implemented.

The editors of this volume have selected the following major issues for analysis—voting rights, equality of education in public schools and colleges, employment and economic opportunities, and fair housing. Several standards of successful implementation are proposed that serve as useful general measures for each analyst without, at the same time, detracting from the dramatic quality of each real-life case. Each chapter applies these standards while introducing the reader to the social and political intricacies of policy development. Thus, one comes to understand what is required for successful implementation, without losing touch with the human effects of failure to achieve it.

In the final chapter Bullock ranks the various areas from the greatest to the least amount of implementation. He also identifies those factors that are most useful in explaining the variation in implementation across policy areas. This important exercise will serve as a baseline for future analysis. The book's contribution, therefore, is not limited to classroom illustrations of the workings of the policy process. It also provides a starting point for future monitoring of progress in this most important field.

The authors of this volume have chosen a difficult and demanding topic. But that fact makes it all the more important that the work be done. It is one mark of progress in guaranteeing ordinary rights to all citizens that a book on implementation can now be written. A work on that topic twenty-five years ago would be more in the form of a pamphlet. Bullock and Lamb have provided students with an opportunity (1) to examine the policy cycle associated with applying ideas "to life and society," (2) to evaluate the results, and (3) to propose new ideas to accomplish common goals. They have every right, therefore, to be pleased with the results of their fine effort.

Charles O. Jones
University of Virginia

Preface

Books, lectures, and courses on policy implementation are a recent phenomenon in political science. The current concern about what happens to policy once it passes out of the hands of those who developed it began with the first edition of Jeffrey L. Pressman and Aaron B. Wildavsky's book *Implementation*.[1] In their book, the authors reviewed social science literature to determine how widespread the concern with implementation was and found it to be virtually nonexistent.

Since the publication of *Implementation* there has been an outpouring of scholarship concerned with the topic. Several brief textbooks devoted to it are now available, such as George Edwards's *Implementing Public Policy*[2] and Robert T. Nakamura and Frank Smallwood's *The Politics of Policy Implementation*.[3] In addition, a multitude of case studies have appeared as books, articles, and conference papers. In this volume, we turn to a number of these studies for guidance in our effort to test hypotheses concerning conditions under which civil rights policy is more likely to be carried out successfully.

A major influence on the development of this book was a conference on implementation set up by Dan Mazmanian and Paul Sabatier at Pomona College and sponsored by the National Science Foundation. In the course of their work on the implementation of coastal zone management policy in California, which preceded the conference, Mazmanian and Sabatier developed a schema for arranging the variables they believed to have an impact on implementation.[4] While preparing a paper for that conference, Bullock[5] began to think about how to evaluate the contributions of a set of variables that were purported to be related to implementation across several programs. Such an exercise would go beyond the case study approach, which, although valuable in identifying potential explanatory variables, is not suited to determining whether the causes of implementation success are broadly applicable or are limited to a unique fact situation.

Somewhat later, we discussed our desire to compare implementation across several areas of civil rights policy, and we came to the conclusion that it would be best to have experts apply a common framework when

[1] Jeffrey L. Pressman and Aaron B. Wildavsky. *Implementation* (Berkeley: University of California Press, 1973).
[2] George C. Edwards, *Implementing Public Policy* (Washington, D.C.: Congressional Quarterly, 1980).
[3] Robert T. Nakamura and Frank Smallwood. *The Politics of Policy Implementation* (New York: St. Martin's, 1980).
[4] Paul Sabatier and Daniel Mazmanian. "The Implementation of Public Policy: A Framework of Analysis," *Policy Studies Journal*, 8, no. 4 (1980): 538-560.
[5] Charles S. Bullock III, "The Office for Civil Rights and Implementation of Desegregation in the Public Schools," *Policy Studies Journal*, 8, no. 4 (1980): 597-616.

examining implementation within the civil rights policy areas in which they specialized. Stuart Scheingold helped in this enterprise by setting up a panel at the 1980 American Political Science Association annual meeting, at which drafts of three of the chapters in this volume were presented. The other two chapters that deal with a particular policy were initially presented later that same fall at the Southern Political Science Association annual meeting.

Civil rights is a policy area particularly well suited to the study of implementation. To determine the influence of potential causal factors on outcomes, it is essential that there be variation in the dependent variable. In this study, there has been anything but uniformity in the dependent variable—that is, in the extent to which the goals of civil rights policy makers have been realized. In voting rights and school desegregation, there have been tremendous changes in the treatment of blacks in the South. Millions of blacks have been added to voter registration rolls as a result of the removal of discrimination pursuant to civil rights laws. In much of the South, particularly in rural communities, the racially segregated dual school systems have ceased to exist. Yet not all civil rights policy goals have been as successfully implemented; for example, discrimination remains widespread in the rental and sale of housing. A major objective of this book is to account for these kinds of differences across areas of civil rights.

Even within the policy areas in which civil rights goals have been most successfully achieved, there have been times when little progress was made. A second aspect of the analysis carried out in this book is therefore longitudinal. Each chapter offers explanations for the success or failure to implement programs from the time the federal courts or Congress initially established goals of equal treatment up into the early 1980s.

In implementing the objectives of this book, we have been helped by several talented readers of earlier drafts of the manuscript. Series editor Chuck Jones is the most significant independent variable in accounting for the length of this volume. When initially sent to Jones, the manuscript was approximately twice as long as it was in its final form. Jones provided helpful suggestions about where to cut. The other two readers—Daniel Mazmanian of Pomona College and Fred Wirt of the University of Illinois—made suggestions that enhanced the clarity of the presentation and the sophistication and accuracy of the treatment. We are most appreciative of the efforts contributed by these skilled colleagues.

Charles S. Bullock III
Charles M. Lamb

Contents

Chapter 1

A Search for Variables Important in Policy Implementation   1

by Charles S. Bullock III and Charles M. Lamb

Civil Rights Implementation   2
Variables   4
Summary   16
Notes   17
References   18

Chapter 2

Voting Rights Act: Implementation and Impact   20

by Richard Scher and James Button

Voting Rights Acts: History and Intent   21
Implementation of the Voting Rights Act   30
Impact of the Voting Rights Act   39
Conclusion   46
References   52

Chapter 3

Equal Education Opportunity   55

by Charles S. Bullock III

Policy Statements   56
Implementation   64

Achieving Equal Education 75
Summary and Conclusions 86
Notes 89
References 90

Chapter 4
**Fair Employment Laws for Minorities:
An Evaluation of Federal Implementation 93**
by Harrell R. Rodgers, Jr.

Formal Antidiscrimination Policies 94
Analysis of Progress Achieved 101
Fair Employment Implementation: Policy, Administration, and
   Enforcement Variables 108
Conclusions 114
References 116

Chapter 5
**Racial Desegregation
in Higher Education   118**
by Q. Whitfield Ayres

Federal Policy 119
Success in Desegregating Higher Education 122
Variation in Policy Success 127
Conclusion 142
Notes 144
References 145

Chapter 6
Equal Housing Opportunity   148
by Charles M. Lamb

Housing Discrimination and Segregation: Historical
   Developments and Continuing Trends 149
Laws Forbidding Housing Discrimination 153
The Federal Government as an Accomplice 158

Implementation Process and Politics   162
Conclusion   177
Notes   178
References   179

Chapter 7
Conditions Associated with Policy Implementation   184
by Charles S. Bullock III

Implementation Success   185
Explaining Variations in Implementation   189
Conclusions   204
Notes   206
References   207

Index   209

Chapter 1

A Search for Variables Important in Policy Implementation

Charles S. Bullock III and Charles M. Lamb

During the 1950s and 1960s, there was widespread hope among civil rights activists and their politically placed supporters that a combination of legislative enactments and judicial decisions would breach the barricades of traditional discrimination. Such faith in the ability of federal initiatives to create a new, better, and more equitable world was not unique to those concerned about the denial of rights to minority Americans. The belief that a combination of education and job training programs, which were to be administered as poor people saw fit, would eradicate poverty derived from the same sort of naivete about the processes through which reformers' dreams are turned into altered realities.

The hope for an easy solution or a quick fix for deeply rooted problems dies slowly. Many Americans continue to believe, and want to believe, that all that is necessary to correct current evils are a few relatively minor modifications. The faith that tinkering with the system will produce the desired results is so strong that when initial adjustments fail to have the intended effect, the response is frequently simply to tinker a bit more, or to maintain that the primary need is for more money to allow the adjustments to be carried out on a grander scale.

Belief that new laws or new court orders will produce substantial change is encouraged by leading public officials. Presidents, legislators, and candidates for public office frequently promise that problems will be resolved by the adoption of their proposals. A classic example occurred during John Connally's unsuccessful 1980 presidential campaign when he boasted, "I could turn this country around in the first 24 hours if I was in office" (*Newsweek*, March 3, 1980, 31).

Experiences of the 1970s, which have been replicated many times over, demonstrate that a pattern of behavior once embarked on has a momentum of its own which is not readily deflected by a single statutory, judicial, or presidential decree. Contrary to the promises of the supporters of the War on Poverty, the antipoverty legislation passed in the mid-1960s did not eliminate want from the American social lexicon. Similarly, the environmental legislation of the early 1970s has not resulted in the full attainment of clean air and water objectives in many areas of the country (Council on Environmental Quality, 1980, chaps. 3 and 4). Nor have Supreme Court decisions holding various religious practices in public schools to be unconstitutional led to their universal discontinuation (Dolbeare and Hammond, 1971, chap. 3). This is not to deny that these policy enactments have had some effect. Yet they have not lived up to the high, at times unrealistic, expectations of their proponents.

Widespread evidence that policy decisions often fail to produce anticipated outputs has recently led to more attention being focused on a long-ignored aspect of the policy process—implementation (Anderson, 1979, chap. 4; Edwards, 1980; Jones, 1977, chap. 7; Nakamura and Smallwood, 1980; Pressman and Wildavsky, 1973). Interest in implementation, or how policy decisions are carried out, has grown as evidence mounts to show that problems at this stage quite regularly account for policies not achieving expectations. Good intentions alone are insufficient to change social realities. For policy statements to overcome the status quo, which is frequently held in place by tenaciously held values, it is essential that careful attention be paid not only to what is included in terms of the policy but also to the environment in which implementation will occur.

While implementation is often difficult, it is not impossible to achieve desired changes. Attention to circumstances surrounding policy implementation has spawned attempts to explain the conditions under which policy goals are not achieved and the reasons for such failures.

CIVIL RIGHTS IMPLEMENTATION

The implementation of civil rights policy has encountered some of the same pitfalls as other reform efforts of the 1960s and 1970s. For example, although equal employment opportunity programs have opened some previously closed jobs to minority workers, the distribution of minorities across job and income categories remains distinctly skewed, with minorities overrepresented in less prestigious and poorer-paying classifications. Minorities still have significantly lower incomes than whites (McCrone and Hardy, 1978), and minority unemployment is much higher than that of whites (U.S. Commission on Civil Rights, 1980, 30). Fair housing efforts provide another illustration of the failure to attain civil rights policy objectives. Although federal legislation has increased the housing options for minorities, residential segregation remains the rule rather than the exception (Danielson, 1976; Lamb, 1978a). Indeed, a series of Burger Court decisions during the 1970s upheld as constitutional exclusionary devices developed by local governments (Lamb and Lustig, 1979, 177–223).

Unlike some other reformist initiatives, certain civil rights objectives have been achieved with considerable success. Some of the more notable changes have occurred in public school desegregation and voter registration. Of course, for many years there was widespread and deeply rooted opposition to racial equality in these areas (Hamilton, 1973; Peltason, 1971; Vines, 1964). Yet by the early 1970s most Southern school districts had been desegregated, and the registration and participation of blacks in the political process had risen substantially (Bullock and Rodgers, 1975). Indeed, the South is now ahead of the rest of the country in school desegregation. Nevertheless, in 1980 the U.S. Commission on Civil Rights reported that "nearly half of the Nation's minority children remain in racially isolated schools" (1980, 14).

In addition to variations in program progress among policies, there have been variations across time even for the more successful policies. During the first half-decade after *Brown* v. *Board of Education* (1954) held de jure school segregation to be unconstitutional, very little changed in the South, and in six Southern states not a single black child attended public schools with whites (Rodgers and Bullock, 1972, 75). The impact of early legislation aimed at reducing impediments to black voter registration in the South resulted in only a 4 percentage-point increase between 1956 and 1962 in the proportion of eligible blacks registered to vote (Rodgers and Bullock, 1972, 25). Thus even for policy decisions that ultimately had notable impacts there was a delay between policy promulgation and significant changes in the behavior of those subject to regulation.

A key consideration for understanding the administrative implementation of civil rights policies and many other programs of the national government is the federalist nature of the American political system. Attempts to implement civil rights depend to a large degree on the response of various state and local officials and, sometimes, of private citizens. Administrative implementation of school desegregation hinged on actions taken by local school boards and superintendents. Equal employment and fair housing implementation is contingent on the responses of a diverse group of public officials (public employers and zoning commissions) and private citizens (private employers, union leaders, realtors, and mortgage institutions, to name a few). It is not uncommon, therefore, for national policy objectives to depend on a number of people not directly answerable to the decision makers who propounded the policy. Consequently, a major prerequisite for successful administrative implementation is that conditions be structured so as to promote the likelihood that support can be obtained from those whose help is essential for effective implementation (Rodgers and Bullock, 1972, chap. 8).

4 Chapter 1

Yet the role of the federal government in civil rights implementation cannot be underestimated. In many instances civil rights compliance flows directly from federal pressures exerted on state and local officials, private businesses, and institutions. Indeed, in equal employment opportunity and fair housing, where full implementation has not been achieved, the role of federal administrative agencies such as the Equal Employment Opportunity Commission and the Department of Housing and Urban Development is becoming more and more necessary.

On rare occasions the national government has completely taken over the implementation of a civil rights program so that the obstinacy of affected officials and the public was negated. One such example occurred under the 1965 Voting Rights Act when federal officials were sent to selected Southern counties to register qualified black voters who had been turned away by white registrars (Hamilton, 1973, chap. 10; Rodgers and Bullock, 1972, chap. 2). When compliance by state and local officials is not forthcoming, the federal government must exercise some form of administrative coercion if national civil rights policy objectives are to be realized.

Leadership by the national government can also be exercised through the judicial branch (Nakamura and Smallwood, 1980, chap. 6; Peltason, 1971). Indeed the judiciary has often upheld unpopular positions (e.g., the need for legislative redistricting and prohibitions on school prayer) when the legislature has failed to respond. Judicial policymaking may involve sweeping, nationwide policy enunciated by the U.S. Supreme Court, or an order directed at only one school district, employer, or housing project. The federal courts, and especially the Supreme Court, were at the cutting edge in declaring various discriminatory practices unconstitutional in the 1940s, 1950s, and 1960s. For instance, *Shelley* v. *Kraemer* (1948), a landmark Supreme Court decision, outlawed enforcement of private restrictive covenants whereby white homeowners agreed not to sell or lease property to blacks. In 1954 the Warren Court declared de jure public school segregation unconstitutional in *Brown* v. *Board of Education*. And in *Shapiro* v. *Thompson* (1969), the Court announced that migrants, most of whom are Mexican-Americans, were not required to maintain a one-year residency in a state before they were eligible to receive welfare benefits.

VARIABLES

In the course of this book, the authors of individual chapters will seek to determine why policies succeeded or failed in terms of both administrative and judicial implementation. In these chapters, a number of variables which may explain why a policy meets with greater success at one time rather than another will be considered.[1] Some of the more critical variables are briefly introduced in the following sections.

Clarity of the Policy

While political scientists who have written on policy implementation have suggested numerous variables which seem to be related to policy success, there is near unanimity about the importance of having policies clearly stated (Rodgers and Bullock, 1972, 164–169; Sabatier and Mazmanian, 1980, 545; Van Horn and Van Meter, 1976; Wirt, 1970, 286–288). There are two aspects of policy which should be explicitly stated by a court, a legislature, or an administrative enforcement agency to enhance the likelihood that policy objectives will be achieved.

First, there should be a clear enunciation of policy goals. This becomes particularly crucial when legislatures sketch out the policy but leave it up to judges and administrators to flesh out the skeletal directives. It must be recognized that, when enacting legislation, Congress does not attempt to anticipate whether its handiwork will apply to the entire range of possible eventualities. Indeed, it would place unreasonable demands on the intellectual capacities of our legislators to expect them to anticipate all the questions that could be raised concerning legislative intent. In addition to overtaxing legislators' powers of foresight, if we demanded that they fully define the intended impact of the laws they pass, it would greatly delay the legislative process. The common pattern, therefore, is for the legislature to indicate in varying degrees of clarity what it expects legislation to accomplish.

Due to uncertainty about legislative intent, judges and bureaucrats play a critical role in determining the extent and conditions under which a piece of legislation is applied. Judges do this as they decide cases; bureaucrats do it in the course of drafting regulations and when applying the law in administrative hearings. To promote the likelihood that a law will be carried out as those who drafted it intended, the original legislation should be as specific as possible. For instance, legislation specifying payments and eligibility standards for participation in the social security and food stamps programs is quite precise, thereby foreclosing opportunities for administrative discretion (Anderson, 1979, 94). In contrast, Title VI of the Civil Rights Act of 1964 broadly states that "No person in the United States shall, on the grounds of race, color, or national origin, be excluded from participation in, be denied the benefits of, or be subjected to discrimination under any program or activity receiving Federal financial assistance." This legislation, central to many forms of civil rights implementation, leaves unresolved many questions over what constitutes illegal discrimination. Before many changes resulted, it was necessary for Title VI enforcement agencies to define what was illegal, a process still underway more than fifteen years after enactment of the statute.

While it is widely recognized that precision in stating policy objectives avoids a number of obstacles during the subsequent implementation stage, precision is often difficult to obtain in civil rights legislation, as was illustrated by the Title VI example. In order to build a legislative coalition sufficient to secure enactment, it has typically been necessary to leave some ambiguity as to the effects of civil rights policy. If it were unequivocally clear what the legislation would and would not do, some potential supporters would withdraw from the coalition, much in the way that some Northern liberals ceased supporting school desegregation when it became apparent that schools in their own districts, as well as those of the South, would be affected. Unfortunately, the actual passage of civil rights legislation is frequently due in part to its vagueness, and civil rights advocates customarily settle for a compromise which provides a partial solution instead of holding out for laws specifically and obviously designed to uproot discrimination completely.

Specificity of Standards

Aside from intent, a second component of clarity in policy statements involves the specificity of the standards to be used in evaluating compliance with the legislation. In the absence of a measure against which to mark progress, it is impossible to determine whether the law is being adequately carried out. For example, if quantitative standards for judging the adequacy of a school desegregation plan are lacking, a district might be able to argue successfully that it no longer practiced segregation once a token black entered a previously all-white school. Or, to offer an illustration from another policy area, if environmental legislation simply contained an admonition to "improve" air quality, this could be marginally accomplished and yet the air might remain hazardous to breathe. Air quality legislation has achieved some measure of success in part because it does specify the level of pollutants which will be tolerated in certain emissions.

Even when decision makers seek to clarify their intent and to precisely define the standards used in assessment, problems may occur in accurately transmitting this information to the regulated parties. Reports on legislative, administrative, and especially judicial decisions may be garbled since those being regulated may learn of the policy from intermediaries who do not fully understand it (Goldman and Jahnige, 1976, 250–253; Nakamura and Smallwood, 1980, 89–94).

In analyzing the implementation of civil rights, we expect that maximum progress toward the objectives of the policymakers will occur when it has been made explicit what is expected of those whose behavior is being regulated. Thus, greater strides toward successful implementation should come when quantitative standards are established for measuring compliance and when it has been made perfectly clear what the objectives of the policy are.

Monitoring

Even with precise standards, progress toward civil rights policy goals cannot be guaranteed since most legislation and court decisions are not self-executing. While we can usually count on some degree of voluntary compliance (Anderson, 1979, 137), it is necessary to provide for monitoring of performance to achieve anything approaching full realization of policy objectives. To illustrate the point, obedience to traffic and tax laws is enhanced by fears that a radar unit may be just over the hill or that one's tax return will be audited. In contrast, no monitoring mechanism has ever been instituted to oversee the implementation of court decisions holding that various forms of classroom devotionals violate the separation of church and state requirements of the First Amendment of the Constitution. In the absence of monitoring, many teachers ignore the Supreme Court's ruling and begin each day with a prayer or Bible reading (Dolbeare and Hammond, 1971, chap. 3).

When objectives are as unpopular as those of civil rights policy have been in some quarters, monitoring is probably essential to achieve more than token compliance. The Supreme Court's 1954 and 1955 *Brown v. Board of Education* decisions (which were not accompanied by systematic monitoring of progress although federal district courts were directed to oversee implementation) triggered massive resistance rather than compliance in the South (Bartley, 1969). Substantial changes in the South's dual system of black and white schools were not achieved until a monitoring mechanism was established in the wake of the 1964 Civil Rights Act, with appropriate federal agencies overseeing the progress of school desegregation (Rodgers and Bullock, 1972, 81–88).

Monitoring is more likely to produce desired changes in policy when there are quantifiable standards with which to measure performance. To be effective, this requires the collection of data. When the monitoring agency can numerically assess progress, or its absence, disputes with those subject to the policy can be reduced. Moreover, to the extent that disagreements cannot be resolved through negotiation, the monitor is more likely to win should it be necessary to go to court if it can be shown that the defendant's performance fails to meet even the minimum on a generally accepted quantitative standard. For monitoring to be useful in promoting policy goals, it is, of course, necessary that the quantitative standards be high enough to force the changes desired in the behavior of those subject to the regulation (U.S. Commission on Civil Rights, 1974a, 84–91).

Another component of effective monitoring is the provision for on-site inspections of a sample of those subject to the policy (Van Horn and Van Meter, 1976, 54). In the sphere of civil rights policy, it has not been uncommon for the regulated parties to file less than complete, wholly accurate reports on their performance. On-site visits present an opportunity to evaluate the quality of the reports received and to identify emerging problems not revealed by current data collection. Another advantage of on-site inspections is the "ripple effect" which influences those not visited. If it is known that the monitor periodically drops in to inspect the records and performance of those being regulated, this will induce compliance with the law's requirements.

Effective monitoring also requires adequate training of whoever carries out on-site inspections. They must be able not only to discern behavior that is in violation of the law but also to be sensitive to any omissions in formal reports or oral interviews that may indicate some requirements are not being followed.

Presence of an Enforcement Agency

Policy decisions may be enunciated by several sources—the courts, the legislature, the chief executive, or the bureaucracy. Policies made by the legislature or through executive decree are dependent on the bureaucracy for implementation. Court decisions may also be carried out by the bureaucracy. A problem arises, however, when there is no administrative structure responsible for carrying out a policy. For example, during the first decade after the Supreme Court's *Brown* decision banning school segregation, there was no federal agency responsible for monitoring progress in the elimination of segregated schools. Although less common, there are instances in which a legislature will establish a new policy objective yet fail to set up an administrative structure necessary for implementation.

Without an agency responsible for seeing that program objectives are accomplished, the desired changes usually come to rest precariously on voluntary compliance. This situation most often occurs when the policy is based on a court decision that has not been endorsed by the other branches of government. It is, of course, possible that private plaintiffs who observe an absence of voluntary compliance will bring suit. For example, between 1954 and 1964 a number of school districts that had ignored the *Brown* decision were sued by black parents. When noncompliance is widespread and when there are relatively few private parties having the resources needed to sue, relatively little change in the direction sought by the policy is likely to occur (Brown and Stover, 1977, 470–471). Moreover, when the policy goal is generally unpopular, as has been typical with many civil rights objectives, voluntary compliance is rare.

When responsibility for attaining policy goals is assigned to an agency, then most of the focus of an implementation study centers on bureaucratic activities. Whereas other decision makers (for example, the legislature) can alter an agency's responsibilities, the agency itself attends to the day-to-day decisions affecting implementation. An agency responsible for a program defines the policy intent and elaborates standards that will be used in evaluating the behavior of those subject to the policy. Federal agencies publish this kind of information in the *Federal Register*; these materials then become a part of the policy. Agency employees seek to apply these standards in their dealings with the regulated parties. The agency may conduct investigations, seek to negotiate with those being regulated, or assess penalties against the noncompliant. Because it is less dependent on voluntarism, administrative enforcement holds greater potential than judicial enforcement for securing compliance with unpopular policies (Lamb, 1978a, 625–633).

Enforcer Commitment

Perhaps of greater significance than the presence of monitors are the attitudes of those responsible for monitoring. Agency personnel who are not strongly committed to promoting equality may only haphazardly investigate complaints alleging discrimination or apply loose standards when reviewing the behavior of those subject to the policy. Commitment to achieving policy goals takes on increased importance as the range of administrative and judicial discretion broadens. When uncertainty exists about what the policy requires and what administrators or judges must do to carry it out, enforcement officials have the option of ignoring all but the most flagrant abuses. For example, some Southern judges interpreted evidence that no blacks were registered to vote in a county with a sizable black population as indicative not of discrimination but of a lack of black political interest. Similarly, federal agencies monitoring the provisions of the Fair Housing Act of 1968 have often assumed that lending institutions do not contribute to discrimination when making home loans, even though these same institutions have been known to encourage realtors to steer minorities away from white residential areas.

The commitment of enforcers to achieving policy goals may be determined by a number of factors. One of these is the enforcers' priorities—either personal or agency priorities. A person will invest more time in and work harder on projects personally interesting or rewarding. All too often, however, monitoring agencies and their employees assign low priority to their civil rights enforcement responsibilities. Of importance, too, are agency decisions about civil rights priorities per se—such as the decision by the Dallas region Office for Civil Rights not to investigate complaints from women and Hispanics until all complaints from blacks had been resolved (U.S. House of Representatives, 1977, 785).

"Agency capture," or co-optation, may be an additional factor in determining the level of commitment to policy objectives. A frequent pattern in the history of regulatory agencies (some would go so far as to characterize it as inevitable) is for those being regulated to gain control over the agency. Examples abound. The Interstate Commerce Commission in time evolved into the protector of the very railroads it was created to regulate (Huntington, 1952). More recently, the Civil Aeronautics Board's chief concern shifted from the air traveler to the air carrier. Such transformations in orientation are not difficult to explain. The interests which were to be regulated are better organized, better funded, and more persistent than those the agency is supposed to protect. Because of these features, and because representatives of the interests being regulated are often more readily identifiable than are representatives of those to be protected, agency members have, at times, been selected disproportionately from the interests being regulated. Even when people who have worked for the regulated do not come to work for the regulator, the regulated may establish indirect lines of influence. The regulated, since they have more at stake, are more likely to be politically active than are representatives of the public interest. This political activity often results in the parties to be regulated developing close ties with legislators who oversee the regulatory agency's activities. The regulated can use their legislative allies to apply pressure on the agency to modify its more strident regulatory impulses.

While agencies newly created to deal with a specific problem may, in time, be co-opted, not all new policies are accompanied by the creation of a new enforcement agency; it just seems that way sometimes. More frequently, new programs are assigned to existing bureaucracies. When this happens, a different impediment to enforcement may exist. Agency personnel are well settled into a routine and already have priorities that do not include the new responsibility. The new program may be subordinated to the previous area of responsibility, which is seen as the agency's primary mission. Thus when the Department of Health, Education, and Welfare's Office for Civil Rights (OCR) was directed to enforce Title IX, which protects women's rights in the field of public education, this task was accorded a lower priority than the agency's initial job of desegregating the schools (Burton, 1979, 37). Or, while not assigning a lower priority to the new policy, an agency may find that its modus operandi conflicts with its new obligations. The Office of Education, which for almost one hundred years had been providing assistance and advice to schools, was unprepared to play a civil rights enforcement role and deny federal funds to schools that refused to desegregate (Orfield, 1969, 48–52).

The point of the preceding discussion is that there are a number of potential factors that may dissuade those to whom implementation is entrusted from vigorously discharging their responsibilities. When this happens, policy objectives are less likely to be realized.

If, however, the enforcers are dedicated to using the tools available to maximize compliance, they can constitute a potent force indeed. Some federal agents involved in early attempts at securing black suffrage and school desegregation performed well beyond what was expected of them. They withstood abusive language, harassment, and threats while working long hours during extended periods away from home. An illustration of the kind of dedication found during that period can be seen from the following comments by a Justice Department lawyer who worked on the *Alexander v. Holmes County Board of Education* case (1969):

> The 19th of August was the date the Fifth Circuit had set for filing [desegregation] plans and the trial in that case. There were four of us [lawyers], two secretaries, and a research analyst who went down there. We were taking affidavits and really working our tails off and then Hurricane Camille hit. We stayed there on the beach in the hotel and weathered it out because we thought we would go to trial there in Biloxi [Mississippi] the next Thursday. In fact, we worked without electricity or food or water for a couple of days. [Interview by Bullock, 1975]

Enforcer commitment of this caliber enhances the likelihood of successful implementation.

Commitment of the Enforcer's Superiors

The extent to which the personnel of federal agencies pursue policy goals entrusted to them in part depends on the cues they pick up from their superiors. If the administrative enforcers perceive that the president and Congress support their efforts, then they will be encouraged to apply standards rigorously. On the other hand, if the president or the Congress opposes the objectives of the policies assigned to a particular agency, this can become a powerful incentive not to apply the law forcefully. In recent years the Environmental Protection Agency, the Federal Trade Commission, and the Office for Civil Rights at the Department of Education are among the federal agencies that have found themselves in charge of what have ceased to be popular mandates.

The course of popular passions can change the administrator's environment much as the force of nature can reshape the physical environment. In both school desegregation and environmental protection, Congress responded to widespread public preferences and enacted sweeping new legislation. During the process of implementation, as the full consequences of these new policies became evident, public preferences shifted. As mentioned earlier, once it became clear that school segregation was not unique to the South, support in the North for the changes needed to eliminate racial isolation declined appreciably. Likewise, higher costs for fuel weakened the popular desire to clean up the environment. Shifts in public attitudes prompt reevaluations among members of Congress.

Augmenting cues from Congress and the public has been presidential opposition to civil rights goals. The president, as head of the executive branch, is ultimately responsible for enforcement of the law. High-ranking officials who actually oversee the carrying out of civil rights guarantees by federal agencies are his appointees. The more dedicated the president is to civil rights, the more likely his administration will be to consider civil rights a high priority. A president who opposes an agency's program can severely impede implementation. *Alexander* v. *Holmes* provides a useful illustration. After the attorneys worked through the hurricane preparing for trial, the Nixon administration capitulated to the defendants' (thirty-three Mississippi school districts) demands for additional time in which to prepare for desegregation. The Justice Department lawyer continued the story:

> The Secretary of Health, Education, and Welfare, from San Clemente, had a letter hand-delivered to the chief judge of the Fifth Circuit stating that the desegregation plans had been drawn too hastily and weren't very good. We had just finished taking affidavits from the men who drew them about how great they were. We were requested on behalf of the government to file a delay. It was pretty outrageous. [Interview by Bullock, 1975]

When an agency encounters continuing negative feedback from the White House and Congress, prudent administrators begin searching for reasons not to enforce the letter of the law. Persistent pursuit of what has become a politically sensitive objective will lead to a rising tide of opposition, political harassment, and job frustration for the besieged bureaucrats. If agency leaders persevere in vigorously enforcing politically unpopular programs, they may encounter hiring freezes and experience difficulties when requesting budget increases. Or the agency may be given new responsibilities which will deflect it from its earlier, now unpopular, course. This happened to HEW's civil rights responsibilities during the Nixon administration (Panetta and Gall, 1971), as well as to the fair housing enforcement duties of the Department of Housing and Urban Development (Danielson, 1976, chap. 8; Lamb, 1978a, 633–640). Therefore, the policy preferences of an agency's superiors may be a key variable in determining whether a program is successfully implemented.

Attitudes of Those Who Benefit from the Policy

The foregoing section discussed a number of elements that singly or in combination may operate to dissuade implementation. A potentially significant counterweight is the attitude of those who would benefit from the policy. In the case of policies surveyed in this book, the beneficiaries are, of course, minorities, especially black Americans. Support of the policy by the potential beneficiaries may offer critical psychological reinforcement for agency personnel who want to continue faithful implementation but are encountering strong opposition from the agency's superiors.

A second function of beneficiaries is more coercive, that is, to monitor the enforcers. Sometimes this involves collusion between the beneficiaries and the enforcers in an attempt to hold the influence of the agency's sovereigns in check. During the height of the Nixon administration's campaign to cut back on civil rights implementation, there were instances in which enforcement officials sabotaged retrenchment efforts by leaking information to allies among private activists, who in turn alerted the press.

At other times minority monitoring of civil rights implementation has been designed to force improved performance by the implementer. A coalition of civil rights groups published an outspoken criticism of the way in which emergency aid was distributed to desegregating school districts (American Friends Service Committee et al., 1970). Similarly, civil rights groups have repeatedly chided the Justice Department for not enforcing voting rights more aggressively (Washington Research Project, 1972).

Beneficiaries also play a role at the local level, where they augment the monitoring capability of the enforcement agency. They may bring local deficiencies to the regulator's attention either through informal means or by filing with the agency a complaint charging local decision makers with violating civil rights requirements. And, as was often the case during the 1950s and 1960s, beneficiaries testified before representatives of the U.S. Commission on Civil Rights who traveled around the country to investigate civil rights conditions.

For beneficiaries to be most effective, it is important that there be some organizational structure. An organization purporting to speak for the beneficiaries will receive more attention from the regulator, local officials being regulated, and the press than will an aggrieved individual. To overcome opposition from Congress or a local school or zoning board, it is probably necessary that the beneficiaries be united in their demand that corrective action be taken. Where there is disunity among the beneficiaries, as for example the conflict among Hispanics over which should have priority, bilingual education programs or a reduction in the ethnic isolation of Hispanic students (Orfield, 1978), the regulators are able to ignore in large part the more politically sensitive issues.

Administrative Coordination

A common obstacle to effective policy implementation is the failure of federal agencies with overlapping responsibilities to coordinate their enforcement activities (Hope, 1976, 16–28; Lamb, 1978b; U.S. Commission on Civil Rights, 1974b; U.S. Commission on Civil Rights, 1975, chap. 6). The basic problem can be traced to the statutes themselves. When the same type of discrimination is addressed by different statutes, this piecemeal approach may create widely varied coverage and overlapping remedies. For instance, several laws, including the Fair Housing Act of 1968,

Title VI of the Civil Rights Act of 1964, and the Housing and Community Development Act of 1974, prohibit housing discrimination. Several federal agencies have been assigned the duty of enforcing these laws, with enforcement occurring in a haphazard manner (Lamb, 1978a).

A different problem of coordination occurs when one statute creates administrative mechanisms for achieving enforcement within an agency's hearing and adjudicatory authority, while another statute is enforceable through the courts with action required by either the Justice Department or private litigants.

Coordination in civil rights implementation avoids duplication of enforcement activities and promotes consistency in federal guidelines. It may also improve the quality and quantity of agency information on minorities, it upgrades and centralizes civil rights training, and it perhaps eliminates confusion among the regulated and the general public concerning rights and obligations (Lamb, 1978b).

Costs and Benefits

While a number of the items discussed could be subsumed under a full-blown cost–benefit approach (Rodgers and Bullock, 1972, chap. 8; Brown and Stover, 1977), a narrower perspective will be adopted in this volume. The costs discussed here are the penalties assessed for failing to comply with the law. The perspective of those who would apply such sanctions is that once the cost of noncompliance becomes too great, the regulated will conform and the program will be implemented. The costs may involve loss of funds—a central factor in desegregating many Southern school systems (Bullock and Rodgers, 1976a)—the threat of punishment, loss of standing in the eyes of one's reference group, or some other penalty. While sanctions directed at funding were instrumental in Southern school desegregation, it is often politically unacceptable to use this tool to force compliance. As Anderson observes, "There appears to be general agreement that policies should be implemented in such a manner as to cause the least necessary material and psychological disturbance to the affected persons. . . . The general objective of public policy is to control behavior [or secure compliance] and not to punish violators except as a last resort" (1979, 142).

Theoretically, inducements also can be strong motivators of behavior. Offering a reward for carrying out a program may suffice to secure compliance. Grant programs operate on the premise that if funding is made contingent upon prescribed behavior, the desired behavior can be obtained. With regard to civil rights, federal grants and contracts now regularly include a provision in which the recipient agrees, as a condition for funding, not to discriminate on the basis of race, color, religion, sex, or national origin.

Whether sanctions (such as threatened loss of federal aid) or incentives (such as grants) are used to prompt compliance, it may prove necessary for federal authorities to adjust the terms to elicit the desired response from all of those subject to the regulation. For example, when termination of federal funds failed to secure desegregation of some Southern schools, the ante was raised and segregated districts were threatened with loss of state education money (Bullock and Rodgers, 1976b). Or an offer of additional grant funds arguably may induce suburban communities to accept more units of low-income housing, which might produce a more racially heterogeneous population. Most civil rights policies have relied more on sanctions than incentives to promote implementation. In the absence of either, compliance becomes highly problematic.

Direct Federal Involvement

The level of federal involvement in promoting equal treatment of minorities can be critical for policy implementation. Frequently, when a right has been newly recognized, the role of the federal government has been mostly passive (Bullock and Rodgers, 1975, 28–46). Under these conditions the federal government acknowledges the existence of a right, but enforcement rests largely with private parties who must sue to force compliance by the reluctant. It is not surprising that when private plaintiffs bear the burden of enforcement, change usually comes very slowly, as was the case for voting rights and school desegregation during the 1950s (U.S. Commission on Civil Rights, 1963, chaps. 1 and 2).

If Congress opts to have the federal government play a more active role in implementing civil rights policy, it can authorize the Justice Department to file suits on behalf of people who are being denied their rights. Or Congress may create a bureaucracy responsible for monitoring compliance and seek to achieve more complete implementation. All other things being equal, active federal involvement is likely to produce implementation more in line with what was expected by those who were active in the adoption of the policy.

One effective method by which federal authorities can promote the likelihood that policy objectives will be achieved is to supplant the authority of local or state officials who would otherwise implement the policy. Foot-dragging by local voter registrars ceased to be an obstacle when federal agents were sent to selected Southern counties to enroll eligible blacks (Hamilton, 1973, chap. 10; Rodgers and Bullock, 1972, chap. 2). As a second example, the discretion of employers, particularly public employers, has been circumscribed by a number of court orders which prescribe that minorities must constitute a specific proportion of all new hires until the employer's labor force ceases to be disproportionately white (U.S. Commission on Civil Rights, 1980, 22–24).

SUMMARY

The previous discussion suggests a number of factors which may be associated with successful implementation of civil rights policy. Accordingly, we may expect that changes in the direction of equality in the treatment of minorities are more likely to occur when:

1. policy goals have been clearly stated
2. precise standards for measuring compliance have been specified
3. a mechanism for monitoring compliance has been created
4. an agency responsible for implementing the policy has been set up
5. personnel responsible for implementation are committed to promoting civil rights
6. those enforcing the policy enjoy the support of their superiors
7. the policy beneficiaries are organized and cohesively support implementation
8. efforts by various agencies responsible for achieving a policy goal are administratively coordinated
9. the cost–benefit ratio of the situation favors compliance
10. the federal government is an active participant on behalf of minorities

The degree to which each of these propositions helps account for differences in implementation success is addressed in the remainder of this book. The next five chapters each focus on the implementation of a specific aspect of civil rights policy—namely, voting rights, equal education opportunity in public schools, equal employment and economic opportunity, desegregation of higher education, and fair housing. Each chapter consists of several sections. Among the items covered is a description of the pertinent policy requirements. In handling this topic, the authors summarize the provisions of legislation, administrative regulations, court decisions, and executive orders which set forth the policy goals. These goals then provide a benchmark for measuring the degree of success achieved in implementation. Thus the second section of each chapter will be devoted to evaluating any changes that resulted from the adoption of the policy and to analyzing the degree to which these changes approximate the objectives of the policy. Along with discussion of goals and implementation toward these objectives, background information is presented to show the conditions that existed before adoption of the policy.

After setting forth the policy objectives and describing the response to these programs, each author examines the reasons for implementation success or failure, seeking to explain why compliance came when it did rather than earlier. It is appropriate in certain chapters to compare the reasons for greater success in achieving some civil rights goals rather than others. The authors refer to the variables outlined in this chapter in assessing the factors relevant to their fields of expertise.

The concluding chapter offers some generalizations about the conditions under which civil rights policy is most likely to flourish, drawing together materials from the five substantive chapters in a cross-sectional analysis. Actors and interactions that are most conducive to successful policy implementation are emphasized there.

NOTES

1. The variables used throughout this book to try to explain implementation have been suggested by a number of scholars. The table below lists some of the major contributors to this field of study and some variables for which they have helped provide refinements.

	Wirt 1970	D & B[a] 1971	R & B 1972	VH & VM 1976	S & M 1980
Clarity of policy	X	X	X	X	X
Specificity of standards	X		X		X
Monitoring			X	X	
Enforcement agency		X	X		
Enforcer commitment	X		X		X
Enforcers' superiors	X				X
Policy beneficiaries	X		X		X
Administrative coordination					X
Costs and benefits	X	X	X		
Federal involvement	X		X		

[a] D & B = Dolbeare and Hammond
R & B = Rodgers and Bullock
VH & VM = Van Horn and Van Meter
S & M = Sabatier and Mazmanian

REFERENCES

Alexander v. Holmes County Board of Education, 396 U.S. 19 (1969).
American Friends Service Committee et al. (1970). *The Emergency School Assistance Program: An Evaluation*. No location. American Friends Service Committee, Delta Ministry of the National Council of Churches, Lawyers Committee for Civil Rights Under Law, Lawyers Constitutional Defense Committee, NAACP Legal Defense and Education Fund, Inc., and the Washington Research Project.
Anderson, James E. (1979). *Public Policy-Making*. 2nd ed. New York: Holt, Rinehart and Winston.
Bartley, Numan V. (1969). *The Rise of Massive Resistance: Race and Politics in the South during the 1950s*. Baton Rouge: Louisiana State University Press.
Brown, Don W., and Robert V. Stover (1977). "Court Directives and Compliance: A Utility Approach." *American Politics Quarterly* 5: 465–480.
Brown v. Board of Education, 347 U.S. 483 (1954).
Brown v. Board of Education, 349 U.S. 294 (1955).
Bullock, Charles S. III, and Harrell R. Rodgers, Jr. (1975). *Racial Equality in America: In Search of an Unfulfilled Goal*. Pacific Palisades, Calif.: Goodyear.
Bullock, Charles S. III, and Harrell R. Rodgers, Jr. (1976a). "Coercion to Compliance: Southern School Districts and School Desegregation Guidelines." *Journal of Politics* 38: 987–1011.
Bullock, Charles S. III, and Harrell R. Rodgers, Jr. (1976b). "Impediments to Policy Evaluation: Perceptual Distortion and Agency Loyalty." *Social Science Quarterly* 57: 506–519.
Burton, Doris-Jean (1979). "Sexual Equality through Title IX: Potential versus Performance." Presented at annual meeting of Midwest Political Science Association, Chicago.
Council on Environmental Quality (1980). *Environmental Quality*. Washington, D.C.: U.S. Government Printing Office.
Danielson, Michael N. (1976). *The Politics of Exclusion*. New York: Columbia University Press.
Dolbeare, Kenneth M., and Phillip E. Hammond (1971). *The School Prayer Decisions: From Court Policy to Local Practice*. Chicago: University of Chicago Press.
Edwards, George C. III (1980). *Implementing Public Policy*. Washington, D.C.: Congressional Quarterly.
Goldman, Sheldon, and Thomas P. Jahnige (1976). *The Federal Courts as a Political System*. 2nd ed. New York: Harper and Row.
Hamilton, Charles V. (1973). *The Bench and the Ballot: Southern Federal Judges and Black Voters*. New York: Oxford University Press.
Hope, John II (1976). *Minority Access to Federal Grants: The Gap between Policy and Performance*. New York: Praeger.
Huntington, Samuel P. (1952). "The Marasmus of the ICC." *Yale Law Journal* 61: 470–509.
Jones, Charles O. (1977). *An Introduction to the Study of Public Policy*. 2nd ed. North Scituate, Mass.: Duxbury Press.
Lamb, Charles M. (1978a). "Presidential Fair Housing Policies: Political and Legal Trends." *Cumberland Law Review* 8: 619–660.
Lamb, Charles M. (1978b). "Administrative Coordination in Civil Rights Enforcement: A Regional Approach." *Vanderbilt Law Review* 31: 855–886.
Lamb, Charles M., and Mitchell T. Lustig (1979). "The Burger Court, Exclusionary Zoning, and the Activist-Restraint Debate." *University of Pittsburgh Law Review* 40: 169–226.

McCrone, Donald J., and Richard J. Hardy (1978). "Civil Rights Policies and the Achievement of Racial Economic Equality, 1948–1975." *American Journal of Political Science* 22: 1–17.

Nakamura, Robert K., and Frank Smallwood (1980). *The Politics of Policy Implementation*. New York: St. Martin's.

Newsweek (March 3, 1980): 31.

Orfield, Gary (1969). *The Reconstruction of Southern Education*. New York: John Wiley.

Orfield, Gary (1978). *Must We Bus?* Washington, D.C.: Brookings Institution.

Panetta, Leon E., and Peter Gall (1971). *Bring Us Together: The Nixon Team and the Civil Rights Retreat*. Philadelphia: Lippincott.

Peltason, J. W. (1971). *Fifty-Eight Lonely Men: Southern Federal Judges and School Desegregation*. Urbana, Ill.: Illini Books.

Pressman, Jeffrey, and Aaron Wildavsky (1973). *Implementation*. Berkeley: University of California Press.

Rodgers, Harrell R., Jr., and Charles S. Bullock III (1972). *Law and Social Change: Civil Rights Laws and their Consequences*. New York: McGraw-Hill.

Sabatier, Paul, and Daniel Mazmanian (1980). "The Implementation of Public Policy: A Framework of Analysis." *Policy Studies Journal* 8: 538–560.

Shapiro v. Thompson, 394 U.S. 618 (1969).

Shelley v. Kraemer, 334 U.S. 1 (1948).

U.S. Commission on Civil Rights (1963). *Civil Rights '63*. Washington, D.C.: U.S. Government Printing Office.

U.S. Commission on Civil Rights (1974a). *The Federal Civil Rights Enforcement Effort: To Provide . . . for Fair Housing*. Washington, D.C.: U.S. Government Printing Office.

U.S. Commission on Civil Rights (1974b). *Toward a More Cooperative and Productive Relationship among Civil Rights Agencies and Officials*. Washington, D.C.: U.S. Government Printing Office.

U.S. Commission on Civil Rights (1975). *The Federal Civil Rights Enforcement Effort: To Eliminate Employment Discrimination*. Washington, D.C.: U.S. Government Printing Office.

U.S. Commission on Civil Rights (1980). *The State of Civil Rights: 1979*. Washington, D.C.: U.S. Government Printing Office.

U.S. House of Representatives (1977). *Committee on Appropriations Hearings, Departments of Labor and Health, Education and Welfare, and Related Agencies Appropriations Fiscal Year 1977*, 94th Congress, 1st Session, Part 6. Washington, D.C.: U.S. Government Printing Office.

Van Horn, Carl, and Donald Van Meter (1976). "The Implementation of Intergovernmental Policy." In Charles O. Jones and Robert Thomas (eds.), *Public Policy Making in the Federal System*, vol. III of *Sage Yearbook in Politics and Public Policy*. Beverly Hills, Calif.: Sage.

Vines, Kenneth N. (1964). "Federal District Judges and Race Relations Cases in the South." *Journal of Politics* 26: 337—357.

Washington Research Project (1972). *The Shameful Blight*. Washington, D.C.: Washington Research Project.

Wirt, Frederick M. (1970). *The Politics of Southern Equality*. Chicago: Aldine.

Chapter 2

Voting Rights Act: Implementation and Impact

Richard Scher and James Button

On August 6, 1965, President Lyndon B. Johnson signed into law the Voting Rights Act. In doing so, the president observed that this piece of legislation would "strike away the last major shackle" of the "ancient bonds" confining blacks to second-class citizenship (Congressional Quarterly Service, 1969, 32). Johnson's words, and indeed the extraordinary congressional consensus which had developed around the bill, can best be understood as a fervent demonstration of the value of the ballot in the American democratic ethos. Voting has long been regarded in this country as the primary mechanism for popular participation in government and the major instrument of social change. To deny citizens of the United States access to the ballot has meant not only deprivation of a basic right but a denial of the legitimate place of individuals or groups in American society. Thus civil rights groups, President Johnson, the Congress, and perhaps ultimately the American public became convinced that unless blacks' right to vote was guaranteed and protected, the civil rights movement remained essentially incomplete.

The importance of the Voting Rights Act was readily apparent at the time of its signing, since there were hundreds of thousands of disenfranchised blacks in the South. President Johnson pledged that implementation and enforcement of the bill would be vigorous and immediate: "We will not delay or we will not hesitate, or will not turn aside until Americans of every race and color and origin in this country have the same rights as all others to share in the progress of democracy" (Lawson, 1976, 329). By August 7, the Justice Department, which was given primary responsibility for enforcement of the bill, began to carry out its provisions. Within three days targeted states and counties in the South were selected for the initial efforts at registering blacks to vote. Because large numbers of blacks were registered relatively quickly, observers in later years called the Voting Rights Act the most effective piece of civil rights legislation ever passed in America (Garrow, 1978, xi).

This chapter discusses the legislative history and intent of the Voting Rights Act of 1965, its subsequent amendments in 1970, 1975, and 1982, and the implementation process of the legislation. We then assess the impact of the act and amendments. The chapter concludes with some theoretical propositions concerning the process of implementation and the determinants of the impact of the act.

VOTING RIGHTS ACTS: HISTORY AND INTENT

From the 1890s until well into the twentieth century, white Southerners, especially in Deep South states and black belt (where the majority of the population is black) counties, used various "Jim Crow" laws to keep blacks, and to some extent poor whites, from the polls. Three of the main techniques (the poll tax, the all-white primary, and literacy tests) are now of historical interest only; but three others (intimidation, discriminatory registration practices, and election law changes) are still present.

Chronology

1870: Fifteenth Amendment to Constitution guarantees blacks the right to vote.
1870 and 1871: Enforcement Acts (later repealed).
1880s–early 1900s: Institution of Jim Crow laws in Southern states.
1944: *Smith v. Allwright.*
1957: Civil Rights Act.
1960: Civil Rights Act.
1964: Civil Rights Act; Twenty-Fourth Amendment to the U.S. Constitution eliminates poll tax in federal elections.
1965: March on Selma, Alabama.
1965: Voting Rights Act.
1966: *South Carolina v. Katzenbach.*
1970: Extension of Voting Rights Act (5 years).
1975: Extension of Voting Rights Act (7 years; inclusion of bilingual requirements).
1982: Extension of Voting Rights Act.

Between 1889 and 1902 the eleven ex-Confederate states initiated a poll tax, which made payment of a fee a prerequisite to voting. The purpose of the tax was to present an economic obstacle to voting by blacks and poor whites. The Twenty-Fourth Amendment to the Constitution, initiated by the Kennedy administration and ratified in 1964, abolished the poll tax (Rodgers and Bullock, 1972, 36–37). The rationale behind the all-white primary was that membership in a political party (and hence the right to participate in the primary) was akin to that of a private organization or club, and therefore membership could be arbitrarily restricted. This notion was overturned by the Supreme Court in *Smith v. Allwright* (1944). The Court held that in the one-party South, primaries were really the only meaningful election, and therefore participation in them could not be limited by race (Key, 1949, 619–625; Rodgers and Bullock, 1972, 18).

Local voting registrars have resorted to many devices to prevent blacks from registering to vote. One of the most common was the literacy test, in which blacks would be required to interpret obscure clauses in state or federal constitutions or statutes. It was not unusual for even educated blacks to fail literacy tests (Key, 1949, 555–577). Registrars could also require applicants to have character references provided by qualified voters. Some registrars rejected applicants for minor flaws in the application, such as failure to write in ink, or miscalculation of one's age. Or registration might be limited to times and places inconvenient to or uncomfortable for blacks.

Intimidation of black voters took a variety of forms in the South. When blacks sought to register, on many occasions they were beaten, tortured, or even murdered by local whites. This violence was meted out by the Ku Klux Klan as well as by groups of self-proclaimed white vigilantes, and sometimes by law enforcement officers. Police and sheriff's deputies frequently arrested blacks seeking to register. Law officers were often aided in their intimidation efforts by local judges who would deny bail, sentence blacks to lengthy jail terms, or affix heavy fines (Watters and Cleghorn, 1967).

Even where physical intimidation did not exist, economic and psychological intimidation were often present. Blacks seeking to register to vote would be fired from jobs, denied credit in stores, or evicted from the land they worked as tenant farmers. Blacks also perceived the white community (especially law enforcement officers and employers) as allied against them, which constituted a severe impediment to registering (Salamon and Van Evera, 1973, 1288–1306; Garrow, 1978, 6–30).

Finally, where blacks could no longer be kept from the polls (especially in large cities), the impact of their vote was often minimized through a variety of election law techniques. In some cases aggregations of blacks were gerrymandered to the extent that no black could win public office. Also, through annexation and the use of at-large elections, the impact of even substantial numbers of black voters could be diluted. These techniques, whose origins go back to the beginning of this century, are still used (Rodgers and Bullock, 1972, 39–40).

Protecting the Right to Vote

Following the Civil War, and continuing through the twentieth century, the federal government made several efforts to enfranchise blacks. The first was the Fifteenth Amendment to the Constitution, ratified after the Civil War, and aimed specifically at former slaves. It was implemented by the Enforcement Acts of 1870 and 1871, but they were repealed. As a result, millions of blacks remained disenfranchised for most of this century. It was not until the beginning of the civil rights movement in the mid-1950s that a concerted effort was again made to provide blacks access to the ballot.

From the very start of the movement, civil rights leaders regarded the right to vote as one of their fundamental goals. They recognized, however, that only through federal action would voting rights be achieved, since Southern election officials seemed unwilling to open voting rolls to blacks. The hopes of black leaders were at least partially realized when President Eisenhower signed into law the 1957 Civil Rights Act. This act was important because it sought to protect black voting rights by allowing blacks to go to court to request injunctions when they felt those rights had been violated. Also the act empowered the U.S. Attorney General to seek court injunctions against practices that deprived blacks of voting rights. Thus, at least symbolically, this legislation demonstrated that the federal government was willing to help blacks secure the right to vote and protect them in their efforts to do so. But substantial change did not occur immediately, in part because President Eisenhower declined to enforce the provisions of the act vigorously (Lawson, 1976, 179–249; Rodgers and Bullock, 1972, 23–24).

Three years later, in 1960, another civil rights bill was passed which extended federal authority to promote voter registration by permitting federal judges or special referees to register qualified blacks who had not been enrolled by local officials. The 1960 Civil Rights Act also permitted access to local voting records by federal officials in the event of prosecution of local officials because of discriminatory practices. The 1964 Civil Rights Act further extended federal authority to ensure voting rights for blacks. It forbade denial of the right to vote even if applications or records contained immaterial or trivial errors. The 1964 act also provided that in those areas where literacy tests were applied, completion of the sixth grade constituted sufficient presumption of literacy. Moreover, the act permitted the empaneling of special three-judge federal district courts to hear voting rights suits if requested by the Attorney General (Rodgers and Bullock, 1972, 24–28).

The importance of these three civil rights bills can scarcely be denied. They provided black citizens with legal remedies to fight discriminatory practices. Perhaps most crucially, these bills provided symbolic support to courageous Southern blacks willing to undergo physical and psychological hardships in their struggle for the franchise. But even the most optimistic assessment of these acts indicates that their effectiveness was limited. Between 1957 and 1962 black voter registration increased by only 4 percent. There was always a shortage of manpower in the Department of Justice to monitor discrimination and file lawsuits. By 1963 the Department of Justice had filed suits against Mississippi and a number of individual counties, but discrimination was certainly present elsewhere.

While undoubtedly the civil rights acts were important factors in the modest black registration increase, other factors had an impact as well, such as increased black militancy, greater attention by the national media to the problems of Southern blacks, erosion of resistance among some Southern election officials, growing voices of moderation among some Southern whites (especially in the business community), and the alleged threat to blacks represented by the Goldwater candidacy in 1964. Limits on the effectiveness of the civil rights acts for increasing voter registration can be seen by comparing the great disparity between figures from the border Southern states and the Deep Southern states, or those with the greatest history of racial discrimination. Just prior to passage of the 1965 Voting Rights Act, black registration in the border states (Arkansas, Florida, North Carolina, and Tennessee) averaged 52 percent. Comparable figures for the Deep South states (Alabama, Georgia, Louisiana, Mississippi, South Carolina, Texas, and Virginia) averaged only 27 percent (Rodgers and Bullock, 1972, 24–28; Garrow, 1978, 6–30).

Unquestionably, however, the greatest weakness of the civil rights acts for improving black voter registration lay in their exclusive reliance on litigation for seeking relief from discrimination. This proved so time consuming and costly that the election in question had usually come and gone by the time a favorable judgment was reached. Also, since the whole procedure rested on a case-by-case approach, there was no comprehensive attack on the widespread traditional patterns of discrimination that existed. Moreover, Southern local and state officials (including judges) proved very imaginative in finding ways of avoiding compliance with the provisions of the law, even to the point of defying court orders. As a result, the House Judiciary Committee noted in the spring of 1965 that progress in voter registration "has been painfully slow. . . . Judicial relief has had to be gauged not in terms of months—but in terms of years" (U.S. House of Representatives, 1965, 2440–2441).

Thus it was evident to civil rights leaders that efforts to provide blacks with full access to the ballot would have to be based on more powerful weapons than existed at that time. Nevertheless, in spite of a growing national sympathy for the civil rights movement and increasing media attention to problems of racial discrimination in the South, there was little political movement for a major piece of legislation aimed specifically at voting rights. The necessary impetus was provided by events in Selma, Alabama, during the early months of 1965 (Lawson, 1976, 307–312; Garrow, 1978, 6–77).

A march on Selma was chosen by Martin Luther King to demonstrate to the nation the extent of racial hatred and discrimination that pervaded the South. The national news media covered in great detail the confrontation between King and his followers on the one hand, and Dallas County Sheriff Jim Clark, who represented the last gasp of a traditional Southern way of life, on the other. Scenes of marches, demonstrations, jailings, beatings, and murders were vividly portrayed in print and on coast-to-coast television. Events reached a climax on March 7, when a peaceful group of civil rights demonstrators was viciously attacked by an army of state and local law enforcement officers.

The violence produced by the lawmen evoked an enormous, vocal response throughout the country. President Johnson, feeling pressure from both outraged whites and increasingly militant blacks, evidently felt he could wait no longer. On March 15, 1965, he went to the Congress to deliver what many felt was the most compelling speech of his presidency. In proposing a voting rights act which would remove obstacles to black political participation, he rebuked his fellow Southerners. He invoked the hymn of the civil rights movement, "We Shall Overcome," and thereby inextricably linked the potential power of the federal government with the goals of King and others committed to civil rights.

1965 Voting Rights Act

In contrast to the earlier civil rights acts, the Voting Rights Act of 1965 focused on specifically designated places where blatant discrimination against blacks existed. It was felt that enforcement of the act would be more effective if the resources of the federal government could be concentrated in relatively limited areas. Places in which a literacy test or similar device was a prerequisite for voting as of November 1, 1964, and in which the Census Bureau found that fewer than 50 percent of the voting-age population was registered to vote or had actually voted in the 1964 presidential election, were automatically subject to the legislation as provided in Section 4 of the act. Originally included under this mechanism intended to automatically "trigger" federal involvement were Alabama, Alaska, Georgia, Louisiana, Mississippi, South Carolina, Virginia, twenty-six counties in North Carolina, and one county in Arizona.

Next, the use of a literacy test, or any device similar to it (such as proof of literacy, educational attainment, or possession of "good moral character") as a determinant of voter eligibility, was suspended for five years. Completion of the sixth grade was to be regarded as proof of literacy, even if the principal language of instruction was not English. This latter provision, which modified the literacy requirement of the 1964 Civil Rights

Act, was aimed primarily at enabling citizens educated in Puerto Rican schools to vote.

Third, the Civil Service Commission, upon a recommendation by the Attorney General, could assign voting examiners in target areas to list eligible voters who had been improperly rejected by local authorities. To prevent the possibility that recently registered blacks would still be denied access to the polls, federal observers could be assigned to areas previously designated by federal examiners.

Finally, any changes in the voting practices of states or local jurisdictions whose voter qualifications had been suspended, or to which the automatic "triggering" mechanism applied, had to be approved either by the Attorney General or the Federal District Court of Washington, D.C. This preclearance provision (Section 5 of the law) was designed to prevent states and counties from passing new voting laws which might still discriminate against blacks, even though literacy and similar tests were removed. The Federal District Court of Washington, D.C., was chosen to circumvent past cooperation between federal district judges in the Deep South and local and state officials to keep blacks off the voting rolls.

The legality of the Voting Rights Act was challenged almost immediately after President Johnson signed it into law. However, the Supreme Court upheld all of the bill's provisions in a major decision, *South Carolina v. Katzenbach* (1966). Chief Justice Earl Warren, who wrote the majority opinion, argued that the continued existence of racial discrimination in voting laws and practices required that Congress assemble an "array of potent weapons" to guarantee blacks access to the ballot. While Warren recognized that some of the provisions of the bill constituted "an uncommon extension of congressional power," he emphatically stated that "exceptional conditions can justify legislative measures not otherwise appropriate."

Central to Warren's defense of the 1965 act were two crucial points. First, the burden of proof was shifted away from blacks, who previously had to demonstrate the existence of discrimination, to state and local voting officials, who now had to demonstrate that their voting qualifications and procedures were not discriminatory. This would allow more immediate redress of discriminatory practices than was possible under previous court proceedings.

Second, implicit in the Court's interpretation of the law was the notion that this legislation, in conjunction with the 1964 Civil Rights Act, sharply changed the focus of federal efforts in this area. Previously the federal government was relegated to a relatively passive role: it could intervene in state and local civil rights matters only as a last resort after voluntary compliance had proven ineffective, and then only through the courts. The Voting Rights Act still permitted, even encouraged, voluntary compliance and court action. But Chief Justice Warren clearly indicated that it was now permissible for federal administrative officers (either the Attorney General or his representatives) to intervene on their own initiative in local counties to force compliance with the law. The act, in Warren's view, propelled federal agents, who presumably could move more swiftly and with more immediate impact than the courts, into a very activist posture. Only such extraordinary measures, Warren concluded, would enable the federal government to help blacks in their efforts to gain full equality.

1970 Renewal

By 1970 the politics of civil rights in America had changed substantially. Richard Nixon was elected in 1968 at least partially because of his "Southern strategy," which was aimed at reducing federal pressure on the South to comply with civil rights laws. He pledged to take a more cautious, slow approach to their enforcement and certainly demonstrated none of Johnson's enthusiasm for the vigorous use of federal authority in dealing with racial problems (Peirce, 1974, 31–34). In this he reflected not just his electoral debt to the South but, perhaps, the attitude of many white Americans who, by the late 1960s, felt mounting fear and resentment toward blacks (Scammon and Wattenberg, 1970, 39–42).

The civil rights stance of the Nixon administration can be seen in its proposals for amending the original 1965 act, which was due to expire in August 1970. By 1969 many civil rights groups were fearful that if it were not renewed, or if it were changed substantially, the gains that the original legislation had wrought would be lost. They pointed especially to the registration of more than one million additional black voters since 1965; while not all of this growth occurred directly because of the Voting Rights Act, civil rights leaders agreed that it was an essential component of the increase.

In June 1969, the administration revealed its proposed changes—proposals that confirmed the fears of civil rights proponents (Congressional Quarterly Service, 1970, 193). There would be a nationwide, five-year ban on literacy tests; the Attorney General would have nationwide, instead of regional, authority to dispatch voting examiners and observers; and he would be given nationwide power to initiate voting rights suits. In addition, the very controversial Section 5 (preclearance) provision of the 1965 Voting Rights Act, which required prior approval of state or local changes in election laws or procedures, would be eliminated. Instead, under the Nixon plan the Justice Department would be able to file suits only against the laws it regarded as discriminatory. Finally, exclusive jurisdiction over voting rights cases would be removed from the Federal District Court of Washington, D.C., and returned to local federal district courts.

The administration's proposals were immediately criticized by liberal legislators and civil rights groups as a "sophisticated but deadly" way to gut the intent of the 1965 law. They feared that broadening the focus of the legislation by making it national would dilute its impact on the South where it was needed most. Moreover, the elimination of the preclearance requirement by the Attorney General and removal of the exclusive authority of the Federal District Court of Washington, D.C., to hear cases would once again force reliance on endless litigation in courts not always friendly to black plaintiffs. The effect of this would undoubtedly be to shift the burden of proof of discrimination back to blacks and away from local voting officials. To many proponents of the Voting Rights Act, the Nixon proposals seemed to promise a return to pre–1965 conditions.

The Nixon plan initially achieved a successful vote in the House of Representatives. Ultimately, however, Republican leadership in the Senate deserted the president and, along with liberal Democrats, insisted on a compromise bill. The new bill extended for five years the suspension of literacy and similar qualifying tests throughout the entire nation, continued Section 5 preclearance, and expanded the Section 4 "trigger" formula by making the bill applicable to all states and counties using a literacy or similar test in which fewer than 50 percent of the voting-age residents were registered on November 1, 1968 or voted in the 1968 presidential election. This change maintained the original coverage of jurisdictions and added one county in Wyoming, five counties in Arizona, two in California, one in Idaho, and the Bronx, Kings (Brooklyn), and New York (Manhattan) counties in New York City.

1975 and 1982 Renewals

By the time of the next renewal (August 1975) other minority groups such as Mexican-Americans and Native Americans had begun to demand federal protection of their voting rights. At first, some blacks were hostile to the idea of expanding coverage of the Voting Rights Act to other groups. They argued that this would dilute the bill, and that controversy surrounding which groups to include might threaten its extension. However, in late January 1975 the U.S. Commission on Civil Rights released a major report evaluating the first ten years of the Voting Rights Act. It called for a ten-year extension of the Voting Rights Act but insisted that the act be broadened to include Spanish and other language minority populations (1975). Congress eventually accepted that proposal; interestingly, black civil rights groups also agreed to support the inclusion of other minority groups (Congressional Quarterly Service, 1977, 669–673).

The 1975 legislation continued for seven years coverage of jurisdictions that had a literacy or similar test in effect November 1, 1964 and where fewer than 50 percent of the entire voting-age population registered or voted in the 1964 or 1968 presidential elections. But it also extended the act to Hispanic, Native American, Asian-American, and Alaskan language minorities. Covered were jurisdictions in which the Census Bureau found that more than 5 percent of voting-age citizens were of a single language minority, in which election materials had been printed only in English for the 1972 presidential election, and in which fewer than 50 percent of the age-eligible citizens had registered or voted in 1972. Bilingual election materials were also required if 5 percent of the area's voting-age citizens were of a single language minority and the illiteracy rate in English of the language minority was greater than the national illiteracy rate (illiteracy was defined as failure to complete the fifth grade). The act required the Census Bureau to collect statistics on registration and voting by race, color, and national origin in each covered jurisdiction following congressional elections. Finally, the power of the Attorney General to send examiners and observers, as well as to require preclearance of changes in voting laws, remained intact.

From 1981 to 1982 Congress debated extension of the act, and controversy over many provisions surfaced once again. The House had overwhelmingly approved a renewal of the act in 1981, but the Senate Judiciary Committee, chaired by Senator Strom Thurmond (R.–S.C.), was hesitant about going along. A compromise version was finally accepted by the committee, however, making it easier to prove voting rights violations. President Reagan endorsed the Senate committee's version of the bill as the White House sought to shore up its standing with the nation's minority groups. Reagan had expressed reservations about the strong voting rights extension passed by the House—but a coalition of civil rights groups, angered by the president's cuts in social programs and by his statements concerning tax exemptions for segregated private schools, made the bill a political test. Indeed, the Senate committee vote and the ultimate renewal of the act in 1982 was a triumph for civil rights groups which had lobbied congressional members intensively, educating them about persistent voting rights problems (*Congressional Quarterly Weekly Report*, May 8, 1982, 1041).

The 1982 extension of the Voting Rights Act contained four major elements. First, it extended Section 5, the preclearance mechanism, for 25 years. Second, as of 1984 covered jurisdictions can bail out from Section 5 if they can prove to a three-judge panel in the District of Columbia that they have had a clean voting rights record for the previous ten years. Third, the act allowed private parties, under Section 2, to prove a voting rights violation by showing that an election law or procedure "results" in discrimination. It specified, however, that a court would have to look at the "totality of circumstances" in determining whether a voting rights violation had occurred. This provision overturned a controversial 1980 Supreme Court decision (*City of Mobile v. Bolden*, see p. 38) which ruled that an "intent" to discriminate must be shown to prove a violation.

Finally, the act extended until 1992 provisions requiring certain areas of the country to provide bilingual election materials (*Congressional Quarterly Weekly Report*, June 26, 1982, 1503).

The Voting Rights Act of 1965 and its extensions gave the federal government unparalleled powers to protect the voting rights of blacks, poor whites, and other minority groups. And yet, like any piece of legislation, the powers provided within the act on paper were only potential ones. Much of the act's promise depended on how it was implemented and enforced. It is to this matter that we now turn.

IMPLEMENTATION OF THE VOTING RIGHTS ACT

As we have seen, the 1965 Voting Rights Act was a complex law with various means of combating different kinds of discrimination in the electoral process. By contrast with previous civil rights acts affecting voting, it not only further strengthened judicial remedies but also provided for direct federal administrative procedures to counter various barriers to effective minority participation. Thus the act was designed as a flexible response to changing circumstances, and some of its features were automatic (like the "trigger" formula of Section 4) while others were discretionary (like the use of federal examiners and observers). Other provisions took effect immediately (such as the suspension of literacy tests and similar devices in covered jurisdictions), and some were designed to have a greater impact in the long run (like the Section 5 preclearance procedures for changes in electoral practices). How, and to what extent, these various provisions have been implemented are the keys to the achievement of the goals of the legislation.

Federal Examiners

Perhaps the most important initial aspect of federal intervention into the electoral process under the Voting Rights Act was the federal examiner and observer programs. Examiners could be sent into specified jurisdictions at the request of the Attorney General as long as one of two conditions applied. First, the Attorney General had to receive written complaints from twenty or more residents claiming voting rights discrimination—and he had to believe these complaints to be "meritorious." Or, the Attorney General might judge that "the appointment of examiners is otherwise necessary to enforce the guarantees of the Fifteenth Amendment" in the absence of a complaint (U.S. Commission on Civil Rights, 1968, 153). In making this judgment, he was authorized to consider, among other factors, whether the ratio of nonwhites to whites registered to vote was a result of continuing racial discrimination or whether the evidence indicated that good faith efforts were being made to overcome the effects of past discrimination.

Evidently believing that the investigation of the merit of each complaint would be too difficult, the Attorney General has acted only under the second condition stated above. However, citizen complaints have been an important part of the Justice Department's information-gathering procedures, often prompting the Department to undertake a field investigation of voting conditions in particular areas (U.S. Commission on Civil Rights, 1965, 40).

The role of the examiners, once appointed, was to enroll all voters who satisfied state voter qualifications which were consistent with federal law and the Constitution. This list of qualified voters was then sent each month to local election officials who were to enter the names on the registration rolls. Regulations also included procedures for challenging listings and for removing names of persons who lost their eligibility to vote. Just three days after the passage of the Voting Rights Act the Attorney General designated nine counties in Alabama, Louisiana, and Mississippi for federal examiners and added five more counties nine days later. Nevertheless, examiners have been used sparingly, and most served during the initial two years after passage of the act in 1965.

The reason for the relatively infrequent use of examiners was that the Justice Department relied primarily on voluntary compliance with the goals of the act. Attorney General Katzenbach expressed federal guidelines for implementation by saying, "Our aim . . . is not the widespread deployment of an army of federal examiners. The purpose, rather, is to insure that every citizen can vote . . . according to normal and fair local procedure" (U.S. Commission on Civil Rights, 1965, 43). The main assumption underlying the Justice Department's position was that the greatest gains in black voter registration were due to local organization and mobilization efforts, not to federal examiners. In addition, by stressing voluntary compliance, Washington hoped to avoid any massive federal intervention which might create a hostile white reaction and thereby make black political activity even more difficult. Other political considerations may also have been important. Thus, a number of Georgia and Mississippi counties with relatively few registered blacks were not designated for federal examiners until almost a year after passage of the act. Several observers have attributed this delay to an unwillingness to offend important Senate committee chairmen such as Senator James Eastland of Mississippi and Senator Richard Russell of Georgia (Garrow, 1978, 185–186; Lawson, 1976, 332–335).

The Attorney General made it clear, however, that if local officials refused to cooperate with voter registration efforts, then the federal government would intervene. Thus early in 1966 Katzenbach sent letters to county officials in the Deep South instructing them to extend regular registration hours and to establish temporary offices in black communities. When some local officials failed to respond, the Justice Department designated examiners for an additional twenty-five counties. Even with the limited use of examiners, the credible threat of a federal presence seemed to prompt many county authorities to register citizens fairly in order to avoid such intrusions into their affairs (Lawson, 1976, 334–335; Watters and Cleghorn, 1967, 261).

Yet a variety of private groups, including the NAACP, the Southern Christian Leadership Conference (SCLC), and the Voter Education Project, consistently urged the Attorney General to assign federal examiners to more Southern counties. As late as mid-1968, examiners functioned in only 58 of 185 counties in which fewer than 50 percent of adult blacks were registered. Civil rights groups lacked the necessary resources to invest time and attention in all these areas of resistance. Moreover, there was still the feeling among many black leaders that federal examiners have "a positive psychological effect in stimulating fearful Negroes to make an attempt to register" (Lawson, 1976, 333).

When examiners were used, they generally proved to be well trained and effective. Almost all of the examiners were college graduates and federal government employees (usually from the Civil Service Commission). They were carefully recruited and underwent three days of training which emphasized the importance of impartiality and knowledge of the procedures for determining voter eligibility. Examiners were also briefed on the backgrounds of areas covered by the 1965 act. Though almost all of the examiners were white Southerners, they reportedly treated most black voter applicants with courtesy and respect. At the same time, they often held preliminary conversations with local officials of the communities to which they were sent in order to avoid misunderstanding and reduce potential friction with whites. Harassment and even bomb threats were dangers a few examiners faced, but they were heavily protected by the Justice Department. Indeed, the only major factor limiting the effectiveness of the examiner program was the lack of publicity in examiner counties. Since the Justice Department opposed the mailing of notices of the opening of examiners' offices to county residents, many blacks never learned of their presence (U.S. Civil Service Commission, 1966, 5; U.S. Commission on Civil Rights, 1975, 15–21).

Architects of the Voting Rights Act were aware that problems associated with the ability of blacks to vote went well beyond registration. It was possible, in fact, for a county to register large numbers of blacks and still not allow them to vote, or to disqualify their ballots. For example, polling places could be placed at sites inconvenient or hostile to blacks. Similarly, assistance could be denied those for whom voting was a strange or difficult procedure (such as for illiterate, handicapped, elderly, or inexperienced voters). Accordingly, the federal observer program was designed to prevent discrimination against blacks beyond the registration process: the Justice Department could place observers in polling places to ensure that local officials permitted blacks to vote, assisted those in need of help, and assured that black ballots were counted.

As in the selection of places to send voting examiners, the Attorney General had considerable leeway in locating observers although they could not be sent to counties not otherwise covered by the Voting Rights Act. Beyond this, flexibility was substantial. Criteria considered by the Attorney General in determining the need for observers were: whether blacks' names had actually been placed on voting rolls (not merely listed by examiners); whether there were enough polling places, favorably located; the extent to which local election officials were prepared to offer assistance to those needing it; and whether officials at polling places were "representative" of the entire community. Attorneys for the Justice Department as well as FBI agents went to some counties to make certain these conditions had been met. They also spoke with local black leaders to find out their views on the ability of blacks to vote (*Report of the Attorney General*, 1966, 191-192).

Between 1966 and 1980, more than 12,000 observers were sent to nine states, six of them Southern states. Mississippi received the highest number by far (more than 6,000), while Alabama was next, followed by Louisiana, Georgia, South Carolina, and Texas, all with more than 300 each. In the first three years, more than one-third of the total number of observers was used (4,487), while the Nixon years saw a noticeable drop in the number of observers. However, there was a moderate increase during the later years (1978-1980) of the Carter administration ("GAO Report," 1978, 182; U.S. Commission on Civil Rights, 1981, 101-102).

Section 5 Preclearance

Section 5 of the Voting Rights Act required that proposed changes in election laws in covered states be submitted to the Attorney General or the Federal District Court of Washington, D.C., for prior approval. Such preclearance was both central to the law's implementation and one of its most controversial features. Prior to 1965, lawsuits were the major weapon available to the Attorney General for combating election laws alleged to discriminate against blacks. Under the Voting Rights Act, however, the Attorney General could require that changes in election laws be submitted to him to ensure they did not discriminate against blacks or other minorities. While Section 5 seemed to give extraordinary discretionary power to the Attorney General, the need for such a provision was firmly recognized by the Supreme Court. In *South Carolina* v. *Katzenbach*, Chief Justice Warren held there was "ample precedent," when Congress felt the need to deal with a "serious problem," for permitting federal action without the need for lengthy "prior adjudication."

Since its inception, the focus of Section 5 has changed considerably.

Preclearance was originally designed to ensure that after blacks were registered to vote, no further devices would be used to keep them from the polls or prevent their ballots from being counted. But legal barriers have now been largely abolished, and blacks can generally register without the overt harassment found earlier. Instead, the willingness of local officials in some areas to try to dilute the black vote through annexation, at-large elections, and redistricting (even gerrymandering) has become a problem. The effect of these devices, of course, is to minimize the impact which even substantial aggregations of black voters have on the outcome of an election. Much of Section 5 preclearance activity today is concerned with preventing this from happening. Now the emphasis of Section 5 has shifted, subtly but critically, from promoting equality of opportunity to a greater concern with equality of results.

Preclearance activity actually began rather slowly. In 1965 only one state, Alabama, proposed an election law change. It was not until 1971 that more than 1,000 proposed changes were submitted. The total number of submissions through 1980 was 35,000, with the overwhelming majority (30,000) having been submitted since 1975 as a result of the bilingual requirements and extension of the act's coverage to additional states (Voting Rights Act Extension, 1981, 11). The Justice Department categorizes the proposed changes according to seventeen different types. Through 1980, election law changes constituted 22 percent of the cumulative total; annexation, 21 percent; polling places, 27 percent; precincts, 9 percent; and (recently) bilingual changes, 5 percent (U.S. House of Representatives, 1981; 2237–2238).

As might be expected, Southern states have had the most submissions. Texas had by far the greatest number (16,208 as of 1980), all of which occurred since 1975 as a result of bilingual and other requirements stemming from the 1975 amendments to the Voting Rights Act. Virginia, South Carolina, Louisiana, Arizona, Alabama, and Georgia each have had more than 1,500 submissions ("GAO Report," 1978, 206; U.S. Commission on Civil Rights, 1981, 66).

In spite of the large number of election change submissions to the Attorney General between 1965 and the end of 1980, relatively few were turned down. Only 811, or 2.3 percent of the cumulative total, were actually rejected (although many proposed changes were withdrawn before the Attorney General ruled on them). While twelve states had proposed changes refused, the number was unequally distributed: Arizona, California, New York, and South Dakota had five or fewer rejected, while Alabama, Texas, Georgia, Mississippi, and Louisiana each had more than sixty rejections as of 1980 ("GAO Report," 1978, 204; Cohen, 1981, 1365; U.S. Commission on Civil Rights, 1981, 68).

Section 5 also permitted the Federal District Court of Washington, D.C., to issue declaratory judgments on proposed changes in election laws. Prior to 1972 only one such change was submitted to this court, and between 1972 and 1977 it issued only thirteen judgments. While reasons for the great disparity between the number of submissions to this court versus the number received by the Attorney General are a matter of conjecture, it may well be that Southern states felt that the office of the Attorney General might be more sympathetic to statutory changes than the Washington, D.C., court. In addition, submitting proposed laws to the Attorney General is considerably cheaper than engaging in expensive litigation through the Federal District Court of Washington, D.C. Also, the Attorney General is required to rule on proposed changes within sixty days of their receipt by the Justice Department. This means that states can receive a relatively prompt ruling on the changes contemplated. Given the understaffed Civil Rights Division and the large number of submissions with which it has to deal, it is also likely that states have hoped that their proposals would receive a less rigorous examination by the Attorney General than in the Washington, D.C., court, which can operate in a more leisurely and perhaps more thorough manner ("GAO Report," 1978, 200).

A number of observers have pointed to several problems in the implementation and enforcement of Section 5. The legislative history of Section 5 makes clear that it was to be used as a weapon to force Southern voting registrars to allow blacks to register. Nonetheless, because of "norms" that developed within the Justice Department, attorneys have not always used Section 5 aggressively and, indeed, have even softened the original intention of the bill's architects. Justice Department officials have often been willing to negotiate changes in state and local laws in a spirit of conciliation and compromise, instead of using Section 5 in a stringent, even punitive, way. This may have resulted from the desire of Justice Department attorneys to avoid conflict, and to work out mutually acceptable agreements without forcing adversary proceedings. Undoubtedly political motives, whereby federal attorneys were unwilling to offend state and local officials, were also present. The result has been approval of some laws and practices which have not necessarily discriminated directly against blacks or other groups, but which may have diluted their vote or otherwise lessened their ability to participate in electoral politics (Ball, Krane, and Lauth, 1980, 4; 14).

A second problem associated with enforcement of the section has been a shortage of manpower. Immediately following the passage of the bill, the budget of the Civil Rights Division (which has primary responsibility for enforcement) increased by 95 percent; this was for fiscal year 1966. About 40 full-time attorneys were employed in the Division, although this staff was also responsible for investigating Southern discrimination in housing, employment, education, and public accommodations, among other areas, in addition to voting rights. In 1967 the Division was reorganized and the number of full-time attorneys who devoted their attention to Southern affairs dropped to 27 (Taylor, 1971). Throughout the 1970s the total number of attorneys and support staff employed by the Division (not just those whose primary attention was focused on the South and who had responsibility in seven other areas besides voting rights) remained relatively constant. In fiscal year 1972 there were 177 attorneys and 180 support personnel; in 1979 there were 173 attorneys and 205 support personnel. However, the number of attorneys available for enforcement of Section 5 has actually decreased, even with the enormous expansion of the Voting Rights Act in 1975. By 1980 just 19 Division attorneys had responsibility for all voting rights violations. They were assisted by a staff of 16, which reviewed changes in the laws of the 7,296 cities, towns, counties, and states affected by the act (Cohen, 1981, 1365).

Adequate and complete information has not always been available to the Justice Department as it makes its determination, since it has few ways of generating its own data and has to rely on information provided by individual states and counties. On occasion, FBI agents have been sent to secure relevant, on-site materials, but these efforts have been sporadic. Minority groups, moreover, have complained that although they might be able to provide information about local conditions, the Justice Department has often failed to consult with them. Also, while much of the decision making about changes in election laws is based on census data, the Justice Department has not employed a professional demographer to help interpret the information (*Report of the Attorney General*, 1966, 191–192; "GAO Report," 1978, 88; U.S. Commission on Civil Rights, 1970, 969–973).

Next, there is no inducement for state and local officials to comply with Section 5 decisions of the Attorney General. Under other federal laws and programs monetary rewards and penalties (sometimes criminal ones as well) can be offered or withheld to force compliance with statutes and regulations. The Attorney General has no such financial inducements to compel compliance. And while the law does specify criminal penalties for failure to heed the Attorney General's decisions, no criminal proceedings have been filed against any state or local official in accordance with Section 5 provisions. Furthermore, the Southern Regional Council estimated that between 1965 and early 1981, jurisdictions in covered states had made over 500 changes in election laws without first submitting them for preclearance. In 1980, the Justice Department sent 124 letters to covered jurisdictions requesting submission where it was believed changes had occurred without preclearance. Of these, 79 responded, with 78 having made changes in violation of preclearance provisions. The implication of these data is clearly that local election officials have not always felt compelled to comply with preclearance requirements even if criminal sanctions can potentially be applied against them (Ball, Krane, and Lauth, 1980, 13; U.S. Commission on Civil Rights, 1981, 72).

Finally, the Justice Department has no monitoring device to discover whether all proposed changes in state and local election laws have been submitted to it. The Department simply assumes that since it has notified state and local officials that their states and counties are covered, changes in laws or procedures will be submitted for preclearance. The only methods used by the Attorney General to identify unsubmitted changes are the unsolicited notification of changes from aggrieved persons and a review of voting rights litigation by private parties. In addition, the Justice Department has very little way of knowing whether rejected changes were put into effect anyway; and if they were, the Department then has to begin a potentially lengthy lawsuit to force their withdrawal ("GAO Report," 1978, 88–89).

Role of Courts

Litigation has played an important role in the implementation of the Voting Rights Act. Not only did it establish the constitutionality of the act, but Department of Justice litigation also secured substantive rights for black voters and candidates. For example, the Department was successful in preventing the Alabama legislature from extending the terms of incumbent white county commissioners in Bullock County, and in thwarting the disqualification on technical grounds of black votes cast in Dallas County, Alabama. In another case, the Department successfully challenged the discriminatory use of absentee ballots designed to defeat a black candidate for the school board in a Louisiana parish. Elsewhere the Justice Department filed suits to relieve overcrowding at the polls, which might delay black voting, to desegregate polling places, and to protect black registrants and voters from harassment and intimidation. In two other cases federal district courts held that local election officials must assist illiterates at the polls. Subsequent court decisions have resulted in orders that bilingual assistance be given voters in districts with substantial non-English-speaking populations (U.S. Commission on Civil Rights, 1968, 162–164).

In the last decade, the primary focus of court litigation concerning the Voting Rights Act has been on the interpretation of Section 5, the preclearance provision. For the most part, the Supreme Court has interpreted the range of subjects covered under Section 5 broadly, and especially included any change by cities to at-large elections (*Allen v. State Board of Elections*, 1969; Binion, 1979). In a 1971 case, the Supreme Court ruled that towns and cities covered by the act cannot annex territory or relocate polling places without federal approval (*Perkins v. Matthews*, 1971). Forcing Section 5 compliance on municipal boundary alterations was important, for annexations of adjacent areas with large numbers of white voters were a frequent ploy for diluting the voting power of minorities. In 1973 in *Georgia v. United States*, the Supreme Court decided that reapportionment plans in states covered by the act may not be used without prior clearance at the federal level. Although this was a potentially important ruling, the fact that it did not occur until some eight years after passage of the act, and that it has been ignored by some local governments, has reduced its impact. Finally, the courts have also declared restrictive filing fees for political candidates and changes in political party practices in elections to be governed by Section 5 (Binion, 1979, 162–164).

Since 1975 there has been a modest change of direction, with courts restricting the potential effectiveness of Section 5 in several areas. The first area was court-ordered reapportionment plans, where confusion reigned for a number of years. However, the Supreme Court has now granted broad immunity from Section 5 for reapportionment plans ordered by a court, implicitly suggesting a distinction between a legislative plan and one ordered by a court (*East Carroll Parish School Board* v. *Marshall*, 1976). In two other cases, the Supreme Court began to limit the substance of changes which could be viewed as violating Section 5 restrictions and began to restrict the discretion of the Attorney General (*Richmond, Va.* v. *U.S.*, 1975; and *Beer* v. *U.S.*, 1976). In *Beer*, for example, the Court held that only new aspects (those created since 1964) of an election system could be reviewed, and only those plans which worsen the electoral position of blacks may be subject to objection by the Attorney General or the U.S. District Court.

Furthermore, there was a controversial 1980 Supreme Court decision, *City of Mobile* v. *Bolden*, which involved Section 2 of the Voting Rights Act. Section 2, a provision allowing private voting rights suits, bars political jurisdictions from adopting election laws or procedures that deny or hamper a person's right to vote because of race. The 1980 decision interpreting the section held that an "intent" to discriminate (not "effect" or results) must be proved to show a voting rights violation. Many civil rights lawyers contended that "intent" would be virtually impossible to prove. Thus, while the Supreme Court has generally rendered decisions supportive of the objectives of the Voting Rights Act, there has been a shift since 1975 to a more restrictive view.

Implementation of Bilingual Requirements

The 1975 amendments to the Voting Rights Act expanded coverage to include minority populations whose native language was not English. Registration and election materials and ballots had to be printed in a second language, as well as English, in areas of language minority concentration. Bilingual assistance also must be given to illiterates and others ill-equipped to deal with the electoral process.

The purpose of the amendments was to increase voting participation among non-English-speaking groups, especially Hispanics in large cities and in the Southwestern states. Data on registration and voting among Hispanics are shown in table 2-1; they clearly demonstrate that rates of electoral participation for this group are substantially lower than for whites and blacks.

As in the case of other portions of the act, implementation and enforcement of the bilingual provisions have been problematic. By 1978 only six states had prepared plans for compliance with bilingual requirements. Another twenty-one had no such plans at all, including Arizona, California, and Texas, each a major target of the bilingual provisions. Moreover, a 1979 survey of U.S. attorneys in a number of covered jurisdictions showed that little effort was being made to enforce bilingual requirements (Congressional Quarterly Service, 1977, 668–673; U.S. Commission on Civil Rights, 1981, 83–88).

Difficulties quickly arose in conjunction with the scope of the formula for coverage. In Hawaii, for example, the 5 percent formula failed to include several thousand people for whom bilingual ballots would have been appropriate, since they did not constitute the minimum population percentage. Also, several thousand Native Americans were omitted from coverage, since their language has no written form and the formula fails to mandate an oral component for bilingual election materials or ballots ("GAO Report," 1978, 106–109). Finally, the Justice Department has not undertaken any comprehensive evaluation of the effectiveness of the bilingual provisions ("GAO Report," 1978, 109–117).

Perhaps most crucial to enforcement of the minority language requirements have been serious attitudinal problems on the part of local election officials. The Federal Elections Commission reported that more than half of the 403 local election officials it sampled in 1979 indicated a lack of willingness to promote bilingual elections. Half claimed they had never received copies of Justice Department guidelines. Fewer than 30 percent of the officials used television, radio, or newspapers to advertise the availability of bilingual registration or election materials and ballots. In many areas the materials were not distributed at the community level but were only available in a central office. In 20 percent of the jurisdictions surveyed, no bilingual assistance was offered at the polls. In some cases faulty translations were printed on ballots. Many officials complained about the added costs of bilingual requirements, but few had records to substantiate their claims. And many exhibited "blatant hostility" to bilingual elections. One official, for example, said that even more money for bilingual election materials "would not overcome apathy and instill civic responsibility" among Hispanics (*New York Times*, July 8, 1979, 5).

IMPACT OF THE VOTING RIGHTS ACT

Various disenfranchisement techniques, both formal and informal, had served to severely restrict black political participation. As late as 1940 only an estimated 250,000 blacks—5 percent of the black voting-age pop-

TABLE 2-1 Estimated Percentage of Voting-Age Population Registered and Voting

	Reported Registration Rates			Reported Voting Rates		
Year	Whites (South)	Blacks (South)	Hispanics	Whites (South)	Blacks (South)	Hispanics
1964	—	38	—	60	44	—
1968	71	62	—	62	52	—
1972	70	64	44	57	48	38
1976	67	56	38	57	46	32
1980	66	59	36	57	48	30

SOURCES: "Voter Registration in the South" (Atlanta: Voter Education Project, 1968); Donald R. Matthews and James W. Prothro, *Negroes and the New Southern Politics* (1966), p. 18; and U.S. Bureau of the Census, *Current Population Reports*, Series P-20, nos. 253, 322, 344, and 359 (Washington, D.C.: U.S. Government Printing Office). All the voting participation estimates, and the 1972–1980 registration estimates, are based on the Census Bureau reports. However, these reports for the Southern region include, in addition to the eleven ex-Confederate states, Delaware, the District of Columbia, Kentucky, Maryland, Oklahoma, and West Virginia. The inclusion of these traditionally non-Southern states most likely serves to inflate actual black registration and voting figures for the ex-Confederate states.

ulation—were registered to vote in the eleven ex-Confederate Southern states. And despite the civil rights movement, the Civil Rights Acts of 1957 and 1960, and favorable Supreme Court decisions, black registration had increased to only 1.4 million, or 28 percent of age-eligible blacks, by 1960. Although this figure jumped to 38 percent by 1964, the most remarkable gains occurred in the first three years following the passage of the Voting Rights Act in August 1965 (table 2-1). During this period, the number of black registrants increased dramatically from just under two million to 3.3 million in 1968.

By far the biggest increases in black registration took place in the seven Southern states covered by the Voting Rights Act (see table 2-2). More than one million new blacks were registered in these states between 1964 and 1972, increasing the percentage of eligible blacks registered from about 29 percent to almost 57 percent. This sharp increase was primarily responsible for the substantial reduction in the gap between white and black registration rates—down from 44 percentage points in 1965 to approximately 11 percentage points by 1971 and 1972. For the entire South (which included the noncovered states of Arkansas, Florida, Tennessee, and Texas), the estimated gap in white–black registration was only 6 percentage points by 1971, and in the states of Arkansas and Texas, the percentage of blacks registered exceeded that of whites. It should be noted, however, that black registration rates in most states not covered by the Voting Rights Act had always been substantially greater than in most covered states, and that increases in black registration rates after 1965 were relatively low in noncovered states (U.S. Commission on Civil Rights, 1968, 12–13).

What role did federal examiners play in furthering black voter registration? Only 73 of the 533 counties and parishes in the seven covered states were designated for examiners, and just 60 counties actually had had examiners by 1975. Between 1976 and 1980, 31 additional counties were designated, but no examiners were actually sent. In the first ten years after the act, only 155,000 of the more than one million new black registrants were originally enrolled by examiners (as were about 12,000 whites), and approximately another 15,000 rejected or later had their names removed from the lists (U.S. Commission on Civil Rights, 1975, 33–34; 1981, 103–104). Thus federal examiners had little direct effect upon minority registration increases.

Nevertheless, the automatic suspension of all previously used tests or devices for registration, plus the threat of examiners being used, were important stimulants to black voter registration in the states affected by the act. Strong evidence of this has been suggested in a recent study comparing black registration and voting in North Carolina in the forty counties covered by the act with a comparable group of counties not legally covered. No federal examiners were ever dispatched to any coun-

TABLE 2-2 Voter Registration Rate by Race in Southern States

	Pre-Act Estimate (March 1965)			Post-Act Estimate (Sept. 1967)			1971–1972 Estimate		
	White	Black	Gap[b]	White	Black	Gap[b]	White	Black	Gap[b]
Covered by Voting Rights Act (1965)									
Alabama	69%	19%	50	90%	52%	38	81%	57%	24
Georgia	63	27	35	80	53	27	71	68	3
Louisiana	81	32	49	93	59	34	80	59	21
Mississippi	70	7	63	92	60	32	72	62	10
North Carolina	97	47	50	83	51	32	62	46	16
South Carolina	76	37	38	82	51	31	51	48	3
Virginia	61	38	23	63	56	7	61	54	7
Not covered by Voting Rights Act									
Arkansas	66	40	26	72	63	9	61	81	−20
Florida	75	51	24	81	64	17	65	53	12
Tennessee	73	70	3	81	72	9	67	66	1
Texas[a]	—	—	—	53	62	−9	57	68	−11

[a] No pre-act voter registration figures by race are available.
[b] Gap is between white and black registration rates.

SOURCES: U.S. Commission on Civil Rights, 1968, Appendix VII; and "Voter Registration in the South, 1971" (Atlanta, Ga.: Voter Education Project, 1972).

ties in North Carolina. This study concludes, after exploring a variety of independent variables, that changes in black registration rates since 1964 are best explained by whether a county was covered by the act and had its literacy tests suspended (Thompson, 1980). It appears that many counties voluntarily registered blacks in order to prevent direct federal intervention and to retain some control over the registration process. The mere presence of federal examiners, whether or not they actually listed many blacks to be enrolled, seemed to inspire private registration campaigns and further encouraged blacks to register.

Since 1968, examiners have been sent to only two new Southern counties. The seven Southern states are still covered by the Voting Rights Act and black registration continues to increase slowly. However, by the late 1970s a moderate gap between white and black voter registration rates in most states was still apparent. This gap was estimated as averaging approximately 12 percentage points in 1976, with the disparity being about 30 percent in rural farm areas (U.S. Bureau of the Census, 1978, 12–21; 1979, 23). While most formal barriers to minority registration were eliminated by the 1965 act, the Voter Education Project (1976) claimed that a variety of informal factors sometimes serve to hamper further increases in black registration. Many of these informal hindrances are related to black poverty and include the lack of affirmative attempts to register eligible voters by local registrars, restrictive times and places for registration, few minority registration personnel, the purging of registration rolls, and the lingering black fear of physical reprisal and economic sanctions by whites. Moreover, civil rights organizations, whose important role in black voter registration has been well documented, were seriously stifled in the 1970s by the decline of race relations as a national issue and by a shortage of funds, part of which was due to a 1969 congressional enactment which limited private foundation contributions to civil rights groups (*New York Times,* Dec. 21, 1974, 23; U.S. Commission on Civil Rights, 1975, 69–70).

Another criterion useful in evaluating the impact of the 1965 Voting Rights Act is Southern black voting rates. While there is little data available on voter turnout by race, statewide turnout figures and survey data indicate that black voting increased at least through 1968 (table 2-1). Yet by the early 1970s black voting rates leveled off, even declining slightly, and it was estimated that black voting in the South lagged behind the white rate by 8 to 12 percentage points. As might be expected, black turnout was generally higher, and the disparity with white turnout usually lower, when blacks ran for office and in metropolitan areas (Campbell and Feagin, 1975, 137; U.S. Bureau of the Census, 1978, 12–21; 1979, 23). An important finding, however, is that by the 1970s most of the disparity in Southern black–white voting rates (and in Hispanic and non-Hispanic white rates) was due to socioeconomic differences between the races or groups, and not to the lingering effects of disenfranchisement techniques (Verba and Nie, 1972, 170–171; Wolfinger and Rosenstone, 1980, 90–92).

To encourage black voting, the 1965 act had stipulated that federal observers could be appointed by the Attorney General to serve in jurisdictions designated for federal examiners. Evaluation of the observer program suggests that it was fairly effective. Many blacks in jurisdictions which had observers believed that federal observers "deter local officials from preventing blacks from voting and, to a lesser extent, from treating black voters discourteously," and that the presence of observers, when known in advance, "encourages blacks to vote because the federal presence can help to alleviate the widespread distrust of local election officials" (U.S. Commission on Civil Rights, 1975, 35–36). Yet the program's impact on black voting was impaired by black complaints that most observers were whites from nearby Southern states who wore no identification tags and were often indistinguishable from local election officials.

Most important, perhaps, was the black criticism that observers were too passive, never taking immediate action against election abuses. In fact, the exact role of the observers was often unclear. Justice Department instructions were that they be "cooperative" with local officials—but this often meant that blacks felt they were not impartial and perhaps were even biased against them. The most frequent problem was that the observers could never decide how far their responsibilities extended when disputes or irregularities occurred. Observers often merely noted difficulties, which they reported to the Justice Department, but did nothing to correct them. And while they were supposed to assist illiterates and others needing help, they did not always do so, nor did they monitor those who did render aid ("GAO Report," 1978, 96–98).

The gains in black registration and voting have resulted in a substantial increase in black Southerners elected to office. Thus far, this is perhaps the most striking outcome of increased black political participation in the South. In 1965 approximately 70 blacks held elective office in the eleven Southern states, but by 1968 their number had increased to 248, and by 1974 the total had risen dramatically to 1,397. The latest figures (1981) indicate the surge in black elected officials has continued, with 2,535 in office, the greatest increases taking place in states covered by the 1965 act (see table 2-3). As of 1981, 42 percent of elective offices won by blacks were in municipal government, and another 22 percent were local school board members. Nevertheless, blacks have recently become more numerous in higher offices, especially in state legislatures and county commissions. Two of the South's largest cities, Atlanta and New Orleans, have black mayors, as do more than one hundred other Southern communities. The mayor of San Antonio, Texas, is Hispanic; in other Southwestern areas first covered in 1975, Hispanics have been elected to office

TABLE 2-3 Black Elected Officials in the South

	TOTAL[a] 1968	TOTAL[a] (1981)	State Legislature 1968	State Legislature (1981)	County Governing Body 1968	County Governing Body (1981)	Judicial or County Law Enforcement 1968	Judicial or County Law Enforcement (1981)	School Board 1968	School Board (1981)	City Mayor 1968	City Mayor (1981)	City Governing Body 1968	City Governing Body (1981)
Covered by Voting Rights Act (1965)														
Alabama	24	(247)	0	(16)	0	(23)	3	(37)	3	(32)	2	(17)	12	(108)
Georgia	21	(266)	11	(23)	3	(20)	0	(13)	3	(55)	0	(8)	4	(139)
Louisiana	37	(367)	1	(12)	10	(80)	16	(30)	4	(94)	1	(12)	5	(122)
Mississippi	29	(436)	1	(17)	4	(27)	15	(72)	1	(80)	1	(20)	5	(162)
N. Carolina	10	(255)	0	(3)	0	(18)	0	(8)	1	(70)	0	(13)	9	(136)
S. Carolina	11	(227)	0	(16)	3	(29)	2	(14)	0	(58)	0	(12)	1	(93)
Virginia	24	(91)	1	(5)	2	(27)	1	(3)	0	(0)	0	(10)	12	(40)
Not covered by Voting Rights Act (1965)														
Arkansas	33	(218)	0	(5)	0	(0)	0	(30)	33	(81)	0	(13)	0	(78)
Florida	16	(110)	0	(4)	0	(2)	0	(5)	1	(13)	0	(6)	14	(78)
Tennessee	28	(123)	6	(13)	10	(52)	2	(10)	2	(17)	0	(1)	8	(28)
Texas	15	(195)	3	(13)	0	(6)	0	(17)	6	(68)	0	(10)	6	(74)
TOTAL (all states)	248	(2535)	23	(127)	32	(284)	39	(239)	54	(568)	4	(122)	76	(1058)

[a]Total includes all black elected officials in the state, not just those categorized here.

SOURCES: U.S. Commission on Civil Rights, 1968, Appendix VI; Joint Center for Political Studies, *National Roster of Black Elected Officials* (1981).

in many cities and counties for the first time ("Voting Rights Act Extension," 1981, 7).

Implicit in the original Voting Rights Act was the assumption that electoral politics could help to redress social and economic inequalities in the South. If this was so, and black elected officials are the most obvious outcome of black voting, what then have these officials been able to accomplish? Empirical evidence on this issue is limited, but it suggests that black officials have been moderately effective. Several studies have indicated that they have been able to increase social welfare expenditures and improve black public services such as streets, water and sewage, recreation, public employment, and police protection. Many Southern black officials have also attained additional federal and state revenue for programs to improve services for blacks (Button and Scher, 1979; Campbell and Feagin, 1975, 150–156; Sanders, 1979; Welch and Karnig, 1979, 115–117). Furthermore, black officials have frequently provided more symbolic kinds of benefits, including securing the appointment of blacks to local boards or committees, breaking down racial stereotypes, and sensitizing white officials to minority problems. Nevertheless, blacks elected to office have frequently been stymied by impoverished conditions, especially in predominantly black communities, and lack of cooperation and support from white officials and sometimes their own black constituents (Bullock, 1975, 735–737; Button, 1978).

The black vote has often had an impact, however, without actually electing blacks to office. Black ballots have increasingly been able to win concessions and appointments from white officials, and the decline in racist campaign rhetoric among Southern governors has been due in part to the growing black vote (Black, 1976; Campbell and Feagin, 1975, 157). Moderate to liberal Southern whites seem relieved at this change because the decline in racial appeals has meant that more attention can be paid to such pressing issues as economic development, tax reform, and environmental protection. Moreover, Southern members of Congress (only two of whom were black in 1981) have increasingly supported civil rights bills in the 1970s; such support is positively related to the black percentage of registered voters in congressional districts (Bullock, 1981; Stern, 1980). Yet, in the long run, perhaps the greatest benefit of the franchise for Southern blacks has been a new pride and a greater feeling of control over their own destiny.

CONCLUSION

The following sections briefly consider the variables that have been critical in implementation of the Voting Rights Act, its amendments, and its renewals.

Federal Involvement

Clearly, active federal involvement was a prerequisite to successful implementation. As mentioned above, prior to the 1965 act the burden of initiating litigation for voting rights was borne by individual blacks and consequently change was very slow. Although the 1957, 1960, and 1964 Civil Rights Acts extended federal authority over voting rights, state and local officials still had primary responsibility in this area. With the 1965 act, however, local election officials could be supplanted by federal agents who were sent to selected Southern jurisdictions to enroll blacks and to observe elections. Although this was an extreme measure and one not often used, it clearly demonstrated a strong federal commitment to enforcing black voting rights.

Clarity of Goals

Having policy goals clearly stated is also important for successful implementation. Considering the legislative history, presidential pronouncements, and Supreme Court decisions upholding the constitutionality of the act, one may conclude that the goals of the 1965 act were relatively clear. Removal of discriminatory barriers to the right of Southern blacks to participate freely in the electoral process was the major goal, and there was the underlying assumption that the removal of such barriers would help to improve social and economic conditions for blacks in the South. Indeed, the primary ideal of the act was the achievement of equality of opportunity in the electoral arena. With the 1975 amendments to the act, especially the bilingual requirements, the emphasis of the original legislation was modified to extend coverage to Hispanics and other language minorities.

In addition to clarity of policy, specificity of standards used in evaluating compliance may affect implementation. In terms of the primary goal of the act, the standards to be used were specific and clear: black registration and voter turnout rates. These rates were then compared with both black rates before the act and the present white rates of registration and voting in order to judge both absolute and relative progress for blacks.

Once the major stress of enforcement shifted to the preclearance provisions and the effective use of the vote, however, the criteria utilized to judge compliance were no longer as clear. In terms of state legislative redistricting, legislatures have been forced to forsake traditional multi-member districts whenever the Justice Department has seen a possibility that the plan might dilute black votes. The impression given by the Justice Department is that the legislature has a duty to maximize the number of majority black districts and therefore the number of black elected officials (Bullock and Rodgers, 1975, 61–62). But, in general, precise measures by which to evaluate possible institutional impediments to the vote were not readily available nor was there always agreement on which measures should be used.

Monitoring Performance

Another major variable in the implementation process is the monitoring of performance, including the collection of data and on-site inspections. Though the 1964 Civil Rights Act stipulated that the Census Bureau should collect minority registration and voting data by jurisdiction, this was not carried out until 1976. Since 1971 only four Southern states (North Carolina, South Carolina, Louisiana, and Florida) have kept voter registration figures by race. Therefore assessments of progress in black registration and voting have had to rely on estimates generated primarily by local election officials, the Justice Department, and the Voter Education Project. Dependable data on the likely impact of electoral system changes submitted under Section 5 are even less available. In these cases the Attorney General has had to rely on information provided by local officials, who are rarely willing to be cooperative, on aggrieved individuals, and on infrequent field investigations by the FBI or Justice Department lawyers.

The use of on-site inspections, especially the actual or threatened intervention of federal examiners, was quite effective, limited only in its relatively infrequent use and lack of publicity. Federal election observers were only moderately effective, since they were almost always white and lacked a well-defined role. Indeed, with the decreasing use of examiners and the modest effectiveness of observers, much of the monitoring of the 1970s was carried out by minority groups with varying degrees of success.

Federal Enforcement Agency Commitment

The Attorney General and the Department of Justice were given the major responsibility for enforcing the Voting Rights Act. Two key provisions of the act provide the Attorney General with discretion to appoint federal examiners and observers, and to approve election system changes under Section 5. With an administrative structure responsible for carrying out this policy, many of the goals of the legislation were achieved. Yet the Attorney General has encouraged voluntary compliance with the law, since the election process is normally a state (and local) function and federal intervention on a massive scale was not seen as the most efficacious method of enfranchising minorities. Bargaining to achieve voluntary compliance and a selective use of more stringent measures, therefore, were viewed as ways to avoid a hostile Southern white reaction while also encouraging private organizations to become more active in the voter mobilization process. In addition, lessened federal intervention served to placate key Southern politicians who might otherwise obstruct important administration proposals in other areas. Certainly it would be difficult to overstate the positive influence on increased voter registration of such voluntary political organizations as the Voter Education Project, Student Nonviolent Coordinating Committee, National Democratic Party of Alabama, Mississippi Freedom Democratic Party, and numerous local voter leagues.

Difficulties in implementation did not arise because the Justice Department was co-opted by Southerners or because an old agency, set in its ways, was given new tasks. Actually, the Division of Civil Rights never gave any serious indication of not being committed to the goals of the act. More significant problems occurred because the Division always had limited manpower, because personnel were willing to bargain with and accommodate Southern interests instead of vigorously applying the law, and because by 1968 the priorities of the Department generally had shifted northward to deal with urban riots, antiwar protests, and rising crime.

Commitment of Enforcer's Superiors

The commitment of the president seems to have been crucial to the enforcement of the Voting Rights Act. Lyndon Johnson, the most enthusiastic supporter of the bill, insisted that target areas be identified and federal examiners be sent to them within days of his signing the original legislation. By his rhetoric and decisive actions he gave clear signals to the South that the federal government was prepared to guarantee blacks the right to vote. Richard Nixon and Gerald Ford had a much more limited view of the act. Nixon's so-called Southern strategy was aimed at reducing federal pressure in that region, so in 1970 he sought to remove key features of the act and accepted its extension only under considerable pressure. Gerald Ford signed the 1975 revision of the Voting Rights Act, but, like his predecessor, he did make vigorous enforcement one of his highest priorities. Data from the Carter years suggest a slightly more motivated enforcement of the major provisions of the act.

Congress has consistently supported extension and expansion of the Voting Rights Act. Reports of the House and Senate Judiciary Committees are among the most eloquent testimonials for continuing the act. On the floor, amendments by Southern Democrats and conservative Republicans designed to weaken the legislation have been repeatedly defeated. The danger, in fact, has been that Congress, in expanding the bill to include language minorities and more states, may have spread the enforcement abilities of the Justice Department so thin as to undercut implementation.

The Supreme Court, for the first ten years after the act, faithfully upheld vigorous enforcement procedures by the Justice Department. Since 1975, however, the Court has to some extent diluted the Department's capabilities, particularly in Section 5 preclearance powers. Undoubtedly this is a result of several combined factors—namely, a national shift in the political climate to the right, Nixon's conservative appointees to the Supreme Court, and a feeling of discomfort by some public officials over the change in emphasis of the Voting Rights Act from equal opportunity (the right of minorities to vote) to equality of results (protecting the minority vote's utility and effectiveness).

Program Beneficiaries

Those who benefited from the legislation had a hand in its successful application; the pressure of civil rights groups on the Justice Department during the implementation phase may have been even more crucial to enforcement than civil rights pressure during formulation of the bill. Because the legal guarantee of the right to vote did not automatically eliminate all forms of discrimination, civil rights groups recognized that continuing federal activity was needed to realize the goals of the act. During the 1970s, however, black pressures on the Justice Department lessened as the civil rights movement fragmented, and bread-and-butter economic issues supplanted concern with voting rights. Also, civil rights organizations have realized that this legislation can only eliminate legal barriers to voting, and these goals have largely been accomplished. More subtle forms of discrimination, and poverty, both of which continue to prevent many blacks from effective political participation, lie beyond the legal remedies available to the Justice Department and must be attacked in other ways. Finally, since 1975, black civil rights organizations have shared the enforcement resources of the Justice Department with other minority groups; this has served to diffuse demands on the Department. Thus black pressure for strong enforcement of the Voting Rights Act is probably not felt as sharply in the Justice Department, and elsewhere in Washington, as it was a decade ago.

Southern opposition also affected implementation of the Voting Rights Act. Even President Johnson seemed ill disposed to offend important Southerners in Congress by forcing examiners and observers on them. The white backlash of the late 1960s and early 1970s, as well as Nixon's Southern strategy, minimized the federal pressure on the South and localized it to just a few counties and states. In fact, recent years have seen Southern public officials finding new ways to dilute the black vote through at-large elections, annexation, and redistricting, while at the same time the Supreme Court has limited the extent to which the Justice Department can combat these practices.

Administrative Coordination

In general, administrative coordination at the federal level has not been a serious impediment to enforcement of the Voting Rights Act. The Civil Rights Division (CRD) within the Department of Justice was given exclusive jurisdiction to implement the act. The relatively small size of the Division and its overall commitment to policy goals have prevented serious coordination problems. A related difficulty, however, has been the expansion of the act in 1970 and especially 1975. These expansions have significantly increased CRD's tasks, although personnel and other resources have not expanded to match widening responsibilities. This blurring of focus and dilution of overall capability have had an impact on the rigor of CRD enforcement.

A more serious problem, however, has occasionally arisen with regard to communication between CRD and state and local election officials, leading to confusion about requirements (for example, in bilingual elections) and about local conditions. Also, the division did not always communicate or coordinate with local private groups which might have been helpful in providing information about or in monitoring local conditions.

Relative Benefits

The Voting Rights Act contained no fiscal "teeth" which could be used either as an incentive or punishment to induce Southern officials to register blacks. Nonetheless, as long as the president, Congress, and Supreme Court showed enthusiasm for even the most stringent measures that the act permitted, it was possible for the Justice Department to pursue enforcement with some vigor. When the focus of the Voting Rights Act was broadened, when presidential commitment became somewhat softer, and as personnel and other resources within OCR were spread more thinly in trying to implement increasingly vague goals, the cost–benefit ratio of enforcement was reduced considerably.

From the point of view of Southern voting registrars, the costs of implementing the Voting Rights Act reached unacceptable levels. Even in areas where federal examiners were not present, local registrars felt resentment toward the federal government for forcing them to act in ways contrary to their traditional patterns. Indeed many local registrars felt that voter registration had been completely taken out of their hands and that the federal government had undercut whatever autonomy they had had as public officials.

But the calculation of costs and benefits should be considered in a wider context. Clearly, the overall political environment, as well as the nature of the act itself, is crucial to a determination of the degree to which implementation is possible. Public opinion has played a key role in the vigor with which the act has been implemented. Initially, when the major goal of the act was the right to vote, public opinion was very favorable (Sheatsley, 1966, 230–231). The vote is, after all, a major element in the American democratic ethos and was difficult even for diehard Southerners to oppose. Public opinion later seemed to become apathetic, once legal barriers to voting were removed. The public sensed little need for more federal involvement. While Americans are willing to provide everyone with the right to vote, they apparently are not as willing to guarantee effective voting power for minority groups.

A related consideration is that giving blacks, or any group, the franchise is relatively cost-free. However, when the *effectiveness* of the vote is protected (not just the right to vote), it may seem to give an unfair advantage to certain minority groups in the quest for scarce public resources. At this point, the franchise is no longer perceived as cost-free by many middle-class Americans. Besides, guaranteeing even the right to vote has not meant instant acceptance of its use; Southerners have often accepted the principle, but not the practice, of minority group voting. Thus, unlike other forms of federal legislation (such as providing for highways or establishing airport safety standards), voting legislation cannot be a "one-shot" federal effort. The repeated federal efforts to enfranchise blacks between 1957 and 1965 are testament to this proposition. Passing a law does not mean the problem has been solved or that it will disappear. To be effective, voting rights legislation requires not just clear goals and good intentions but constant monitoring. At best, the Justice Department has been sporadic and inconsistent in its monitoring efforts.

Also, unlike other forms of federal activity (such as revenue sharing or aid to education), voting legislation has no built-in, well-organized, powerful constituency that can keep implementation moving forward. In short, voting rights legislation cannot avoid the slings and arrows of changing political fortune but rather is very sensitive to political shifts and transformations. Hence, it is reasonable to conclude that unless high-level federal officials, especially the president, Supreme Court, and Attorney General, are all committed not only to ensuring access of minority groups to the polls but also to preserving the meaning of their vote, the well-intentioned goals of the Voting Rights Act will not be fully realized.

REFERENCES

Allen v. State Board of Elections, 393 U.S. 544 (1969).

Ball, Howard; Dale Krane; and Thomas P. Lauth, Jr. (1980). "Accountability and Discretion in a Federal System: The Politics of Compliance with the 1965 Voting Rights Act." Presented at Symposium on Southern Politics, Charleston, S.C., March 27–29, 1980.

Beer v. U.S., 425 U.S. 130 (1976).

Binion, Gayle (1979). "The Implementation of Section 5 of the 1965 Voting Rights Act: A Retrospective on the Role of Courts." *Western Political Quarterly* 32: 154–173.

Black, Earl (1976). *Southern Governors and Civil Rights*. Cambridge, Mass.: Harvard University Press.

Bullock, Charles S. III (1975). "The Election of Blacks in the South: Preconditions and Consequences." *American Journal of Political Science* 14: 727–739.

Bullock, Charles S. III (1981). "Congressional Voting and the Mobilization of a Black Electorate in the South." *Journal of Politics* 43: 662–682.

Bullock, Charles S. III, and Harrell R. Rodgers, Jr. (1975). *Racial Equality in America.* Pacific Palisades, Calif.: Goodyear.
Button, James (1978). "Impact of Black Elected Municipal Officials: A Descriptive Analysis." Presented at annual meeting of Southern Political Science Association, Atlanta, Ga., November 9–11, 1978.
Button, James, and Richard Scher (1979). "Impact of the Civil Rights Movement: Perceptions of Black Municipal Service Changes." *Social Science Quarterly* 60: 497–510.
Campbell, David, and Joe R. Feagin (1975). "Black Politics in the South: A Descriptive Analysis." *Journal of Politics* 37: 129–162.
City of Mobile v. Bolden, 446 U.S. 55 (1980).
Cohen, Richard E. (1981). "Will the Voting Rights Act Become a Victim of Its Own Success?" *National Journal* (August 1, 1981): 1364–1368.
Congressional Quarterly Service (1969). *Congress and the Nation*, vol. II, 1965–1968. Washington, D.C.: U.S. Government Printing Office.
Congressional Quarterly Service (1970). *1970 Congressional Quarterly Almanac*, vol. 26. Washington, D.C.: U.S. Government Printing Office.
Congressional Quarterly Service (1977). *Congress and the Nation*, vol. IV, 1973–1976. Washington, D.C.: U.S. Government Printing Office.
Congressional Quarterly Weekly Report 40, no. 19 (May 8, 1982): 1041–1043.
Congressional Quarterly Weekly Report 40, no. 26 (June 26, 1982): 1503–1504.
East Carroll Parish School Board v. Marshall, 424 U.S. 636 (1976).
"GAO Report on the Voting Rights Act" (1978). Hearings Before the Subcommittee on Civil and Constitutional Rights of the Committee on the Judiciary. House of Representatives, 95th Congress, 2nd Session.
Garrow, David J. (1978). *Protest at Selma.* New Haven: Yale University Press.
Georgia v. U.S., 351 F. Supp. 444 (1973).
Joint Center for Political Studies (1981). *National Roster of Black Elected Officials*, vol. 11. Washington, D.C.
Key, V. O., Jr. (1949). *Southern Politics.* New York: Knopf.
Lawson, Steven F. (1976). *Black Ballots.* New York: Columbia University Press.
Matthews, Donald R., and James W. Prothro (1966). *Negroes and the New Southern Politics.* New York: Harcourt, Brace, and World.
New York Times (Dec. 21, 1974): 23; (July 8, 1979): 5.
Peirce, Neal R. (1974). *The Deep South States of America.* New York: W. W. Norton.
Perkins v. Matthews, 139 U.S. App. D.C. 179 (1971).
Reports of the Attorney General of the United States (1966, 1971–1980). Annual Reports. Washington, D.C.: U.S. Government Printing Office.
Richmond, Va. v. U.S., 422 U.S. 358 (1975).
Rodgers, Harrell R., Jr., and Charles S. Bullock III (1972). *Law and Social Change: Civil Rights Laws and Their Consequences.* New York: McGraw-Hill.
Salamon, Lester M., and Steven Van Evera (1973). "Fear, Apathy, and Discrimination: A Test of Three Explanations of Political Participation." *American Political Science Review* 67: 1288–1306.
Sanders, M. Elizabeth (1979). "New Voters and New Policy Priorities in the Deep South: A Decade of Political Change in Alabama." Presented at annual meeting of American Political Science Association, Washington, D.C., August 31, 1979.
Scammon, Richard M., and Ben J. Wattenberg (1970). *The Real Majority.* New York: Coward, McCann and Geoghegan.
Sheatsley, Paul B. (1966). "White Attitudes toward the Negro." *Daedalus* 95: 217–238.
Smith v. Allwright, 321 U.S. 649 (1944).
South Carolina v. Katzenbach, 383 U.S. 301 (1966).

Stern, Mark (1980). "Assessing the Impact of the 1965 Voting Rights Act: A Micro Analysis of Four States." Presented at annual meeting of Midwest Political Science Association, Chicago, April 23–26, 1980.
Taylor, William L. (1971). "Federal Civil Rights Laws: Can They Be Made to Work?" *George Washington Law Review* 39, no. 5: 971–1007.
Thompson, Joel A. (1980). "The Voting Rights Act in North Carolina: A Quasi-Experimental Analysis of Policy Effectiveness." Presented at Symposium on Southern Politics, Charleston, S.C., March 27–29, 1980.
U.S. Bureau of the Census (1978). *Current Population Reports*, Series P-23, no. 74, "Registration and Voting in November 1976—Jurisdictions Covered by the Voting Rights Act Amendments of 1975." Washington, D.C.: U.S. Government Printing Office.
U.S. Bureau of the Census (1979). *Current Population Reports*, Series P-20, no. 344, "Voting and Registration in the Election of November 1978." Washington, D.C.: U.S. Government Printing Office.
U.S. Civil Service Commission (1966). *Annual Report*. Washington, D.C.: U.S. Government Printing Office.
U.S. Commission on Civil Rights (1965). *The Voting Rights Act—The First Months*. Washington, D.C.: U.S. Government Printing Office.
U.S. Commission on Civil Rights (1968). *Political Participation*. Washington, D.C.: U.S. Government Printing Office.
U.S. Commission on Civil Rights (1970). *The Federal Civil Rights Enforcement Effort*. Washington, D.C.: U.S. Government Printing Office.
U.S. Commission on Civil Rights (1975). *The Voting Rights Act: Ten Years After*. Washington, D.C.: U.S. Government Printing Office.
U.S. Commission on Civil Rights (1981). *The Voting Rights Act: Unfulfilled Goals*. Washington, D.C.: U.S. Government Printing Office.
U.S. House of Representatives (1965). *Judiciary Committee Report, U.S. Code, Congressional and Administrative News* 2, 89th Congress, 1st Session, Legislative History. Washington, D.C.: U.S. Government Printing Office.
U.S. House of Representatives (1981). "Extension of the Voting Rights Act." Hearings before the Subcommittee on Civil and Constitutional Rights of the Committee on the Judiciary, 97th Congress, 1st Session. Washington, D.C.: U.S. Government Printing Office.
Verba, Sidney, and Norman H. Nie (1972). *Participation in America*. New York: Harper and Row.
Voter Education Project (1968). "Voter Registration in the South." Atlanta, Ga.: Voter Education Project, Inc.
Voter Education Project (1972). "Voter Registration in the South, 1971." Atlanta, Ga.: Voter Education Project, Inc.
Voter Education Project (1976). "Barriers to Minority Political Progress in the South." Atlanta, Ga.: Voter Education Project, Inc.
"Voting Rights Act Extension" (1981). Report from the Committee on the Judiciary. U.S. House of Representatives, 97th Congress, 1st Session.
Watters, Pat, and Reese Cleghorn (1967). *Climbing Jacob's Ladder*. New York: Harcourt, Brace, and World.
Welch, Susan, and Albert K. Karnig (1979). "The Impact of Black Elected Officials on Urban Expenditures and Intergovernmental Revenue." In Dale Rogers Marshall (ed.), *Urban Policy Making*, Beverly Hills, Calif.: Sage, pp. 101–126.
Wolfinger, Raymond E., and Steven J. Rosenstone (1980). *Who Votes?* New Haven: Yale University Press.

Chapter 3

Equal Education Opportunity

Charles S. Bullock III

From one perspective antidiscrimination policy has been more successfully implemented in public education than in many other areas of civil rights. In most Southern school districts black and white children have attended the same facilities since the early 1970s. The creation of unitary schools with biracial facilities and the participation of a biracial student body in a full range of academic and extracurricular activities is an impressive example of the ability of federal policy to achieve sweeping changes against long odds.

It would, however, be naive to assert that the goals of equal education opportunity have been fully realized. Racial isolation remains high in many urban school systems, North and South; blacks continue to be underrepresented on faculties and especially in high administrative positions. Even in desegregated schools, local policy decisions may reduce contact across racial lines. Classroom assignments may result in racial proportions varying widely from class to class. Separation of the races may be furthered by special education programs in which nonwhites are overrepresented in classes for the educable mentally retarded but rarely found in classes for the gifted and talented.

In this chapter evidence of the changes produced by antidiscrimination policy, as well as of the persistence of discrimination in public schools, will be presented after a discussion of policy statements outlining the obligations of school systems to educate students in a nondiscriminatory environment. In the third section, the focus shifts to an analysis of causes for differential rates of compliance.

POLICY STATEMENTS

Numerous guidelines, admonitions, and directives issued by a number of federal policymakers must be considered to understand what constitutes a nondiscriminatory education environment. Major court orders, legislation, and regulations issued by the Department of Health, Education, and Welfare (HEW is now the Department of Education) and its component charged with overseeing equal education opportunities, the Office for Civil Rights (OCR) will be reviewed. In discussing policy requirements, the presentation will be broken down into three topics: school desegregation, postdesegregation treatment of minorities, and bilingual education programs for non-English-speaking minorities.

School Desegregation

Prior to 1954, school desegregation was left to state discretion. In *Plessy v. Ferguson* (1896) the Supreme Court held that the Fourteenth Amendment's equal protection clause allowed states to separate blacks and whites so long as the facilities for each were equal. By 1954 the eleven Southern states, six border states, and the District of Columbia forbade school desegregation. Kansas and three other states permitted local communities to decide whether to segregate.

Contrary to the blind assumption of the doctrine of "separate but equal," the facilities attended by blacks did not come close to equaling those attended by whites. Almost all segregated schools discriminated against blacks in the facilities provided, with Southern states spending from two to ten times as much per student for whites as for blacks (Kluger, 1976, 134).

In *Brown v. Board of Education* (1954), the Supreme Court overturned *Plessy* with the statement, "We conclude that in the field of public education the doctrine of 'separate but equal' has no place." The Court, well aware of the unpopularity of its decision, took the unusual step of not directing the defendants to come into immediate compliance. Rather than set a specific date for compliance, it ordered segregated schools to desegregate "with all deliberate speed."

The *Brown* decision evoked differing responses from Southern and border states. In the latter, some districts began implementation relatively soon. In contrast, the eleven ex-Confederate states devoted their resources to fashioning an interlocking barricade of legislation known as "massive resistance." On the theory that desegregation could be delayed by enacting numerous laws, each of which would have to be challenged in court, Southern legislators boasted that "As long as we can legislate, we can segregate" (Rodgers and Bullock, 1972, 72).

Working against these impediments was the judicial system to which challenges to the South's resistance were brought. Few Southern schools desegregated during this period until ordered to do so by a court. Even when trial courts ruled in favor of black plaintiffs, local school boards typically sought to display their commitment to "the Southern way of life" and pursued all possible appeals before desegregating. The events in New Orleans are not atypical of what occurred in many districts. Black parents sued the school district in 1952. Nine years and $96,000 later, after seven appeals to the Supreme Court and five appearances before the Fifth Circuit Court of Appeals, 12 of the school system's 55,000 black children were enrolled in white schools (Scheingold, 1974, 120). Desegregation at this pace, while of undeniable symbolic benefit, had a negligible impact on the racial composition of Southern schools.

Support for the courts from the other branches of government was slow in coming. President Eisenhower displayed a noticeable reluctance to uphold his oath to "preserve, protect, and defend the Constitution of the United States" when it came to desegregation. He justified his laissez faire approach to *Brown* on the basis that government policy could not force people to change their attitudes about social issues. President Kennedy also avoided pushing for desegregation legislation, fearing that to do so would jeopardize his other policy objectives.

Not until 1964 did Congress, at President Johnson's urging, overcome the objection of most of its Southern members and endorse school desegregation. The Civil Rights Act of that year included three sections applicable to public schools. The new legislation contained provisions that

1. authorized the Justice Department to sue school districts on behalf of black students (Title IV)
2. authorized the Justice Department to join school desegregation suits filed by private plaintiffs (Title IX)
3. directed that institutions that segregated be denied federal funds (Title VI)

The 1964 act actively involved the federal government on the side of black plaintiffs. Prior to 1964, Southern schools were desegregated only when local parents braved white hostility and filed suit. Thereafter Department of Justice attorneys handled the litigation to desegregate many communities. This change largely eliminated the financial burdens and physical, economic, and psychological intimidation which had deterred many blacks from challenging segregation. The Justice Department resources—its ranks of well-trained attorneys, research assistants, and FBI agents—expedited the development of successful litigation.

Also of great significance was the authority to cut off federal aid to segregated schools. In 1965 the Department of Health, Education, and Welfare set out to negotiate desegregation plans with local school districts. Some schools adopted freedom of choice plans under which children continued to attend a segregated school unless their parents requested a transfer. In some systems, freedom of choice was implemented one grade at a time so that twelve years would elapse before all grades were affected. In others, HEW attempts at negotiation were rebuffed.

HEW and the courts reacted to stratagems for delay in 1968 by clarifying schools' obligations. In unmistakable language, schools that had practiced de jure segregation (that is, segregation required by law) were told that they had "the affirmative duty to take whatever steps might be necessary to convert to a unitary system in which racial discrimination would be eliminated root and branch" (*Green v. New Kent County School Board*, 1968). A precise deadline was set with schools being directed to establish unitary school systems no later than the fall of 1970.

After years of dealing with Southern schools, federal officials developed set routines for bringing the remaining recalcitrant districts into compliance. The superintendents of these districts were invited to their state capitol to meet with representatives of the Justice Department and HEW. Following a presentation in which legal requirements were outlined, the schools were given a choice. They could sign up with HEW for a round of no-nonsense negotiating, or they could register with the Justice Department and prepare to be sued.

The last attempt at widescale avoidance in the South was turned back in *Alexander v. Holmes* (1969). Inspired by Richard Nixon's opposition to desegregation, some thirty Mississippi school districts sought to have the deadlines for full desegregation extended. As noted in chapter 1, the White House ordered the Justice Department to side with the request for more time. The Supreme Court, however, ordered that desegregation be carried out immediately. In language designed to clear up uncertainties caused by *Brown*, the *Alexander* decision held that "the obligation of every school district is to terminate dual school systems at once and to operate now and hereafter only unitary schools."

The Supreme Court elaborated on the need for full desegregation in *Swann v. Charlotte-Mecklenburg Board of Education* (1971), which upheld the necessity of a district-wide busing plan in order to achieve racially balanced student bodies among Charlotte, North Carolina's 109 schools. The Court recognized that replacing neighborhood schools with busing would cause inconvenience for some. Nonetheless it ruled that busing was necessary to achieve racial balance in formerly de jure segregation districts.

At about the time that major breakthroughs in Southern desegregation were occurring, the scope of HEW's efforts was being significantly expanded. In 1968 Congress directed the agency to begin desegregating Northern schools. Attempts to implement desegregation outside of the South encountered numerous obstacles. Foremost among these was the question of whether racial separation in the North and West was illegal. Non-Southern school officials explained to federal authorities that whatever segregation existed was not a product of law (as in the South) but resulted from choices of blacks and whites to live apart (de facto segregation).

It was not until 1973 that the Supreme Court, in *Keyes v. School District No. 1 of Denver* acknowledged a possible remedy for segregated minorities in states where segregation was not required by law in 1954. *Keyes* did not, however, hold that all non-Southern segregation was unconstitutional. Instead the distinction between illegal de jure and legal de facto segregation was allowed to remain.

The consequences of this distinction are significant. In the South after 1968, all that was necessary to prove that a school system was unconstitutionally segregated was to show that there was substantial racial imbalance among the schools. In the North, there is a more demanding standard. To show that Northern segregation is de jure, it is necessary to prove that the local government was at least partially responsible for it. In *Keyes* this was done by proving that the school board had drawn and redrawn school attendance zones and located new schools and mobile classrooms so as to keep black and white children apart. In other non-Southern districts, findings of de jure segregation have rested on evidence that optional attendance zones, which allowed whites to transfer from predominantly black schools, or housing policies (the location of public housing) contributed to segregation.

Although it is now possible to win suits against non-Southern districts, the road to success winds through a complex maze of old school board minutes and census figures. These have to be carefully analyzed to prove that over the years *intent* to promote racial separation guided policy decisions. The extra effort notwithstanding, it is possible to prove that Northern school systems are guilty of de jure segregation. If the plaintiff shows that a board of education is guilty of "action and practices that could not 'reasonably be explained without reference to racial concerns' and that 'intentionally aggravated, rather than alleviated' racial separation in the schools," it will be ordered to institute a district-wide corrective (*Columbus Board of Education v. Penick*, 1979). The director of HEW's Office for Civil Rights testified before an appropriations subcommittee that "about 15 times more man-hours are needed to establish discrimination in the North than in the South" (U.S. House of Representatives, 1970, 1061).

Changes in the dominant attitudes in the White House and Congress have further impeded school desegregation efforts. Pressures from President Nixon and his chief lieutenants were brought against the Justice Department and HEW staffers responsible for implementing school desegregation. During the Nixon administration, the Justice Department became less vigorous in pursuing noncomplying districts. HEW lost its ultimate power of cutting off federal aid and was directed to refer cases it could not resolve to the Justice Department for prosecution that frequently never came.

In Congress a series of legislative checks on the use of busing were proposed. Although the most extreme remedy, a constitutional amendment prohibiting mandatory busing, has not been adopted, Congress has restricted administrative correctives. In 1977 Congress prohibited HEW from requiring schools to use busing to promote racial balance. Congress came down in favor of the neighborhood school concept, which in many cities, resulted in mostly segregated schools.[1] Legislation has been introduced which would impose similar limitations on the remedies that Justice Department lawyers can seek. In 1980 a busing prohibition directed at the Justice Department passed both houses but was removed when President Carter threatened to veto it. With the support of President Reagan, conservatives in the Senate have approved legislation which would (1) ban the Justice Department from asking judges to require busing, (2) prohibit federal judges from using busing as a remedy, and (3) open the way for districts which are now implementing court-ordered busing to have a rehearing on the issue. The House of Representatives refused to enact these proposals during 1982.

Table 3-1 shows major policy decisions and court cases that have influenced equality in education. The chilling effects of presidential and congressional opposition on bureaucratic implementation of the 1964 Civil Rights Act have once again isolated the judiciary in its support for desegregation. There have continued to be a trickle of cases, usually brought by private parties, which have forced individual school districts to develop desegregation plans. In some, such as Boston, busing is required even though it has disappeared from the list of remedies sought by the Department of Education.

Although the courts are more likely than other arms of government to demand further desegregation, the judicial branch has limited the change necessary to comply with constitutional requirements. Once a school district has corrected previous discrimination and established a unitary system, it has no constitutional obligation to perpetuate racial balance among its schools. Therefore, if resegregation occurs but school board policies have in no way contributed to it, there is no obligation to take further corrective action (*Pasadena v. Spangler*, 1976). Since whites often leave neighborhoods as blacks move in, the meaning of *Spangler* seems to be that racial balance is something that need occur only once in a district's history. Thereafter some schools can become all black if that reflects the racial composition of the neighborhoods they serve.

The Supreme Court has also become increasingly concerned with the slippery issue of intent. Lower courts have been advised as follows:

TABLE 3-1 Major Policy Provisions Affecting Equal Education Objectives

School Desegregation	
Brown v. Board of Education, 1954, 1955	Called for schools segregated by state or local statutes to be desegregated with all deliberate speed
Civil Rights Act of 1964	Authorized Justice and HEW to actively pursue desegregation through litigation, negotiation, and fund termination
Green v. County School Board, 1968	Elimination of dual schools required
Swann v. Charlotte-Mecklenburg, 1971	Busing cited as an acceptable remedy
Keyes v. School District No. 1, 1973	Supreme Court finds illegal segregation in a non-Southern school
Busing limitations, 1977	Congress begins using its appropriations powers to prohibit federal authorities from requiring busing
Postdesegregation Discrimination	
Emergency School Aid Act, 1973	HEW establishes thresholds for evaluating school policies
Bilingual Education	
Lau v. Nichols, 1974	Court orders that districts educate their non-English-speaking students
"Lau Remedies," 1975	Established standards for bilingual education programs
Reagan Administration, 1981	Killed proposed tougher federal regulations for bilingual education programs

The duty of both the district court and the court of appeals in a case such as this, where mandatory segregation by law of the races in the schools has long since ceased, is to first determine whether there was any action in the conduct of the business of the school board which was intended to, and did in fact, discriminate against minority pupils, teachers or staff. [*Dayton Board of Education v. Brinkman*, 1977]

In addition to restricting the scope of the remedy, the Supreme Court has been reluctant to order desegregation plans involving more than a single district. The effect is to allow racial separation in metropolitan areas where the central city is predominantly black and the suburbs overwhelmingly white.

The Supreme Court has been unwilling to order cross-district busing plans which would produce more racially balanced schools throughout a metropolitan area unless it has been proven that *all* of the districts involved previously practiced segregation (*Milliken v. Bradley*, 1974). The Supreme Court did allow a lower court order requiring the desegregation of Wilmington, Delaware, along with ten surrounding districts (*Evans v. Buchanan*, 1978) to stand when it was shown that the de jure system that had characterized all eleven districts had never been dismantled.

To summarize, the obligations of school districts to desegregate are currently somewhat uncertain. Activism by the Departments of Education and Justice has receded so substantially since the late 1960s that now these departments rarely seek to implement more demanding requirements.

Postdesegregation Discrimination

Now, more than a quarter of a century after *Brown* v. *Board of Education* (1954), many schools still have symptoms of racial discrimination. This discrimination, which occurs in legally unitary school systems, is frequently referred to as second-generation discrimination. It is manifest in several forms. It may involve unfair personnel practices, with blacks being passed over for jobs and promotions in favor of less qualified whites, or qualified blacks being fired and replaced by whites.

Other aspects of second-generation discrimination include intentionally reducing racial contact within desegregated schools. Some districts which had never operated special education programs implemented them coincident with eliminating racially dual schools. By underrepresenting whites in classes for the educable mentally retarded, and overrepresenting them in classes for the gifted and talented, black and white classroom contact was reduced. The designation of ability groups, or tracking, also frequently separates the races by producing a predominantly white top or college-preparatory track, and a predominantly black low or remedial track, with sizable numbers of both races represented only in the intermediate track.

In developing protections for minority rights against second-generation discrimination, it has been recognized that by no means are all assignments of blacks to special education or all firings of black teachers racially motivated. Indeed, if special education programs are operated as they should be, they will better serve the needs of students placed in them than will regular classrooms. Therefore, it has been necessary to distinguish carefully between those practices which are acceptable and those which are not.

Much of the federal policy relating to second-generation discrimination was developed by HEW, although the lower federal courts have played some role. HEW established thresholds beyond which it is presumed that a school is practicing discrimination. These requirements were enforced primarily through the evaluation of school districts applying for 1973 Emergency School Aid Act (ESAA) funds. For example, if black representation in classes for the educable mentally retarded (EMR) exceeded black representation in the school system's total enrollment by more than 20 percentage points, it was presumed that the district was discriminating. If the school district could not provide an explanation that refuted the presumption of bias, corrective action was demanded. The same presumption applied if the review revealed that the proportion of blacks on the applicant's faculty or administrative staff had declined by more than 10 percent since before desegregation began. The necessary remedial action may include retesting children with bias-free instruments to see if their placement in EMR classes was correct. Schools may also be required to rehire improperly dismissed black staff and provide back pay.

In addition to quantitative standards, OCR also makes qualitative assessments of district practices. Thus, for the EMR component of a district's special education program to be acceptable, the district is supposed to show that the participants are taught by specially trained teachers who provide a curriculum designed to meet the students' special needs, and that enrollees make more progress than if they had been left in regular classrooms. Evidence that student–teacher ratios are larger in EMR than in regular classes will raise doubts as to the academic merit of a program. Federal courts have also found some ability grouping programs to be discriminatory (*Moses v. Washington Parish School Board,* 1971). To refute presumptions of discrimination in personnel practices, districts must show that they provide equal employment opportunities and are affirmative action employers. This can be demonstrated, in part, by making recruiting visits to predominantly black colleges and universities. In evaluating both personnel and punishment practices, the Department of Education checks to see if the district has established procedures that are bias-free on their face and if these have been applied equally to blacks and whites.

The courts have set standards for equal employment opportunities for black teachers and administrators. Faculty desegregation was required as early as 1965 *(Rogers v. Paul).* In 1969 the courts held that the percentage of black teachers in an individual school could not be less than 75 percent of the proportion for the district as a whole or more than 125 percent of the district proportion *(Singleton v. Jackson Municipal Separate School District).*

Bilingual Education

In response to a suit filed on behalf of Chinese-speaking children in San Francisco *(Lau v. Nichols,* 1974), school districts were directed to provide instruction in the native language of non-English-speaking pupils. As a result of *Lau,* 334 districts were identified in which there were enough language minorities to obligate a district to establish a bilingual program.

Rather than requiring districts to take specific steps in order to comply with *Lau,* HEW specified objectives that districts had to meet. Ostensibly districts had great latitude in deciding how to go about honoring the terms of the court order. In reality the range of acceptable responses was fairly narrow, so the ambiguity of HEW's approach may have caused confusion and delay.

Upon receipt of a plan for implementing *Lau,* HEW would compare it with the standards for acceptance. Components that must be contained in all bilingual education plans include the identification of students' primary or home language, diagnosis of the educational needs of students not proficient in English, and a program to bring these students to the level of English proficiency enjoyed by other students. The ultimate objective is for every child whose native or home language is not English to be enrolled in a bilingual education curriculum. The Department of Education's OCR measures the acceptability of programs that include the requisite components in terms of whether they serve all of the eligible children. The extensiveness of a program is often more critical in a review than the quality of the education provided.

There are two basic approaches that may be incorporated into a bilingual education program. The one apparently most often favored by Hispanics calls for an extensive program to deal with aspects of students' cultural backgrounds as well as teaching courses in the students' native tongue. Programs of this type are intended to develop fluency in English while maintaining fluency in the native tongue. In contrast, Orientals seem more in favor of intensive programs which will prepare their children to handle English as soon as possible. This approach, which teaches English as a foreign language, lacks a maintenance component for the student's native tongue. It is expected that once a student's English proficiency is adequate she or he will move into regular classes. The second approach conforms more to the American melting-pot tradition. During the Carter administration the emphasis was on the former, more extensive program. The Reagan administration, in keeping with its philosophy of giving more authority to the states, is more tolerant of local variations in approach.

IMPLEMENTATION

School Desegregation

Responses to the declaration that separate but equal schools were unconstitutional differed along regional lines. In Washington, D.C., and the border states there was relatively little delay in taking steps toward compliance. Many districts, including a number of large urban ones, removed legal obstacles which had separated the races. In smaller border state districts racial balance among schools was frequently achieved soon after the *Brown* orders.

Table 3-2 traces the increase in the actual proportion of black pupils attending school with whites in the South and border areas. Delaware and West Virginia, border states with the fewest black students, took the lead and desegregated while Oklahoma and Maryland hung back. By

TABLE 3-2 Percentage of Black Students Attending School with Whites, 1954–1973

	1954–55	55–56	56–57	57–58	58–59	59–60	60–61	61–62	62–63	63–64	64–65	65–66	66–67	68–69	70–71	72–73
AL	0.0	0.0	0.0	0.0	0.0	0.0	0.0	0.0	0.0	*	*	0.4	4.7	14.4	79.9	83.6
AK	*	*	*	0.1	0.1	0.1	0.1	0.1	0.2	0.3	0.8	4.4	15.1	28.9	91.4	98.4
FL	0.0	0.0	0.0	0.0	0.0	0.3	*	0.3	0.7	1.5	2.7	9.8	20.8	40.9	90.2	96.5
GA	0.0	0.0	0.0	0.0	0.0	0.0	0.0	*	*	0.1	0.4	2.7	9.9	23.6	83.2	86.8
LA	0.0	0.0	0.0	0.0	0.0	0.0	*	*	*	0.6	1.1	0.7	3.5	18.1	76.0	83.0
MS	0.0	0.0	0.0	0.0	0.0	0.0	0.0	0.0	0.0	0.0	*	0.6	3.2	11.8	89.2	91.5
N.C.	0.0	0.0	0.0	*	*	*	*	0.1	0.3	0.5	1.4	5.2	15.6	41.0	93.2	99.5
S.C.	0.0	0.0	0.0	0.0	0.0	0.0	0.0	0.0	0.0	*	0.1	1.5	6.0	20.7	92.7	93.9
TN	0.0	0.1	0.1	0.1	0.1	0.1	0.2	0.8	1.1	2.7	5.4	16.3	31.7	41.3	74.2	80.0
TX	*	1.1	1.4	1.4	1.2	1.2	1.2	1.3	2.3	5.5	7.8	17.2	47.3	56.5	85.9	92.9
VA	0.0	0.0	0.0	0.0	*	0.1	0.1	0.2	0.5	1.6	5.2	11.5	24.8	42.0	89.7	99.4
South	.001	.115	.144	.151	.132	.160	.162	.241	.453	1.17	2.25	6.1	16.8	32.0	79.0	86.0
DE	2.0	11.0	28.5	36.2	43.7	44.1	45.0	53.7	55.9	56.5	62.2	83.3	100.0	100.0	100.0	98.8
D.C.	NA	NA	97.0	88.5	81.5	81.9	84.1	85.6	79.2	83.8	86.0	84.8	86.3	72.2	67.5	64.3
KY	0.0	0.8	20.9	28.4	27.5	38.9	47.7	51.2	54.1	54.4	68.1	78.4	88.5	94.8	96.7	92.6
MD	5.1	15.9	19.1	22.1	32.4	29.3	33.6	41.5	45.1	47.8	50.9	55.6	64.0	68.8	74.3	76.0
MO	NA	NA	NA	NA	NA	42.7	41.7	41.4	38.9	42.1	42.3	75.1	64.2	66.6	69.8	69.4
OK	0.0	NA	8.7	18.2	21.2	26.0	24.0	25.6	23.6	28.0	31.1	38.3	55.7	82.7	89.2	100.0
WV	4.3	NA	NA	38.7	39.8	50.0	66.6	62.0	61.4	58.2	63.4	79.9	84.3	95.9	99.1	99.1
Border	NA	NA	NA	NA	NA	45.4	49.0	52.5	51.8	54.8	58.3	68.9	71.7	74.8	50.4	53.5

*Less than 0.05 percent
NA = Not Available
SOURCE: *Statistical Summary and Southern Education Report*, various issues (Nashville: Southern Education Reporting Service).

the fall of 1966 all of Delaware's black pupils attended desegregated schools and, in the border states, seven of ten blacks were in desegregated schools.

Except for a handful of districts on the periphery of the South, school officials in the ex-Confederate states took no steps to implement *Brown*. Instead leaders of these states concentrated on defiant rhetoric and the creation of obstacles to federal authority.

Amid the general defiance, the mass meetings of angry whites, the covert gatherings of armed klansmen, the threats and bombings, it is easy to overlook the initial steps toward compliance. Those who had rejected *Brown* with promises of "Never" and boasts of "No, not one" had complete control of the situation in only five states of the Deep South. When fifty-seven black children enrolled in white schools in four Mississippi districts in 1964, desegregation had begun in all Southern states.

The token nature of the changes in the South is readily apparent in table 3-2. In 1959 fewer than 25 blacks per 10,000 had white classmates. Not until 1963 did Southern desegregation reach even one percent.

The miniscule progress in the South during the first decade after *Brown* had several causes. Southern whites were more resolutely committed to racial separation than were even neighboring border-state whites. Racist attitudes among the masses and ambition among their leaders fed upon one another. In many communities politicians vied with one another in trying to prove greater commitment to the concept of white superiority. Some political figures who might have played down racial issues concluded that this component of the political world was so salient to so many voters that anything but an extremist stand risked defeat. For example, George Wallace lost his first bid to become Alabama's governor while running as a relative moderate. He decided never to be defeated again by a more strident opponent of desegregation, vowing that "They out-niggered me that time, but they'll never do it again" (Sherrill, 1968, 314). With the moderates silenced, the field was largely abandoned to those who mouthed the racial hatred of the revitalized Ku Klux Klan and its country-club cousin, the White Citizens Council.

In the face of such opposition the only way to challenge school district policy, prior to 1964, was to sue the school board. Since there were more than 2,200 school districts in the South and since almost none of them were willing to desegregate until ordered to do so by a judge, tremendous amounts of litigation would have been needed.

The NAACP Legal Defense Fund and other civil rights organizations matched the lawyers with local black parents serving as plaintiffs. However, in a number of rural communities social and economic pressures against potential black plaintiffs proved unbearable. The price for suing the school board might be loss of a job, loss of credit, or threatened loss of life. These tactics, not surprisingly, dissuaded some potential litigants. However, blacks in urban areas were less susceptible to such pressures because of the anonymity afforded by a city, and also less likely to be faced with such pressures because of greater white tolerance in cities. Consequently, the initial desegregation in the Deep South came following court orders directed at city schools in Atlanta, Charlotte-Mecklenburg, New Orleans, and other urban areas.

Initial desegregation successes are impressive in magnitude only when viewed against the history of total segregation. School boards, more often than not, delayed the process by pursuing every possible appeal. Once avoidance became impossible, some districts narrowly construed court orders directed at them, thereby minimizing their impact. In some well-publicized instances the few children allowed to enter white schools were subjected to harrowing experiences as they ran a gauntlet of jeering whites.

The authors of the Civil Rights Act of 1964 recognized that if school desegregation was to advance beyond tokenism, implementation could not be restricted to private litigation. The pace of desegregation quickened after the cutoff of federal education funds and federally sponsored litigation were authorized in 1964.

Passage of the Elementary and Secondary Education Act in 1965 and the subsequent increase in federal aid to education provided HEW with the leverage necessary to negotiate plans with most Southern schools. The negotiation strategy was made easier as the criteria for what constituted an acceptable school district response were escalated gradually. For example, a district could sign a commitment in 1965 pledging that it no longer segregated and receive the new federal funds even if there was little—or even no—desegregation. Having received the money, there was an incentive to do whatever was necessary, that is, to step up efforts to desegregate, in order to continue the activities inaugurated with the initial round of federal funding. The gradualism of the mid-1960s, unlike that of previous years, had advantages because schools were actually making changes when faced with unrelenting federal pressures.

School districts could still delay implementation, but the outer limits of delay were much more distinct than before 1964. Once it became obvious that a district would not negotiate a desegregation plan, the district would be sued by the Justice Department. Even the 200 districts that had been unwilling to negotiate a final desegregation plan in order to qualify for federal dollars did not stand long against unfavorable court decisions (Rodgers and Bullock, 1976).

The three-pronged attack on school segregation (HEW's threat of fund cut-offs, suits by the Department of Justice, and private suits) produced noticeable desegregation during the late 1960s. Data in table 3-2 show massive changes in each Southern state between 1968 and 1970. By 1972 more than 90 percent of the blacks in seven states were in schools with some whites. While many still attended predominantly black schools, the changes registered in table 3-2 for every state are impressive.

By the early 1970s most Southern and border districts with 10,000 or fewer pupils had implemented plans which produced approximately the same racial proportions throughout the district. Typically this was accomplished through combining what had been separate black and white schools, closing some which were in poorest repair, and enlarging others.

Particularly in big-city districts, however, some virtually all-white and virtually all-black schools were likely to remain even under the final desegregation plan accepted by federal authorities. While research by Lambda Corporation (1971) disputes the validity of this explanation, urban schools have claimed that travel time, distance, and the location of black and white neighborhoods preclude anything approaching racial balance.

In cities such as Atlanta and Washington, D.C., the number of white students is too small to permit anything more than a sprinkling of white faces in overwhelmingly black schools should a plan for racial balance be implemented. The futility of such a move, which might trigger further white withdrawals from the city's public schools, has been widely accepted by school desegregation implementers. Indeed in Atlanta the local NAACP chapter dropped its demands for additional desegregation in return for a guarantee that the next superintendent and a share of the other top administrators would be black. The terms of this agreement have now been honored.

While Southern big-city schools tend to be less desegregated than those in rural areas and small cities, schools in Northern cities typically have higher levels of racial isolation than in comparable Southern cities. For example, the public school enrollments of Jacksonville, Florida, and Milwaukee, Wisconsin, are almost identical and the percentage of the black population is similar, yet racial isolation is more pronounced in the Northern city. The same pattern (see table 3-3) emerges for other comparisons: Tampa and San Diego; Pinellas County, Florida, and Clark County, Nevada; Charlotte and Boston. There are some instances to the contrary—for example, Seattle and San Antonio, San Francisco and Palm Beach.

A comparison of the figures for 1970 and 1976 on the proportion of blacks in majority black schools shows that racial isolation increased most often in border state districts. In 44 percent of the border state districts shown in table 3-3, racial isolation increased—both in predominantly black districts (Baltimore City) and in those with few blacks (Baltimore County). Approximately one-quarter of the Northern and Southern districts experienced increased racial isolation.

If we look at table 3-3 from a different perspective, we see that Southern districts were more likely to substantially reduce racial isolation than were other districts. Of the Southern districts, 38 percent reduced racial isolation by more than 20 percentage points between 1970 and 1976. This compares with 26 percent of the Northern districts and none of the border districts.

Table 3-4 shows that the South has been the nation's least segregated region since 1970. In 1976, the last year for which complete data are available, the South has a larger share of its black pupils in majority white schools and a smaller share in the most racially isolated black schools. The border states are the least desegregated.

District composition is a possible factor in explaining regional differences. Southern school districts are frequently county-wide, while in the North they are more commonly subunits of counties. Southern urban districts are therefore more likely to include not only the central city but some share of the suburbs (Orfield, 1978). For example, a single district serves all of Miami and surrounding Dade County. In geographically larger districts it is more difficult for whites to move out of the city to avoid schools with higher black enrollments.

To summarize the results of desegregation policy, we see that after years of almost imperceptible change, the pace of Southern desegregation accelerated rapidly beginning in the mid-1960s. Within five years, the South had not only caught up with the border states that had begun desegregating earlier, it had eclipsed them. Indeed, by 1970 what had been unthinkable to many had come to pass. The South was less segregated than the North. The racial isolation that remained was an urban phenomenon. But even in the largest cities, the South had done a more thorough job of desegregating than had other regions.

Postdesegregation Discrimination

The reluctance of school officials to accept the directions implicit in *Brown* has, not infrequently, been manifest in the treatment accorded blacks once facilities were desegregated. Postdesegregation discrimination has been directed at both black students and staff. In assessing trends in second-generation discrimination, two aspects will be considered: assignment of pupils to classes for the educable mentally retarded (EMR) and staffing.

EMR classes were frequently the first type of special education established by a school system, and their inauguration often coincided with the creation of a unitary system. EMR programs which consist disproportionately of black youngsters and are underfunded create a strong presumption that the motivating factor was not to meet student needs but rather to perpetuate second-class educations for blacks (American Friends Service Committee et al., 1970). Specialists at the Department of Education's OCR who have monitored assignments to special education classes perceive that the EMR classification allows teachers and admin-

TABLE 3-3 Selected Characteristics of the Nation's 50 Largest School Districts

	Enrollment 1976	% Black in System 1970	% Black in System 1976	% Black in Majority Black Schools 1970	% Black in Majority Black Schools 1976	2nd-Generation Discrimination, 1976 EMR	% Bilingual Being Served 1976
New York	1,076,325	34.5	37.9	51.5	57.6	0.50	51.8
Los Angeles	601,703	24.1	24.5	86.0	74.7	1.05	I
Chicago	520,742	54.8	59.6	94.3	95.4	1.00	39.7
Philadelphia	260,857	60.5	62.4	90.9	92.4	0.65	100.0
Dade County (Miami)	240,023	25.4	27.9	64.2	57.3	1.80	5.6
Detroit	238,209	63.8	79.3	93.0	91.7	0.30	25.7
Houston	204,843	35.6	43.1	84.3	77.1	0.70	50.4
Baltimore City	159,781	67.1	75.0	90.6	94.8	0.65	24.3
Prince Georges County, MD	143,720	19.9	37.5	57.8	41.5	1.40	100.0
Dallas	138,926	33.8	46.7	93.7	69.6	0.95	52.1
Broward County, FL	136,576	23.2	21.5	47.9	25.3	2.90	87.7
Fairfax County, VA	134,507	3.2	4.6	0.0	0.0	1.00	23.5
District of Columbia	125,058	94.6	95.1	98.8	99.6	0.20	56.0
Memphis	121,155	51.5	70.6	93.5	88.9	0.75	10.9
Baltimore County, MD	120,731	3.8	7.6	0.0	20.5	0.60	55.4
San Diego	119,988	12.4	14.5	53.9	35.3	0.85	63.6
Cleveland	119,520	57.6	58.2	95.6	94.8	0.55	78.4
Jefferson County, KY	118,718	3.6	24.7	M	M	1.20	8.4
Montgomery County, MD	116,816	5.1	9.5	0.0	5.5	0.35	100.0
Hillsborough County (Tampa)	114,911	19.4	19.6	71.6	5.3	1.75	13.9
Duval County (Jacksonville)	109,536	29.4	33.2	74.4	42.0	2.15	19.7
Milwaukee	108,798	26.0	37.5	87.8	56.5	0.75	28.2
Columbus, OH	96,993	26.9	32.3	74.1	62.6	0.80	7.3
New Orleans	92,202	69.5	80.3	90.9	91.7	0.70	47.1
Pinellas County, FL	89,787	16.2	16.4	54.5	3.8	2.35	16.1

	1976	1970	1976	1970	1976	EMR	1976
Dekalb County, GA	85,162	6.3	20.4	23.0	73.5	1.75	24.7
Saint Louis	84,524	65.6	71.8	97.5	94.9	0.35	0.0
Orange County (Orlando)	83,792	18.1	20.7	59.3	41.6	2.40	25.2
Clark County, NV	82,881	13.0	14.8	37.7	10.3	2.25	87.0
Albuquerque	82,825	2.4	2.9	10.1	0.0	0.15	41.0
Atlanta	82,438	68.7	88.3	93.4	95.6	0.20	61.7
Indianapolis	81,936	35.8	45.6	79.5	60.9	1.05	40.5
Jefferson County, CO	80,296	0.1	0.4	0.0	0.0	*	15.6
Charlotte-Mecklenburg	79,731	30.8	35.6	8.5	10.9	2.20	7.9
Nashville	77,649	24.6	30.4	75.0	43.6	1.65	13.7
Anne Arundel, MD	77,647	13.0	13.0	17.6	9.7	1.25	78.8
Denver	74,783	14.7	20.8	38.2	16.1	0.90	100.0
Boston	73,782	29.8	42.6	72.0	46.7	I	95.8
Fort Worth	72,206	26.7	34.6	M	M	0.65	72.0
Newark	71,692	72.2	72.6	91.2	94.7	0.60	99.9
Palm Beach	70,900	27.5	29.8	69.7	33.0	2.25	98.3
Jefferson Parish, LA	69,662	20.8	23.5	51.3	6.9	1.25	37.3
East Baton Rouge	68,134	38.6	38.8	78.0	73.8	2.05	13.7
San Francisco	67,704	28.5	29.1	57.6	11.6	1.30	30.5
Cincinnati	65,651	45.0	52.8	83.1	87.0	0.35	2.1
San Antonio	65,475	15.3	15.8	48.1	53.1	0.15	35.9
Mobile	65,419	44.5	44.3	81.8	71.5	1.35	13.0
El Paso	64,531	3.0	3.3	0.0	0.0	0.20	38.1
Seattle	61,819	12.8	17.4	40.7	33.3	0.80	77.9
Tulsa	61,147	13.7	18.8	72.5	67.9	1.65	0.0

*Too few blacks

I = Impossible to calculate from data available
M = Missing data

SOURCES: HEW, *Directory of Elementary and Secondary School Districts and Schools in Selected Districts, 1970–1971 and 1976–1977*, vols. 1 and 2 (Washington, D.C.: U.S. Government Printing Office, 1972 and 1979).

TABLE 3-4 Proportion of Black Students in Schools with Fewer than 50 Percent Blacks, and 99–100 Percent Blacks, 1968–1980

	1968	1970	1972	1974	1976	1980
National						
0–49.9% Black	23.4	34.0 (33.1)	37.9 (36.3)	39.2	40.0	37.1
99–100% Black	39.7	24.2 (14.0)	20.5 (11.2)	19.5	17.9	NA
South						
0–49.9% Black	18.4	40.1 (40.3)	46.3 (46.3)	47.1	47.1	42.9
99–100% Black	68.0	21.0 (14.4)	14.0 (8.7)	12.1	11.6	NA
Border & D.C.						
0–49.9% Black	28.4	21.8 (28.7)	25.7 (31.8)	30.1	29.8	40.8
99–100% Black	25.2	49.6 (24.1)	46.6 (23.6)	42.5	38.1	NA
North						
0–49.9% Black	27.6	37.2 (27.6)	41.5 (31.8)	42.4	42.5	NA
99–100% Black	30.9	22.6 (11.7)	17.2 (10.9)	15.8	14.4	NA

NA = Not Available

SOURCES: Data not in parentheses for 1970–1976 are from Office for Civil Rights, "Users' Guide and National and Regional Summaries" (Washington, D.C.: HEW, 1978). This is a smaller sample of districts than was used in 1968. Data in parentheses for 1970–1972 are from a larger sample which is more equivalent to the 1968 figures. The larger sample includes many small districts in which there is little racial isolation; therefore the numbers in parentheses indicate more extensive implementation of desegregation requirements. These data are from "Fall 1972 Racial and Ethnic Enrollment in Public Elementary and Secondary Schools" (Washington, D.C.: Office for Civil Rights, 1973). Data for 1968 from *HEW News*, June 18, 1971. Data for 1980 from Gary Orfield, "Desegregation of Black and Hispanic Students from 1968 to 1980" (Washington, D.C.: Joint Center for Political Studies, 1982).

istrators great potential for abuse. EMR children's scores on standardized tests may be only marginally lower than those of students in regular classes. The discretionary nature of assignments to EMR classes is captured in this statement by an experienced OCR staffer.

> There's not much reason for the EMR category. . . . There's no decent way to measure potential. . . . These kids' potential is not limited, they've been denied experiences. You're just measuring what they've been exposed to, like working with blocks and scissors. Stanford-Binet and the revised version of WISC [IQ tests] are typically used in classifying kids for EMR. These tests measure where you've been [i.e., your experiences]. [Interview by Bullock]

Some scholars agree that the tests used by school systems to determine who should be placed in EMR classes tap previous experiences rather than ability (Clement, Eisenhart, and Wood, 1976; Mercer, 1974). Tests of experience tend to favor children from upper- or middle-class homes.

All of this is not to deny that a properly designed and administered EMR program can be a useful educational tool. The judgment voiced by OCR specialists and nongovernment civil rights monitors, however, is that all too often EMR does more harm than good (American Friends Service Committee et al., 1970). The caliber of the teachers and materials may not provide EMR children with an education superior to what they would receive in regular classrooms. Contributing to the harmful aspects of EMR, assignment to these classes carries the stigma of retardation. This may result in teachers expecting less and students trying less, leading to a self-fulfilling prophecy.

A second aspect of second-generation discrimination is black representation on faculties. When desegregation made it impossible to restrict black faculty members to contact with black students exclusively, some black teachers were fired and many black administrators were demoted. Subsequently there have been charges of discrimination in hiring and promotions.

For both types of postdesegregation discrimination, violation of ESAA thresholds simply creates a presumption of discrimination, which a school district may be able to refute. Where the distribution of blacks and whites diverges greatly from what would be expected through chance or random assignment, the presumption of intentional discrimination may be difficult to refute. The Emergency School Aid Act of 1973 set thresholds of a 20 percentage-point overrepresentation of blacks in EMR classes or a 10 percent decline in the proportion of black educators as the maximum deviation which needs no justification.

The means presented in table 3-5 are calculated so that scores in excess of 1.0 indicate black overrepresentation in EMR classes or underrepresentation on faculties.[2] The data indicate extensive black overrepresentation in EMR classes and that blacks are generally underrepresented on faculties. Data from nine Southern states for 1973 show that in at least three-fourths of each state's school districts, blacks constitute more than twice as large a share of the EMR enrollment as of the total student enrollment (Bullock and Stewart, 1979). Table 3-5 shows conditions have worsened in EMR. A sawtoothed pattern exists for the faculty data, with lower scores for the even years in which more comprehensive surveys

TABLE 3-5 Second-Generation Discrimination Means in South, 1968–1974

	1968	1969	1970	1971	1972	1973	1974
Educable Mentally Retarded	3.26 (245)	3.26 (180)	4.27 (418)	4.78 (351)	4.78 (450)	4.75 (847)	5.43 (1,021)
Faculty	1.81 (1,236)	2.40 (437)	2.23 (1,435)	2.38 (716)	2.19 (1,148)	2.39 (801)	2.22 (981)

Number of districts are in parentheses.
SOURCE: Joseph Stewart, Jr., *Second Generation Discrimination: Unequal Educational Opportunity in Desegregated Southern Schools*, Ph.D. dissertation, University of Houston, 1977 (p. 56). Reprinted by permission.

were carried out. This suggests that blacks may be slightly less equitably represented in larger districts that constitute a larger share of the odd than the even year surveys.

Second-generation discrimination is not just a Southern problem. Figures in column 6 of table 3-3 show that black overrepresentation among EMR placements occurs nationwide. Using data for the nation's fifty largest school systems, in only ten is black overrepresentation in EMR programs less than 50 percent greater than the percent of blacks in the system's enrollment (i.e., scores of 0.50 or lower).[3]

While all sections of the country are represented among the districts having strong evidence of discrimination, the incidence is highest in the South. Of Southern districts less than 70 percent black in 1976 for which data are available, 68 percent exceed 1.0 on EMR.[4] The incidence of border districts is second—67 percent on EMR—and approximately a quarter of the Northern districts score above 1.0.

Bilingual Education

Statistics with which to assess the development of bilingual programs are hard to find. From the information available it appears that most districts with sizable enrollments of students for whom English is not the primary language have established some form of program. On the other hand, figures suggest that not all students who need bilingual education are being served.

Once it began to take bilingual education seriously, OCR's initial focus was on 334 districts which were identified as having large populations of national origin minority students. About 20 percent of these districts were found to already have acceptable programs. The remaining districts have now developed adequate programs, according to the senior OCR staff who work in this area. In all, almost 500 districts have developed plans acceptable to OCR. Districts implementing programs must file progress reports for three years with OCR. The agency has also done on-site monitoring in approximately 20 percent of these districts. The results of the on-site checks and desk audits indicate that the guidelines set out in the "Lau Remedies" (1975) are being honored.

In addition to districts required to have a bilingual education program because they have large numbers of limited-English-speaking or non-English-speaking students, a number of districts with smaller concentrations of national origin minority pupils have set up some form of a program. Districts having fewer than twenty pupils in a single language group can get by without meeting all of the terms of the "Lau Remedies."

If we shift the evaluation perspective from the *existence* of programs to the *extent* to which the programs serve the eligible, then it appears that implementation is incomplete. As table 3-3 shows, there is wide variation in the extent to which the nation's largest school districts were meeting the needs of students for bilingual education. Four districts were serving all of the pupils who had been identified in 1976 as needing bilingual education and another three districts were serving in excess of 90 percent of the pool. At the other end of the scale, neither Saint Louis nor Tulsa had established programs as of 1976. In five other districts, fewer than 10 percent of the eligible students were receiving training in a language other than English.

ACHIEVING EQUAL EDUCATION

This section evaluates the degree to which the variables discussed in chapter 1 are appropriate for understanding school districts' willingness to implement equal education opportunity programs. Some variables help explain implementation of some programs but not others, while other variables seem unrelated to implementation.

Clarity of Policy

The need for program goals to be stated clearly seems obvious. Greatest progress in school desegregation came when policy objectives were least ambiguous (Bullock, 1980a, 606–607). As the courts and HEW defined with increasing precision what federal law required of Southern school systems, the amount of racial isolation declined (Rodgers and Bullock, 1976).

The importance of clearly defining policy objectives is pointed up by the sluggish pace of desegregation after *Brown* but before the elimination of dual schools was required in 1968 (Rodgers and Bullock, 1972, 96). While clarification of what was expected of Southern schools was necessary for achieving substantial desegregation, it was insufficient in many of the region's more populous school districts (Giles, 1975, 86–87; Rodgers and Bullock, 1976, 35; U.S. Commission on Civil Rights, 1976).

It does not appear that the 1968 federal goal in the South of unitary schools has been set as the goal in other regions. Moreover, the evolutionary pattern that characterized development of case law for Southern desegregation has been missing elsewhere. Decisions involving Southern districts gradually increased the amount of desegregation necessary to demonstrate compliance. In contrast, in the North, the Supreme Court has provided conflicting cues. For example, in *Dayton I* (1977) the Court seemed to say that a district need do only what was necessary to undo the segregation caused by official actions—seemingly a withdrawal from the system-wide remedy required in *Keyes* (1973). However, in a rehearing of the Dayton case (*Dayton II*, 1979), the Court again called for system-wide desegregation plans. These decisions have produced confusion over what steps Northern districts must take.

The great increase in bilingual education programs also came only after HEW, responding to a Supreme Court decision, specified the conditions under which such a program was necessary. An earlier HEW directive extending coverage of the 1964 Civil Rights Act to national origin minorities failed to get schools to institute the necessary programs. Given the vague terms in which the directive spelled out schools' obligations (a "district must take affirmative steps to rectify the language deficiency in order to open its instructional program to these [national origin minority] students") it is not surprising that it was largely ignored.

Only with the identification of 334 potentially deficient districts and the promulgation of a set of steps which districts were to follow in identifying and serving the clientele group did the requisite programs become common. The extent to which confusion persists over what kind of program must be offered is partially due to failure by federal policymakers to specify obligations with greater precision. Federal officials have intentionally allowed some ambiguity to permit latitude in dealing with school districts having varying numbers of mixes of national origin minorities.

The Department of Education was moving to clear up these ambiguities and had released proposed regulations for educating students with limited English competence. The proposed regulations were withdrawn by the Reagan administration. Since then the obligations of school districts have become so uncertain that a seasoned OCR bilingual specialist commented in late 1981 that "in effect, OCR has no policy on bilingual education" (interview by Bullock). It is unlikely that districts will institute new programs while federal policy is so clouded by ambiguity.

There is also confusion over the objectives of the Emergency School Aid Act—the policy statement under which second-generation discrimination was most often challenged. ESAA's goal—to facilitate desegregation and to alleviate racial isolation—was never convincingly linked to a set of actions which schools must unequivocally carry out. A review of the uses of ESAA funds suggests several goals: to facilitate desegregation, to help slow students catch up through remedial work, or to promote parental involvement in education policymaking. There is some commonality in that ESAA guidelines were based on the presumption that equitable treatment of black students and faculty would promote these goals. However, inclusion of multiple goals typically reduces the likelihood of successful implementation.

While there were precise standards for some parts of ESAA, there does not always appear to be a causal linkage between the standards and the policy objectives. Some ESAA objectives, such as helping slow students catch up through special programs, may even cause greater racial isolation, at least in the short run.

Precision of Standards

Confusion over ESAA objectives is not offset by the inclusion of quantitative standards for funding. The ESAA regulations established quantitative standards for assessing the racial equity of procedures for placing students in EMR classes, for racial isolation, and for personnel policies. Applicant districts that scored above the tolerance levels established for these policies received funding only if they agreed to take corrective action.

The presence of quantitative standards for assessing applicants' treatment of black faculty and students has not prevented a number of ESAA recipients from taking actions that appear to have produced inequities. Although conditions are somewhat better in ESAA districts than in districts that have not participated in the program, the figures strongly suggest that the carrot of ESAA money is unable to fully prevent discrimination. Indeed, the evidence suggests growing discrimination in the South in EMR class assignments.

The apparent precision of ESAA standards is misleading since districts could exceed these by offering a nondiscriminatory rationale. Full adherence to both the letter and the spirit of equal employment opportunity policy may still leave black faculty underrepresented in a system if prospective black educators can earn substantially more by pursuing alternative careers. Racial imbalances in classes may be due to clusters of whites selecting a course at one hour while clusters of blacks choose the same course but at another hour. Students of both races may be motivated by a desire to be in classes with their friends. There are, thus, alternative explanations for patterns which could be attributable to discriminatory policies. Consequently the issue of intent must be resolved. This is often a slow procedure and one not conducive to precise measurement.

Quantitative standards had a greater influence in desegregating the South than in restricting second-generation discrimination. The incorporation of numerical goals into the 1966 HEW desegregation guidelines coincided with increased desegregation. As shown in table 3-2, after the 1968 regulations called for total desegregation, the greatest change of all occurred.

No uniform standards for measuring compliance have been developed for schools outside of the seventeen de jure states. A combination of quantitative guidelines specifying the degree of desegregation to be achieved and a policy statement which clearly indicated that most non-Southern schools were obligated to substantially reduce racial isolation might produce widespread changes in the North.

Further hampering Northern desegregation has been the need to prove that school officials actually intended to segregate. Education policymakers opposed to reducing racial isolation can refuse to act until they have exhausted judicial appeals, since it is only through litigation that "intent" can be demonstrated.

There are now quantitative standards for assessing implementation of bilingual education. The adequacy of a district's bilingual program is determined in part by how many students "who speak or use a language other than English more often than English" are not in a bilingual program (Office for Civil Rights, 1979, 11–1). OCR's national office recommends that its regional offices concentrate their bilingual education enforcement efforts in the one hundred districts with the highest scores on this measure.

Quantitative standards may be useful in determining the extent to which school systems are implementing programs. They are, perhaps, not necessary in establishing a program. Thus expansion of bilingual education prior to 1978 came in the absence of a quantitative standard. Many of even the one hundred least compliant districts already have sizable numbers of their national origin students in bilingual programs. At least half of the students needing this service are in bilingual programs in twenty-three of the hundred most deficient districts.

Enforcement Agency Presence

An enforcement agency currently exists for all of the programs considered here. Given the variation in implementation across programs, it is clear that presence of an enforcement agency alone is insufficient in the absence of clarity of program objectives and standards for measuring change. Indeed the existence of an enforcement agency in the absence of some other considerations may produce little change. Thus HEW's OCR did little to oversee the establishment of bilingual programs during the early 1970s, other than apprise districts of their obligations. The incidence of second-generation discrimination seems to have increased despite the presence of an agency responsible for preventing this. Nor has OCR been able to significantly reduce segregation in recent years. Instead the agency has largely foresaken this, its initial raison d'être (Bullock and Stewart, 1978b).

The single instance in which presence of an enforcement agency has seemed to make some difference was in pre-Nixonian desegregation. Even here, however, it is difficult to sort out the independent effects of clearer goals, more precise standards, and the presence of an enforcement agency. OCR's creation in 1967 coincided closely with the ultimate desegregation guidelines issued the next year.

We can only speculate that the impact of the 1968 guidelines was heightened and the rate of change accelerated by the presence of the new blood found in OCR. With many of its employees recruited from the ranks of civil rights activists and answerable directly to the Secretary of HEW, OCR staff went into the South committed to desegregating schools.

So long as the Secretary of HEW supported these efforts, OCR was able to apply sufficient pressure to secure desegregation agreements from most Southern school districts.

Monitoring

The 1964 Civil Rights Act assigned responsibility for school desegregation jointly to HEW and the Justice Department, and both played important roles. HEW, through OCR, had a monitoring capacity; the Department of Justice did not.[5] The larger staff at OCR enabled it to do more on-site work than the Justice Department. OCR's monitoring capability may account for the greater desegregation achieved in its districts than in those desegregated through litigation (Giles, 1975). Visiting districts, inspecting their schools, and talking to pupils, parents, and staff made OCR more aware of progress and problems and facilitated quicker adjustments to new obstacles.

OCR's monitoring capability may partially account for the lower incidence of second-generation discrimination in schools desegregated by OCR than in those handled by the Department of Justice. While both sets of districts give strong evidence of inequitable EMR assignments and personnel policies, conditions have worsened more in Justice than OCR districts (Stewart and Bullock, 1981). OCR enforcement is more successful in districts where compliance with civil rights requirements is reviewed as part of an application for Emergency School Aid. An analysis of three states' school systems found less evidence of discrimination in districts that received ESAA funds (Bullock, 1980a, 601).

OCR monitoring of bilingual education has a less extended history than its work with the other programs. Data for estimating the degree to which schools were meeting the needs of national origin minority students were not collected until 1976. On-site visits and desk audits of plans have been conducted in districts identified as potentially not in compliance with *Lau*. *Lau*-related monitoring seems to have made little difference in whether districts ignored smaller shares of their bilingual students in 1978 than in 1976 (Bullock, 1980b).

Commitment of the Enforcing Agency

An advantage of assigning a new program to a new agency is that the personnel will be able to devote their full attention to achieving the program's goals. Downs (1967) has noted the tendency of agencies to become increasingly conservative as they age. It is, therefore, not surprising that OCR pursued school desegregation more aggressively during its early years than later or that the importance of this variable is clearest in its relationship with desegregation.

In time the zealots[6] either leave an agency or become co-opted. By the time that OCR Director Leon Panetta was forced to resign in 1970 for pushing for Title VI enforcement (that is, the use of federal fund cut-offs to force desegregation) in the face of the White House opposition (Panetta and Gall, 1971), OCR's orientation had changed. Those whose chief concern was to maintain the agency took over and, in time, acceded to their superiors' demands to go slow on desegregation. This changed orientation may help explain the persistence of high levels of racial isolation in some urban Southern districts and in the North (Mills, 1974, 105).

As OCR withdrew from the struggle to desegregate schools, it acquired as a rationale for its continued existence the conducting of civil rights compliance reviews in districts applying for emergency funds to help facilitate desegregation (Bullock and Stewart, 1978b). Interviews with OCR regional staff indicate that when OCR was first given responsibility for reviewing the civil rights records of districts applying for ESAA money, the tendency was to require full compliance with the regulations. Subsequently some newer staff members adopted a different view of their role in reviewing ESAA applications. They placed a higher priority on helping districts secure funding than on forcing compliance with the regulations. This orientation was promoted by OCR policy under which only denials of funding, and not approvals, were reviewed by the Washington office. This shift in emphasis may account for the growing evidence of second-generation discrimination.

Seeing that adequate bilingual education opportunities are available seems never to have been OCR's primary objective. Bilingual education has been subordinated, successively, to school desegregation, ESAA reviews, and expeditious processing of complaints.

Commitment of Enforcer's Superiors

During the Johnson presidency, the chief executive and Congress were aligned with the Supreme Court in support of federal desegregation initiatives. Immediately on taking office the Nixon administration began throwing sand into the gears of the desegregation machinery (Orfield, 1978, chap. 9; Panetta and Gall, 1971). Within a few months, HEW had been stripped of its authority to cut off funds, and the Justice Department was siding with Mississippi districts that were requesting additional delays before desegregation. HEW employees who tried to secure busing plans from school districts were threatened with firing (*Congressional Quarterly*, 1971, 1829).

The timing of the decline in presidential support for desegregation helps explain why Southern urban schools typically remain more segregated than rural ones. Urban districts are larger and typically have more political power. School officials in urban districts could more often use their contacts and their electoral significance to induce members of Congress to intercede on their behalf with the administration. Urban overtures to members of Congress were more successful, in part, because they came when the administration was less committed to school desegregation. During the Johnson administration when enforcement efforts were more likely to be directed at rural districts, OCR and White House officials were less easily cowed by demands for exemptions from congressional offices. Support from superiors was a critical factor in determining the vigilance and aggressiveness directed toward achieving desegregation.

OCR was further handcuffed when Congress limited its power to require busing. After restricting the use of busing as a remedy, Congress prohibited it altogether in 1977. The Department of Justice, although not yet covered by this legislation, has acknowledged changed attitudes among its superiors and now demands less from districts it sues.

As already noted, the Supreme Court has been more reluctant to find actionable segregation in the North than in the South. And even in the South it has become less demanding. Nonetheless the courts are more supportive of desegregation than recent presidents or congressional majorities. Recent major desegregation efforts, as in Boston, Los Angeles, and Louisville, have all come at the behest of the courts, rather than the Department of Education or Justice.

Congress registered its opposition to second-generation discrimination and, over President Nixon's objections, put teeth into the Emergency School Aid Act (Orfield, 1975, 173-182). Congress extended the life of this legislation for a number of years and, unlike the case of school desegregation, did not seek to curb enforcement of the administrative regulations. Congressional support, however, might have been due to the fact that ESAA had come to be seen as an aid program which required little compliance in return for the money.

Indifference characterized congressional attitudes on bilingual education, until the early 1980s. Congress and the Reagan administration have responded to those in the public who believe that the school's obligation is simply to acculturate new immigrants to English. President Reagan's Department of Education has responded to the patriotic fervor summed up by the statement that "I don't want to be in the trenches with someone who doesn't speak English" (statement of a witness at OCR hearing on bilingual education as related by OCR staffer to Bullock). The administration in effect terminated OCR efforts at bilingualism although it continued to express its support for the concept.

Beneficiaries' Attitudes

When Southern schools were negotiating desegregation plans, blacks almost unanimously favored the change. Granted, there was hesitancy in some quarters about openly challenging segregation, but there were few who preferred the status quo to desegregation. Black parents were active in filing suits which advanced desegregation standards. In some Northern communities, black pride and concern about the quality of education in desegregated schools divided black attitudes about the utility of desegregation. Some blacks were willing to accept greater racial isolation in return for more influence in setting education policy and a larger number of black administrative appointments.

That support for desegregation among blacks would be a correlate of desegregation progress conforms with the hypothesis frequently found in policy implementation research (see Sabatier and Mazmanian, 1980, 551; Wirt, 1970, 305). While the pattern of black attitudes vis-à-vis desegregation seems to show that actions and attitudes of those who could benefit from a program are important determinants of success, multivariate analyses have found little independent role for beneficiaries' attitudes. Once other factors were considered, black efforts were not important in desegregating schools in Georgia (Rodgers and Bullock, 1976) or Northern cities (Crain, 1969, 114, 159; Kirby et al., 1973; Rossell and Crain, 1975).

Black efforts to challenge second-generation discrimination have taken the form of complaints filed with federal agencies and litigation. Local school policymakers may be more responsive to efforts on behalf of black faculty than on behalf of students. An analysis of three Southern states found that black faculty were significantly less underrepresented in districts where a complaint had been filed with OCR than in districts where no complaint had been registered (Bullock and Stewart, 1978a, 16). In contrast, black pupils in districts in which complaints had been filed were overrepresented in EMR classes. Despite some exceptions, it does not appear that efforts by blacks have had a significant impact on the implementation of OCR's postdesegregation policy.

Potential beneficiaries of bilingual education disagree about the purpose of such programs. As mentioned earlier, Mexican-Americans often prefer full bilingual-bicultural education that supports maintenance of students' ancestral language and culture, while Oriental immigrants assign a higher priority to rapid acquisition of English and American acculturation. Although we have no evidence, we can speculate that in communities in which there is disagreement about the proper function of bilingual education, school officials will have greater latitude to procrastinate or carry out only partial programs.

Coordination of Enforcement Agencies

The consequences of administrative coordination for equal education opportunity cannot be readily determined, in part because there has been relatively little actual coordination. From the early days of Title VI, OCR adopted a hands-off approach toward Justice districts and vice versa. If the Department of Justice sued a district, OCR ceased trying to negotiate an administrative solution. Nor would Justice sue a district while it was still negotiating in good faith with OCR.

Interviews with staff members in the two agencies reveal some rivalry (Bullock and Rodgers, 1976b). Justice attorneys disparage OCR investigators for not developing the information needed for successful prosecution. The staff at OCR criticizes the Justice Department for timidity when given an opportunity to establish new precedents and a general unwillingness to sue districts referred by OCR.

While interdepartmental conflict is long-standing, there are instances of past cooperation. Once the courts demanded desegregation plans from all Southern districts, the two departments united to bring the last recalcitrant districts into compliance. OCR's director and the assistant attorney general for civil rights met with the superintendents of districts which had refused to desegregate. After each agency explained its approach, the noncompliant superintendents were allowed to opt for litigation or negotiation. Since these events of the early 1970s, each department has gone its own way, but with neither strongly committed to school desegregation.

No coordination has existed between the Departments of Justice and Education in rooting out second-generation discrimination or in pursuing the goal of bilingual education opportunities, since Justice has taken no steps in these areas. Nor has OCR worked closely with funding units in the Department of Education to use ESAA regulations to combat second-generation discrimination. Instead the relationship between these two units has been sequential, with money doled out once OCR certifies which applicants comply with civil rights requirements.

Cost–Benefit Analysis

Much of the research into correlates of school desegregation has dealt with variables which may affect the costs perceived by education policymakers in coming into compliance (Rodgers and Bullock, 1976).[7] One of the most frequently used variables in cost–benefit estimates has been the *proportion of blacks* in the school district. The assumption has been that whites, fearing black dominance, will be most reluctant to extend equal rights to blacks where they are numerous.

In keeping with this expectation, many studies have found that, from the beginning of desegregation through 1970, districts with larger percentages of blacks were less willing to desegregate than were districts with few blacks (Bullock, 1976; Bullock and Rodgers, 1976a; Dye, 1968; Farley, 1975; Fitzgerald and Morgan, 1977; Giles, 1975; Giles and Walker, 1975; Vanfossen, 1968). These findings apply to the North as well as the South. Once the bulk of the desegregation had occurred, the proportion of blacks in a school system bore less relationship to the extent of desegregation that a city had carried out (Farley, 1975; Fitzgerald and Morgan, 1977).

District size is another cost factor, since larger districts tend to face greater logistical problems—such as time and distance of busing—than do small ones. It has generally been found that in all regions, less desegregation occurs in large districts (Dye, 1968; Farley, 1975; Fitzgerald and Morgan, 1977; Giles, 1975; Rossell and Crain, 1975).

A related factor is the extent of *residential segregation* in a community (Farley, 1975; Fitzgerald and Morgan, 1977). As with the size of the black population, however, there is evidence that residential segregation is now less of a factor in determining the amount of school segregation than it once was.

The *attitudes of local white school officials* affect costs because they are in positions from which they can facilitate or impede the process. Not surprisingly, when they personally oppose desegregation, implementation is made more difficult (Bullock and Rodgers, 1976a; U.S. Commission on Civil Rights, 1972; 1976, 73–75, 89–93). Policymakers who lacked the courage to act on their convictions expedited desegregation by working sub rosa with HEW or the Department of Justice to facilitate desegregation. A former OCR employee reports that

> We would go in and see the superintendent and see that his legs were not strong enough. We'd talk to the board of education and they'd say, 'If you'll tell us, then we'll do it. We're reluctant because the election is coming up' or for whatever reason. So then you'd rattle off something that sounded like jargonese, but said the same thing, which they could show to the citizenry. [Interview by Bullock]

Similar observations come from Department of Justice attorneys who worked on school desegregation. "A lot of local officials had always said, 'Look, I know what the right thing to do is and I would like to do it, but I need a court order to insulate me from committing political suicide'" (interview by Bullock).

In the more recalcitrant Northern districts, such as Boston, white officials do not acknowledge an obligation to desegregate. They continue to believe that segregation in their schools is de facto and, therefore, not illegal.

The *method by which top school officials are chosen* may influence their willingness to desegregate. Appointed school officials are somewhat insulated from popular passions, and therefore desegregation has come more rapidly in Northern and Southern districts which appointed boards in 1967 (Dye, 1968; Crain, 1969, 171–173). In a Georgia study, Bullock and Rodgers (1976a) found that where the superintendent was appointed, schools were more readily desegregated.

Finally, the *amount of change necessary* to implement a program may constitute a form of cost (Bullock, 1980a, 606). Desegregation in the North may require greater change than in the South. Southern urban districts, because they often include less densely populated areas on the urban fringe, had traditionally transported many of their pupils to school. Some desegregation could be achieved by rerouting buses and eliminating the overlapping network which had taken black pupils to black schools and whites to white schools. While some children who, in the past, had walked to school might now be bused out of their neighborhoods, this change was not as novel in the South as in Northern cities that, because of higher density, were served either exclusively by neighborhood schools or left it up to families to arrange transportation. Either way, a busing component to a desegregation plan was a greater break with tradition in Northern than in Southern urban districts.

Another aspect of costs—which blends in with the next variable to be considered—is the *penalties* that are threatened or imposed on a district. Although not universally successful, the threat to cut off federal aid was sufficient to extract desegregation agreements from many schools, especially those which had few blacks. While loss of federal funds was not a sufficiently high cost to obtain compliance from some districts, the threatened loss of state funding was intolerable, and this sufficed to desegregate even the most adamant districts (Rodgers and Bullock, 1976). Civil rights activists contend that had financial penalties been used in the North, there might be less segregation there.

The use of funding to attack second-generation discrimination is quite different than its use in school desegregation. Additional federal funds can be obtained by districts that are not guilty of second-generation discrimination. This approach has been only partially successful. Second-generation discrimination has generally become more prevalent in districts which received the additional funds, but the increase has been less than in unfunded districts.

District characteristics such as size and proportion black are not clearly linked to the incidence of second-generation discrimination (Bullock, 1976; Bullock and Stewart, 1979). Nor is difficulty in desegregating a system a useful predictor of postdesegregation policies. The only linkage is that districts which have more racial isolation tend to have less evidence of second-generation discrimination (Bullock and Stewart, 1979). This may mean that where greater segregation remains, there is less inducement to manipulate class assignments so as to reduce black–white contact. Such a finding conforms to a cost–benefits interpretation.

In contrast with the extensive literature on desegregation that can be placed in a cost–benefit context, no such analyses have been done on bilingual education.

Federal Involvement

In the desegregation of thirty-one Georgia districts, Rodgers and Bullock (1976) found that pressure from the federal government was essential. Fitzgerald and Morgan (1977) report that in both Northern and Southern cities the amount of federal activity was related to changes in the level of desegregation between 1968 and 1972, but by 1974 the pattern holds up only in the North (Morgan and Fitzgerald, 1980). The major increase in the number of bilingual programs also came after federal authorities began actively reviewing current conditions to determine whether national origin minority children were being taught.

Remediation for second-generation discrimination could come about in two ways. One role of the federal government is that of an active opponent, while the other is largely passive. Refusal to fund ESAA applicants because of discrimination turned up during OCR reviews constituted an active effort on behalf of blacks. However, in districts which did not seek ESAA funds, it was necessary for those who believed they had suffered discrimination to lodge a complaint. Evidence from selected Southern states indicates that in districts in which the federal government assumed an active role, there is less evidence of second-generation discrimination (Bullock, 1980a, 601). On the other hand, when districts are dichotomized based on whether a complaint has been filed, only for employment practices is there evidence of less discrimination in the complaint districts. This may indicate that when federal authorities adopt a passive approach, little is done to protect the rights of black pupils.

SUMMARY AND CONCLUSIONS

This chapter gives some insight into the conditions associated with successful implementation. The degree to which equal education opportunity programs have been carried out has varied. For desegregation and postdesegregation discrimination, implementation has fluctuated across time. Of the programs considered here, implementation has been most complete for Southern desegregation—particularly in smaller districts. Less change has been produced in the schools of the North. In contrast, postdesegregation discrimination is most severe in the South. This is in keeping with the hypothesis that second-generation discrimination emerged as a means of perpetuating racial separation once this objective could no longer be pursued by segregating students.

Longitudinally within the South there have been variations among the aspects of second-generation discrimination. Black overrepresentation in EMR classes has grown appreciably. An oscillating pattern has been found for black representation on faculties. As with EMR, implementation of bilingual education requirements seems to be far from complete, with conditions beginning to deteriorate between 1976 and 1978 in many communities.

Perhaps not surprisingly, it appears that there is substantial variation across programs in the variables which are linked to implementation (see table 3-6). Policy clarity and federal involvement are the only variables

TABLE 3-6 Importance of Potential Correlates of Implementation Success in Three Equal Education Policy Areas

	Policy Clarity	Precise Standards	Enforcement Agency	Monitoring	Agency Commitment	Superiors	Program Beneficiaries	Administrative Coordination	Cost/Benefit	Federal Involvement
Desegregation	Important	Important	May have been important	Important	Very important	Very important	Evidence mixed	Unimportant	Very important	Important
Second-generation discrimination	Potentially important	Unimportant	Unimportant	Important	Important	Evidence mixed, but seems unimportant	Little	Unimportant	Unimportant	Important
Bilingual education	Important	Unimportant thus far	Unimportant	Unimportant	Uncertain	Uncertain	May be important	Unimportant	Unknown	Important

that seem to influence implementation for all programs considered. Greater efforts to secure desegregation in the South and to establish bilingual education came once policy objectives were clarified. ESAA goals were uncertain, which may help account for the extensive postdesegregation discrimination which remains.

Increasingly active federal involvement was a factor in expediting Southern desegregation, and a return to passivity has meant less pressure on Northern districts to desegregate or on urban ones in the South to complete the task. Federal reviews have also spawned large numbers of bilingual programs—although most do not fully serve the potential clientele. A more active federal approach also seems to pay greater dividends than a passive one when it comes to postdesegregation discrimination.

Two variables appear to be useful in understanding implementation in two policy areas but not in bilingual education. Where there has been federal monitoring, there has been more desegregation and less evidence of second-generation discrimination. The evidence here, however, suggests that monitoring stemming from the *Lau* decision is not associated with more complete bilingual programs.

A commitment to desegregation by those responsible for implementation coincides neatly with the increase and subsequent leveling off in desegregation. As OCR staffers became less conscientious in demanding compliance with ESAA regulations before approving applicants, conditions in EMR assignments worsened. This decline and the absence of improvement in black faculty may also be partially due to the supplanting of ESAA reviews as OCR's top priority by other responsibilities, primarily complaint monitoring. Implementation of bilingual education may be partially a product of this program's priority with OCR staff, although there is no clear evidence.

Three variables are related to change in one program but not the other two. Desegregation increased when the president, Congress, and the courts were united behind implementers' efforts, as the standards by which compliance was judged became more precise, and when the costs–benefits of compliance outweighed the costs–benefits of noncompliance. Two of these variables appear unrelated to what has happened in post-desegregation discrimination. The evidence on the impact of OCR's superiors' attitudes is at best mixed. The impact of two of these variables on the implementation of bilingual programs is unclear at present. Precision of standards seems not to have resulted in a better record of implementation.

Creation of enforcement agencies coincided with increased school desegregation. It is even more difficult to assess the impact of an enforcement agency on the implementation of other programs since there was no period in which federal policy pursued these goals in the absence of an agency. The role of program beneficiaries seems not to explain the implementation of policies aimed at second-generation discrimination, and the evidence relating this variable to desegregation is mixed. The evidence on bilingual programs is less clear. Splits within and between ethnic communities over what kind of bilingual program should be operated may be a factor in the slowness of implementation in some communities.

The final variable, administrative coordination, has not been a factor largely because it has been frequently absent. Of course, it is possible that had there been some coordination it might have facilitated implementation.

It is possible that some variables cited here as important may actually make little independent contribution to the explanation of differences in implementation. The relationship glimpsed in rough outline here might prove spurious once the effects of other variables are held constant. Yet another possibility is that implementation is affected by the interaction of two or more variables. Moreover, factors beyond the control of school districts may affect implementation. Thus it is possible that blacks are underrepresented on the faculty in some districts, not because of discrimination, but because the demand for those with college degrees is such that they can earn much more in fields other than teaching.

NOTES

1. The effect of this legislation was mostly symbolic since HEW had already bowed to political pressures and was no longer demanding busing plans.
2. Means in table 3-5 are based on figures for individual districts which are calculated using the following formula:

$$\frac{\text{Blacks in EMR/Black student enrollment}}{\text{Whites in EMR/White student enrollment}}$$

   Calculation of scores on the faculty index divided the black student–teacher ratio by the white student–teacher ratio.
3. The measure used for the equity of black representation in EMR classes in table 3-3 is designed to indicate whether the district exceeds the 20 percentage point threshold used by OCR in evaluating the civil rights compliance of ESAA applicants. The measure is the proportion black of those in EMR classes minus the proportion black in the system. This figure is divided by 20. Scores of 1.0 or less are within the 20 percentage point tolerance acceptable to OCR.
4. A 70 percent black cut-off is used here because in districts with this many blacks, OCR would not find almost totally black EMR unacceptable. Districts which are at least 80 percent black cannot exceed the OCR plus 20 percentage point threshold.

Chapter 3

5. While the Justice Department was not staffed to periodically visit districts it was desegregating in order to check on implementation, some courts ordered that the school system file periodic reports indicating what changes were being made.
6. Downs (1967, 109–110) describes zealots as those in a bureaucracy who are deeply committed to promoting certain policies and who will stop at nothing in trying to achieve their objectives. The zealots' role tends to decline as a bureau ages.
7. See Brown and Stover (1977) for a theoretical treatment of this issue.

REFERENCES

Alexander v. Holmes, 396 U.S. 19 (1969).

American Friends Service Committee et al. (1970). *The Status of School Desegregation in the South 1970*. No location: American Friends Service Committee, Delta Ministry of the National Council of Churches, Lawyers Committee for Civil Rights Under Law, Lawyers Constitutional Defense Committee, NAACP Legal Defense and Education Fund, Inc., and the Washington Research Project.

Brown, Don W., and Robert V. Stover (1977). "Court Directives and Compliance: A Utility Approach." *American Politics Quarterly* 5 (October): 465–480.

Brown v. Board of Education, 347 U.S. 483 (1954).

Bullock, Charles S. III (1976). "Defiance of the Law: School Discrimination before and after Desegregation." *Urban Education* 11 (October): 239–262.

Bullock, Charles S. III (1980a). "The Office for Civil Rights' Implementation of Desegregation Programs in the Public Schools." *Policy Studies Journal* 8: 597–616.

Bullock, Charles S. III (1980b). "Implementation of Selected Equal Education Opportunity Programs." Presented at the annual meeting of American Political Science Association, Washington, D.C., Aug. 28–31, 1980.

Bullock, Charles S. III, and Harrell R. Rodgers, Jr. (1976a). "Coercion to Compliance: Southern School Districts and School Desegregation Guidelines." *Journal of Politics* 38 (November): 987–1011.

Bullock, Charles S. III, and Harrell R. Rodgers, Jr. (1976b). "Impediments to Policy Evaluation: Perceptual Distortion and Agency Loyalty." *Social Science Quarterly* 57 (December): 506–519.

Bullock, Charles S. III, and Joseph Stewart, Jr. (1978a). "Complaint Processing as a Strategy for Combatting Second Generation Discrimination." Presented at annual meeting of Southern Political Science Association, Atlanta, Ga., Nov. 9–11, 1978.

Bullock, Charles S. III, and Joseph Stewart, Jr. (1978b). "When You Can't Do Everything at Once: Policy Implementation under Conditions of Growing Responsibilities." Presented at the annual meeting of American Political Science Association, New York, N.Y., Aug. 31–Sept. 3, 1978.

Bullock, Charles S. III, and Joseph Stewart, Jr. (1979). "Incidence and Correlates of Second-Generation Discrimination." In Marian Lief Palley and Michael B. Preston (eds.), *Race, Sex, and Policy Problems*. Lexington, Mass.: Lexington Books, pp. 115–129.

Clement, Dorothy C.; Margaret Eisenhart; and John Wood (1976). "School Desegregation and Educational Inequality." In *The Desegregation Literature: A Critical Appraisal*. Washington, D.C.: National Institute of Education.

Columbus Board of Education v. Penick, 443 U.S. 449 (1979).
Congressional Quarterly Weekly Report (August 28, 1971): 1829.
Crain, Robert L. (1969). *The Politics of School Desegregation.* New York: Anchor-Doubleday.
Dayton Board of Education v. Brinkman, 433 U.S. 406 (1977).
Dayton Board of Education v. Brinkman, 443 U.S. 526 (1979).
Downs, Anthony (1967). *Inside Bureaucracy.* Boston: Little, Brown.
Dye, Thomas R. (1968). "Urban School Desegregation: A Comparative Analysis." *Urban Affairs Quarterly* 4 (December): 141–165.
Evans v. Buchanan, 447 F. Supp. 982 (1978).
Farley, Reynolds (1975). "Racial Integration in the Public Schools, 1967 to 1972: Assessing the Effect of Governmental Policies." *Sociological Focus* 8 (January): 3–25.
Fitzgerald, Michael R., and David R. Morgan (1977). "Changing Patterns of Urban School Desegregation." *American Politics Quarterly* 5 (October): 437-464
Giles, Micheal W. (1975). "H.E.W. versus the Federal Courts: A Comparison of School Desegregation Enforcement." *American Politics Quarterly* 3 (January): 81-90.
Giles, Micheal W., and Thomas G. Walker (1975). "Judicial Policy Making and Southern School Segregation." *Journal of Politics* 37 (November): 917–936.
Green v. New Kent County School Board, 391 U.S. 430 (1968).
Keyes v. School District No. 1 of Denver, 413 U.S. 189 (1973).
Kirby, David et al. (1973). *Political Strategies in Northern School Desegregation.* Lexington, Mass.: Lexington Books.
Kluger, Richard (1976). *Simple Justice.* New York: Knopf.
Lambda Corporation (1971). *School Desegregation with Minimum Busing.* Arlington, Va.: Lambda Corporation.
"Lau Remedies" (1975). Mimeograph. Washington, D.C.: Office for Civil Rights.
Lau v. Nichols, 414 U.S. 563 (1974).
Mercer, Jane R. (1974). "A Policy Statement on Assessment Procedures and the Rights of Children." *Harvard Educational Review* 44: 125–141.
Milliken v. Bradley, 418 U.S. 717 (1974).
Mills, Roger (1974). *Justice Delayed and Denied.* Washington, D.C.: Center for National Policy Review.
Morgan, David R., and Michael R. Fitzgerald (1980). "Desegregating Urban Schools," *American Politics Quarterly* 8: 87–208.
Moses v. Washington Parish School Board, 330 F. Supp. 1340 (1971).
Office for Civil Rights (1979). Mimeograph. *Analysis of Selected Civil Rights Issues.* Washington, D.C.: Office for Civil Rights.
Orfield, Gary (1975). *Congressional Power.* New York: Harcourt Brace Jovanovich.
Orfield, Gary (1978). *Must We Bus?* Washington, D.C.: Brookings Institution.
Panetta, Leon E., and Peter Gall (1971). *Bring Us Together.* Philadelphia: Lippincott.
Pasadena v. Spangler, 427 U.S. 424 (1976).
Plessy v. Ferguson, 163 U.S. 537 (1896).
Rodgers, Harrell R., Jr., and Charles S. Bullock III (1972). *Law and Social Change: Civil Rights Laws and Their Consequences.* New York: McGraw-Hill.
Rodgers, Harrell R., Jr., and Charles S. Bullock III (1976). *Coercion to Compliance.* Lexington, Mass.: Lexington Books.
Rogers v. Paul, 382 U.S. 198 (1965).
Rossell, Christine H., and Robert L. Crain (1975). Mimeograph. "The Political and Social Determinants of School Desegregation Policy."
Sabatier, Paul, and Daniel Mazmanian (1980). "The Implementation of Public Policy: A Framework of Analysis." *Policy Studies Journal* 8: 538–560.

Scheingold, Stuart A. (1974). *The Politics of Rights*. New Haven: Yale University Press.
Sherrill, Robert (1968). *Gothic Politics in the Deep South*. New York: Ballantine Books.
Singleton v. Jackson Municipal Separate School District, 419 F. 2nd 1211 (1969).
Stewart, Joseph, Jr., and Charles S. Bullock III (1981). "Implementing Equal Education Opportunity Policy: A Comparison of the Outcomes of HEW and Justice Department Efforts." *Administration and Society* 12 (February): 427–446.
Swann v. Charlotte-Mecklenburg Board of Education, 402 U.S. 1 (1971).
U.S. Commission on Civil Rights (1972). *Five Communities: Their Search for Equal Education*. Washington, D.C.: U.S. Government Printing Office.
U.S. Commission on Civil Rights (1976). *Fulfilling the Letter and Spirit of the Law*. Washington, D.C.: U.S. Government Printing Office.
U.S. House of Representatives (1970). *Committee on Appropriations Hearings, Departments of Labor and Health, Education and Welfare and Related Agencies Appropriations for Fiscal Year 1970*, 91st Congress, 1st Session, Part 6. Washington, D.C.: U.S. Government Printing Office.
Vanfossen, Beth (1968). "Variables Related to Resistance to Desegregation in the Public Schools." *Social Forces* 47 (September): 39–44.
Wirt, Frederick M. (1970). *The Politics of Southern Equality*. Chicago: Aldine.

Chapter 4
Fair Employment Laws for Minorities: An Evaluation of Federal Implementation

Harrell R. Rodgers, Jr.

During most of the twentieth century minority Americans were systematically and blatantly discriminated against in the job market. Most of the better-paying jobs in the private sector, and even in the federal, state, and local governments, were reserved for whites—mostly for white males. One of the central thrusts of the civil rights movement was to end this discrimination and overcome its legacy.

This was, and is, an extremely complicated goal. As late as 1964 black Americans were only very modestly represented in middle- and upper-income jobs; as a result, black median family income was only 50 percent of white median family income. To bridge this awesome gap would require better education and training for millions of black Americans, an end to discriminatory employment practices on the part of thousands of businesses and employers, and a healthy growing economy vigorous enough to provide opportunities for the labor force. The last point needs to be stressed: even a superbly designed and vigorously enforced job discrimination program can have only a limited impact if the economy is not healthy and growing. Thus progress requires a very high degree of coordination between federal, and even state, policies.

During the 1960s the federal government took the first major steps toward ending job discrimination. In the sections below we will describe the policy approaches employed, assess their impact on black Americans, and attempt to isolate those factors that have impeded progress.

FORMAL ANTIDISCRIMINATION POLICIES

Office of Federal Contract Compliance Programs (Department of Labor)

Equal employment policy can be traced back to Franklin Roosevelt's World War II executive order (E.O. 8802) prohibiting job discrimination on the part of defense contractors. The Fair Employment Practices Commission was created to enforce the order, but it did little and was allowed to expire once the war ended. President Truman issued Executive Order 9980 calling for fair employment throughout the federal government, but the order was never enforced.

In 1961, President Kennedy issued Executive Order 11114 forbidding racial discrimination in all federally financed construction projects. President Johnson extended the order in 1965 (E.O. 11246) to all private contractors, subcontractors, and unions doing work under or related to a federal contract (Bullock, 1975; Rodgers and Bullock, 1972, 113–137). Those found guilty of discrimination could be punished by a loss of present and future contracts. Each federal agency was required to enforce the nondiscrimination standards among its contractors. Contractors were required to obtain pledges of compliance from subcontractors and unions. The Office of Federal Contract Compliance Programs (OFCCP) was created to supervise the enforcement of the standards by the twenty-six federal agencies responsible for contracts. The potential sweep of the executive orders is suggested by the fact that about one-third of the total work force is employed directly or indirectly by the federal government (U.S. Commission on Civil Rights, 1970, 12). Table 4-1 outlines the policy provisions that have affected equal employment goals since World War II.

In 1968, OFCCP published guidelines for federal contractors that required not only nondiscrimination but affirmative action programs. The OFCCP guidelines noted that

> A necessary prerequisite to the development of a satisfactory affirmative action program is the identification and analysis of problem areas inherent in minority employment and an evaluation of opportunities for utilization of minority group personnel. The contractor's program shall provide in detail for specific steps to guarantee equal employment opportunities keyed to the problems and needs of members of minority groups, including when there are deficiencies, the development of specific goals and timetables for the prompt achievement of full and equal employment opportunities. [U.S. Commission on Civil Rights, 1971, 173]

Contractors, then, were expected to play a very active role, including the establishment of numerical goals for minority employment to be achieved within specific time-frames. In 1970, OFCCP required federal

Fair Employment Laws for Minorities 95

TABLE 4-1 Major Policy Provisions Affecting Fair Employment Practices

Executive Order 8802, 1941	President Roosevelt prohibits job discrimination by defense contractors
Executive Order 9980, 1948	President Truman calls for fair employment practices throughout the federal government
Executive Order 11114, 1961	President Kennedy forbids discrimination in all federally financed construction
Executive Order 11246, 1965	President Johnson bans discrimination from all work sites of contractors who work on federal jobs and creates the Office of Federal Contract Compliance Programs (OFCCP) to carry out enforcement
Civil Rights Act of 1964	Equal Employment Opportunity Commission created to prohibit job discrimination by private employers
Civil Rights Act of 1972	EEOC authorized to sue on behalf of workers suffering discrimination
Regents v. Bakke, 1978	Supreme Court strikes down racial quota for medical school admissions
Administrative Reorganization, 1978	EEOC given jurisdiction over job discrimination within the federal government
United Steelworkers v. Weber, 1979	Supreme Court approves voluntary affirmative action plans
Fullilove v. Klutznick, 1980	Supreme Court approves earmarking a share of federal contracts for minority businesses
OFCCP Guidelines, 1981	Federal jurisdiction over private contractors' personnel practices is rewritten to exclude all but very large concerns

contractors to provide the data needed to evaluate their programs. However, in 1973 the U.S. Commission on Civil Rights charged that OFCCP had failed to require sufficient data from contractors and failed to develop the guidelines necessary to evaluate compliance.

In the early 1970s OFCCP did take two significant steps. In Philadelphia and some fifty other cities, contractors were required to bring increasing numbers of blacks into the skilled trades. Contractors were required to survey the number of minorities and women in each occupation group within their business. If the numbers were less than those in the community's labor force, the contractors were required to establish numerical hiring goals and a compliance timetable. OFCCP also required federal agencies to carry out compliance reviews in at least half of the contracts let, rather than the usual 10 percent. Generally, agencies are required to evaluate contractors' recruitment, promotion, and training policies.

Throughout most of the 1970s OFCCP depended primarily on voluntary cooperation from contractors. Disbarments and suits against contractors were rare, totaling only twenty-seven through 1980. OFCCP selectively audited agency supervision of contractors, sometimes requiring additional on-site inspections. In reality, however, the procedures looked better on paper than they actually were. One study (Derryck, 1972, 16) concluded that contractors often only pretended to comply with fair employment standards, knowing that OFCCP rarely cracked down. In the mid-1970s OFCCP reported that it was holding more administrative hearings and was more often applying sanctions against recalcitrant contractors (U.S. Commission on Civil Rights, 1977, 330).

Equal Employment Opportunity Commission

Employment discrimination by private employers was prohibited by Title VII of the 1964 Civil Rights Act. Title VII prohibited discrimination by employers or unions with twenty-five or more employees, which included about 75 percent of the labor force. To enforce Title VII, the five-member Equal Employment Opportunity Commission (EEOC) was created.

For most of its life, EEOC has proven inadequate to fulfill its mandate. Its problems have been numerous. First, EEOC adopted the mostly passive approach of complaint processing. From the beginning EEOC received far more complaints of discrimination than had been anticipated. During its first seven years, the EEOC received 110,000 complaints of employment discrimination. The EEOC did not have enough employees to investigate all the complaints, many of its employees were poorly trained, and the general disorganization of the Commission caused a rapid turnover in personnel and a great deal of internal tension. As Bullock (1975, 83) notes:

> During its first half decade, four chairmen, five general counsels, and six executive directors passed through the EEOC's revolving door. Indicative of restlessness in the ranks was the filing of 220 charges of discrimination against the Commission by its employees, a rate of complaints 28 times greater than was generally found in federal offices.

The result was that by the end of 1972 only about half of the 80,000 complaints the Commission had recommended for action had been investigated. By 1976 the rate of complaints had increased to around 80,000 a year, causing the backlog to mushroom. Instead of clearing complaints within the required sixty days, processing averaged two years.

Even when EEOC did investigate a complaint, its success rate was extremely low. Of the 41,000 investigations EEOC conducted in its first seven years, only 6 percent were successfully resolved (U.S. Commission on Civil Rights, 1971, 29). Bullock (1975, 82) points out that this "miserable batting average appears even worse—if that is possible—when compared with the opinion of an EEOC chairman that 80 percent of the complaints are valid."

While EEOC was fumbling, the Justice Department prosecuted a number of important cases that it felt had industry-wide implications. Among corporations sued were United States Steel, Household Finance, Roadway, AT&T, and several unions. In these cases the courts upheld the use of statistical data on racial distributions in job categories as a method of proving discrimination and upheld the suits against the industries (Rosenthal, 1973). The courts also ruled against employment tests that excluded more blacks than whites (*Griggs* v. *Duke Power Co.*, 1971), and seniority systems that excluded blacks from better-paying jobs (*U.S.* v. *Local 189, United Paperworkers,* 1970). The courts also ordered specific unions to adopt affirmative action plans in compensation for their past discriminatory behavior (Bullock, 1975, 88).

Even with this type of court backing, EEOC continued to make minimal progress. In 1972, Congress responded by expanding EEOC's enforcement powers. Prior to 1972 EEOC was only authorized to negotiate with discriminating employers through conferences, conciliations, and persuasion. If EEOC found a pattern of discrimination, it could refer the matter to the Attorney General for possible prosecution. In 1972, Congress gave the EEOC the authority to take cases directly to the federal district courts. EEOC jurisdiction was also extended to state and local government employees and to employers and unions with fifteen or more employees.

EEOC's effectiveness still proved to be limited. The major problem that continued to plague it was that it failed to approach job discrimination in a systematic manner. Rather than develop industry-wide plans or undertake class action suits, it continued to spend most of its time processing individual complaints. Not until 1974 did EEOC reluctantly formulate voluntary nondiscrimination plans for entire industries. In 1974, EEOC also began to initiate more federal suits, a policy it continued throughout the 1970s. EEOC began to collect data on firms with one hundred or more employees, and began to put pressure on some of these companies for greater compliance. Industry-wide plans were adopted for several fields, including the airlines, the trucking industry, and some construction trades. In one of its most successful cases, EEOC convinced AT&T to pay $15 million in back wages and raises totaling $23 million to women and minorities who had suffered discrimination. The United Steelworkers Union and nine of its affiliate companies also agreed to end dual seniority systems based on race, and to pay back wages to minority workers affected by discrimination. Dozens of other cases involving coal mines, cities, specific city departments, grocery chains, and manufacturers have also been won in recent years.

Two major developments between 1977 and 1980 further consolidated EEOC's powers and converted it into the nation's major fair employment agency. The first development concerned the constitutionality of affirmative action plans—programs designed to overcome the impact of discrimination by giving preference in hiring and training to minorities and women. Affirmative action plans had been the core of the field strategies used by EEOC after 1973. Under such plans employers might, for example, set aside a certain percentage of all job openings for qualified blacks. While very effective, such programs were always controversial. White males began to argue that Title VII's prohibition of racial discrimination included discrimination against white males, thus making affirmative action plans unconstitutional.

The first case on this topic to reach the Supreme Court involved college admissions rather than employment. It produced rather ambiguous results. In *Regents of the University of California v. Bakke* (1978) the Court held that Title VI of the Civil Rights Act of 1964, which prohibited discrimination in any program receiving financial assistance, barred a state university from setting aside a fixed quota of seats in a medical school's entering class for minorities. Five of the justices ruled that it would be constitutionally permissible for admission officers to consider race as one of the complex of factors that determine class admission. These judges seemed to be saying that a quota of seats for minorities could be set aside but that the minority applicants would have to have admission scores that were higher than those of rejected applicants. The lack of precision in the decision left employers, educators, and policymakers without clear guidelines.

Some of the ambiguity was cleared up with the 1979 case of *United Steelworkers v. Weber*. The case raised the question of whether a company could voluntarily establish an affirmative action program even though it had never been officially charged with racial discrimination. In an effort to bring more of its black employees into skilled jobs, the Kaiser Aluminum Company had established an affirmative action program at its Gramercy, Louisiana, plant. The program, with union backing, set aside 50 percent of the slots in a training program for black employees. Weber, a white employee, charged that he had been discriminated against because he had more seniority than some of the blacks admitted to the program.

Confused perhaps by the *Bakke* decision, both the District Court and the Fifth Court of Appeals ruled in favor of Weber. The Supreme Court, however, reversed these decisions and upheld the plan. The Court ruled that a literal reading of Title VII's prohibition of racial discrimination might sustain Weber's complaint, but that the purpose of the act, not its literal language, was the issue. The Court said:

> It would be ironic indeed if a law triggered by a nation's concern over centuries of racial injustice and intended to improve the lot of those who had been "excluded from the American dream so long" constituted the first legislative prohibition of all voluntary, private, race-conscious efforts to abolish traditional patterns of racial segregation and hierarchy. [p. 2728]

By emphasizing the need to enhance minority opportunities, the Court thus interpreted Title VII as encouraging voluntary and local remedies for employment discrimination. It is equally important, however, that the Court decided that Title VII prohibits the government from requiring employers to formulate affirmative action plans unless they are federal or state agencies, a federal contractor, or operating under a compensatory program to rectify past bias.

The Court's decisions then were only a partial victory for the government, but they did leave government agencies with the power to negotiate affirmative action plans under some circumstances or to encourage voluntary affirmative action plans among private employers. In 1979, the EEOC published a set of affirmative action guidelines that employers and policymakers could follow and still stay within the boundaries established by the Court's interpretation of Titles VI and VII (U.S. Commission on Civil Rights, 1980, 24).

Affirmative action programs were given a further boost in early July 1980, when the Supreme Court upheld a provision of the Public Works Employment Act which set aside 10 percent of all contracts under the $4 billion federal public works program for minority-owned businesses. In a 6 to 3 decision the Court said that such racial quotas were necessary to remedy past inequities (*Fullilove* v. *Klutznick*, 1980). The decision bolstered OFCCP's authority and indirectly upheld a number of other compulsory affirmative action programs for federal contractors.

The second major development affecting EEOC was congressional approval in 1978 of the reorganization of federal equal employment agencies (Lamb, 1980). This reorganization created a "Super-EEOC" by transferring to EEOC the Office of Personnel Management's jurisdiction over job discrimination within the federal government, the Department of Labor's responsibilities for enforcing the Equal Pay Act and the Age Discrimination in Employment Act, and the Equal Employment Opportunity Coordinating Council's duty to coordinate all federal employment activities (this latter agency was later abolished). The OFCCP, located in the Department of Labor, was left with the responsibility of overseeing federal contract compliance, and the Department of Justice retains the authority to bring suit against state and local governments that discriminate in their employment practices.

The newly bolstered EEOC also reorganized its national office and established new procedures designed to process complaints more quickly, reduce its backlog, and eliminate patterns of discrimination in smaller companies. In 1978, all EEOC offices adopted the "rapid charge processing system." In this new two-step system an intensive interview is scheduled with a complainant immediately after the complaint is filed. In the second step, a face-to-face conference between the complainant and the respondent is scheduled as soon as possible. At the conference, the EEOC representative attempts to gather the facts and work out a conciliation. If evidence of discrimination is uncovered and no conciliation is achieved, EEOC then initiates a lawsuit in federal district court. If an employer is taken to court, its hiring and promotion policies are monitored after the suit to make certain that discriminatory behavior has ended.

EEOC also adopted two other procedures—the "backlog charge processing system" and the "early litigation identification" program. The first program is designed to clear up the agency backlog so that attention can be focused on current complaints. The second is designed to identify small companies with a pattern of discriminatory behavior. Once identified, EEOC will bring a class action suit if necessary. This strategy is designed to enhance EEOC's impact by broadening its approach and by replacing the time it spends on the more passive complaint processing approach (Lamb, 1980, 90–91).

EEOC representatives have been quite optimistic about the impact of the new programs and procedures but so far there is no empirical data by which to judge the effect of these efforts. It is a safe guess, however, that evidence will show that EEOC has been more effective in recent years.

Discrimination within the Federal Government: Office of Personnel Management

As noted above, the reorganization plan of 1978 transferred the Office of Personnel Management's (OPM) jurisdiction over racial discrimination within the federal government to the EEOC. OPM's loss of jurisdiction over these cases resulted from its poor performance in handling such cases. While OPM was willing to address direct cases of agency discrimination, it never supported the concept of affirmative action. The reason was that OPM had always promoted strict merit hiring, and affirmative action suggested a need for special training programs or qualification exceptions for minorities and women.

Thus, OPM adopted an extremely limited concept of affirmative action. As Rosenbloom (1980, 171) notes, "Affirmative action was to be confined to situations in which a federal agency had failed to hire substantial proportions of numbers of minority groups who were: (1) in possession of the requisite employment skills and (2) within the organization's normal recruitment area." In reality this only required agencies that had engaged in blatant discrimination, and which had a pool of qualified minorities to draw upon, to end discriminatory practices and meet certain minority hiring goals by specified deadlines. But the evidence indicates that OPM did a poor job of monitoring the practices and progress of even these affected agencies (Rosenbloom, 1980, 172). The result was that OPM's limited emphasis was on agency avoidance of discrimination in hiring, not on efforts to overcome the effects of past discrimination.

ANALYSIS OF PROGRESS ACHIEVED

What have been the consequences of fair employment legislation? This question can be addressed from two perspectives—black employment gains and improvements in black incomes relative to white incomes.

Table 4-2 shows the percentage of black males and females employed in various types of jobs between 1958 and 1977. During this period, blacks represented about 9.8 percent of the total work force. Even a very cursory review of the data shows that a great deal of change has occurred. In 1958 black males were very poorly represented in professional and managerial jobs. Most black males were employed in low-paying blue-collar service and laborer jobs. In 1958 most black women were employed as domestics and service workers.

Progress between 1958 and 1968 was slow but steady. By 1968 black representation in white-collar jobs had increased significantly, and a smaller proportion of black women were working as domestics. Still, over half of all black males were employed in low-paying blue-collar jobs, and most black women were still employed as domestics or service workers.

The contrast between black job representation in 1958 and 1977 is quite striking. By 1977 black males were much better represented in white-collar and skilled blue-collar jobs, and significantly less likely to be laborers and operatives. Black women had moved into white-collar jobs in large numbers, especially in clerical and technical jobs. Only 8.9 percent of all black women worked as domestics in 1977, compared to 37.2 percent in 1958.

On the negative side the data for 1977 and 1979 (see table 4-3) show that while blacks have made considerable gains over the years, they are still underrepresented in the professions and better-paying jobs and overrepresented in low-income occupations. In some job categories such as managers, administrators, and sales workers, the underrepresentation is severe; and, at the current rate of progress, the gap will not be bridged for a long time. Notice that table 4-3 shows that in 1979, 52.5 percent of all white workers were employed in white-collar jobs compared to only 35.2 percent of all black workers. Blacks were also underrepresented in skilled craft jobs and substantially overrepresented among service workers.

The figures in tables 4-2 and 4-3 also mask an important point. While blacks have moved into white-collar jobs, they are still severely underrepresented in the most prestigious professions and the high-income white-collar jobs. For example, blacks are more likely to be nurses than doctors, hygienists than dentists, paralegals than lawyers, school teachers than professors, office managers than branch or district managers, supervisors than vice-presidents. Thus, while blacks have made a great deal of progress, they have a long way to go before obtaining parity in most of the more prestigious and better-paying occupations.

TABLE 4-2 Black Occupations by Sex, 1958–1977

	1958 Black and Other		1960 Black and Other		1964 Black and Other		1968 Black and Other		1972 Black and Other		1976 Black and Other		1977 Black and Other	
	Males	Females	Males	Females	Males	Females	Males	Females	Males	Females	Males	Females	Males	Females
Professional and technical	3.2	5.4	3.9	6.2	5.7	8.2	6.6	9.5	8.2	11.2	9.6	14.2	9.6	14.3
Managers and administrators	2.8	1.8	3.0	1.9	3.3	1.6	3.6	1.6	5.8	3.4	5.8	2.8	6.4	2.9
Sales workers	1.0	1.5	1.4	1.5	1.5	1.9	1.7	2.2	1.8	2.8	2.4	2.5	2.6	2.6
Clerical workers	5.2	7.4	5.9	9.3	5.2	11.3	7.1	18.3	7.4	23.3	7.6	26.0	7.7	26.0
Craftsmen and kindred	9.4	0.7	9.7	0.5	11.6	0.6	13.4	0.8	14.7	0.9	15.3	1.1	15.5	1.3
Operatives	24.1	14.3	24.5	14.3	25.1	14.0	28.2	17.4	16.5	15.0	15.9	15.3	14.8	15.5
Nonfarm laborers	24.0	0.8	22.5	0.6	21.6	0.6	18.1	0.6	16.8	0.9	14.3	1.4	14.4	1.2
Private household	0.5	37.2	0.3	34.8	0.4	32.5	0.3	22.1	0.2	15.2	0.2	9.4	0.2	8.9
Other service workers	14.3	21.6	14.0	21.5	14.5	23.3	14.2	25.1	15.6	26.8	16.6	26.0	16.3	26.0
Farmers and farm managers	5.8	0.6	4.8	0.6	2.9	0.6	2.0	0.2	1.0	0.1	0.9	—	0.7	—
Laborers and foremen	8.9	8.6	9.2	8.7	7.2	5.3	4.8	2.3	2.4	1.1	2.6	0.8	2.5	0.9

NOTE: All figures are percentages.
SOURCE: *Handbook of Labor Statistics 1978* (Washington, D.C.: Superintendent of Documents, 1979), pp. 75–81.

TABLE 4-3 Occupations by Race, 1979

Labor Force and Occupational Group	Total	White	Black	Hispanic
Employed: Number	96,945	86,025	9,160	4,604
Percent	100.0	100.0	100.0	100.0
White-collar workers	50.9	52.5	35.2	32.6
Professional and technical	15.5	15.9	10.5	7.6
Managers and administrators	10.8	11.6	4.6	6.0
Sales workers	6.4	6.8	2.4	3.9
Clerical workers	18.2	18.2	12.6	15.1
Blue-collar workers	33.1	33.6	38.4	47.3
Craft and kindred workers	13.3	13.8	9.6	13.9
Operatives, except transport	11.3	10.8	15.4	21.5
Transport equipment operatives	3.7	3.6	5.3	4.0
Nonfarm laborers	4.8	4.5	8.1	7.8
Service workers	13.2	12.0	25.3	16.3
Private household workers	1.1	.8	3.8	1.5
Other service workers	12.1	11.1	20.5	14.8
Farmworkers	2.8	2.9	2.1	3.8

SOURCE: *Employment and Training Report of the President* (Washington, D.C.: Superintendent of Documents, 1980), p. 10.

The evidence on black employment by the federal government suggests a form of progress that parallels that in the private sector. Data on federal employment by race go back to 1962 (U.S. Civil Service Commission, 1962–1969). The data for the 1960s show blacks substantially overrepresented in the lowest-paying federal jobs (GS 1-4), modestly overrepresented in low- to medium-level jobs (GS 5-8), and substantially underrepresented in the better-paying to top-rank positions (GS 9-11 and GS 12-18). For example, in 1967 blacks were 20.5 percent of all employees in GS 1-4 positions, 11.6 percent in GS 5-8 positions, 4.3 percent in GS 9-11 positions, and only 1.8 percent in GS 12-18 positions (Rosenbloom, 1980, 180).

In 1976 blacks were still substantially overrepresented in GS 1-4 and GS 5-8 grades (21.1 percent and 17.4 percent respectively), approaching parity in GS 9-11 grades (8.4 percent), but still substantially underrepresented in the super grades GS 12-18 (4.4 percent) (U.S. Civil Service Commission, 1976). While blacks are still overrepresented in the lowest-paying jobs and underrepresented in the better-paying positions, there is no doubt that much progress has been made. Still, at the current rate of progress it will take decades for blacks to obtain parity in the top positions within the federal government.

Another serious problem is the high rate of black unemployment. In early 1982 the unemployment rate for blacks was 17.4 percent, compared to about 8.0 percent for whites. The ratio of black to white unemployment in early 1982 was rather typical of the ratio over the last twenty years.

Between 1958 and 1981 the white unemployment rate averaged about 5.1 percent. During the same period the black unemployment rate averaged almost 11.0 percent, never falling below 6 percent. White unemployment exceeded 7 percent only twice during this period, while black unemployment was 10 percent or more in fourteen of the twenty-four years. In fact, between 1972 and 1981 the black unemployment rate averaged over 12 percent. Thus, unemployment is, and has long been, an extremely serious problem for the black population.

Examining the impact of employment progress on black income gains requires a rather complex analysis. Traditionally such analyses are based on comparisons of either black and white males (McCrone and Hardy, 1978), or black and white family income. While both approaches yield interesting insights, they fail to show the dynamics of employment and income gains and losses among the black population. Comparisons of only males are distorted by the extremely high black teenage unemployment rate and by the fact that the mean age of the black population is considerably lower than the mean age of the white population. Comparisons of families obscure the fact that the impact of civil rights laws has affected various types of families in very different ways.

Table 4-4, for example, comparing median family income by race between 1964 and 1980 provides a traditional comparison. The data suggest that little progress has been made. In 1964 black median family income was only 50 percent of white median family income, and after sixteen years of struggle the black median had increased by only about 8 percentage points. These data clearly tell us that blacks as a group have a long way to go to achieve income parity with whites, and that black median family incomes are on the average still extremely low. But the data do not yield any insight into the impact of civil rights laws on different types of families.

If the aggregate figures for black families are broken down they provide some very interesting and important information. The first is that husband-and-wife black families have made very significant gains. These gains are reflected in the fact that the income gap between two-parent black and white families is not anywhere near as large as for black families generally. Table 4-5 compares husband–wife families by race in 1959, 1969, and 1980. The gains for these families over this period are quite apparent.

In 1959 black husband–wife families in which only the husband worked earned only 58 percent of the income earned by similar white families. By 1980 the ratio for these families was 74 percent. The gains for two-spouse black families with both the husband and wife employed have been even more substantial. In 1959 black husband–wife families with both partners in the workplace earned 64 percent of the earnings of similar white families. By 1978 these families earned 88 percent of the earnings of similar white families.

TABLE 4-4 Median Income of Families by Race, 1964–1980

	Black	White	Black as Percent of White
1964	$3,724	$6,858	50%
1965	3,886	7,251	50
1966	4,507	7,792	58
1967	4,875	8,234	59
1968	5,360	8,937	60
1969	5,999	9,794	61
1970	6,279	10,236	61
1971	6,440	10,672	60
1972	6,864	11,549	59
1973	7,269	12,595	58
1974	7,800	13,400	58
1975	8,780	14,270	61.5
1976	9,240	15,540	59
1977	9,560	16,740	57
1978	10,880	18,370	59
1979	11,650	20,520	57
1980	12,670	21,900	58

SOURCES: Bureau of the Census, "Social and Economic Status of the Black Population in the United States in 1974," *Current Population Reports*, Series P-23, no. 54, p. 25; "Money, Income and Poverty Status of Families and Persons in the United States: 1976 (Advance Report), September 1977, p. 1; 1977 (Advance Report); *Current Population Reports*, Series P-60, no. 116, July 1978, p. 1; 1978 (Advance Report); *Current Population Reports*, Series P-60, no. 120, November 1979, p. 1; 1979 (Advance Report); *Current Population Reports*, Series P-60, no. 125, October 1980, p. 7; 1980 (Advance Data from the March 1981 Current Population Survey); *Current Population Reports*, Series P-60, no. 127, August 1981, p. 1.

Black family incomes are greater relative to white family incomes since more wives work in black two-spouse families than in similar white families. In 1980, 69 percent of black wives in such families were employed, compared to 57 percent of white families. While the average earnings of women are low, black women earn almost as much as white women. In 1980 black women employed year-round earned $10,915, compared to $11,703 for similarly employed white women.

The increase in the number of black families that have joined the middle class is also reflected in black representation in upper-income earning families. In 1970, 4 percent of all black families had earnings of $15,000 or more. By 1980, 5 percent of all black families had comparable earnings ($27,500 or more). This one percent represents an additional 300,000 or so more black families joining the middle class.

While a significant number of two-spouse black families, and even many single black adults, have made great strides in the last two decades, some blacks have made little or no progress, and some have even suffered reversals. Those making the least progress have been older blacks,

TABLE 4-5 Median Income for Husband–Wife Families, 1959, 1969, and 1980

Husband–Wife Families	1959 Black	1959 White	1959 Black as Percent of White	1969 Black	1969 White	1969 Black as Percent of White	1980 Black	1980 White	1980 Black as Percent of White
Husband only employed	$3,025	$5,233	58%	$5,792	$8,805	66%	$18,799	$25,287	74%
Husband and wife employed	$3,845	$6,013	64	$8,423	$9,926	85	$26,432	$29,842	88

SOURCES: Bureau of the Census, "The Social and Economic Status of Negroes in the United States, 1970," *Current Population Reports*, Series P-23, no. 38, July 1971, p. 31; Bureau of the Census, "Money, Income and Poverty Status of Families and Persons in the United States: 1980," *Current Population Reports*, Series P-60, no. 127, August 1981, pp. 11-12.

including many older black couples. Single black women, like single white women, have made steady but only very modest progress. Black teenagers have also found job opportunities very limited. During the 1970s the black teenage unemployment rate averaged about 37 percent.

One factor among the black population has canceled out many gains and has kept the mean black family income figure low—namely, the very substantial increase in black female-headed families. Between 1970 and 1980, the number of black female-headed families increased from 1.4 million to 2.6 million, an increase of over 80 percent (U.S. Bureau of the Census, 1981, 9). While the number of female-headed families increased by more than 70 percent between 1960 and 1980, and affected all racial groups, the rate of increase was highest for blacks. For example, between 1970 and 1980 white female-headed families increased by 41 percent.

The significance of the great increase in black female-headed families is that women generally, and black women particularly, have a very difficult time earning enough to adequately support their families. For example, in 1980 only 5.2 percent of all two-spouse families lived in poverty. However, 33 percent of all female-headed families were poor (26 percent of all white female-headed families and 51 percent of all black female-headed families).

As further indication of the impact of the rising numbers of female-headed families, in 1959 only 23 percent of all poor families were headed by a female. By 1980, 50 percent of all poor families had a female head. Of the 4.2 million poor white families, 38 percent were headed by a female. Of the 1.8 million poor black families, 72 percent had a female head.

The increasing instances of black female-headed families just since 1970 have added almost one million families to the low-income ranks, about one-third joining the poverty ranks. Thus, in 1970 black families accounted for only 22 percent of all poor families in the nation, but by 1980 they accounted for 29 percent of all poor families.

The discrepancy between black and white incomes, then, is not just a matter of job discrimination, although this is still a very serious problem. Several researchers (Garfinkel and Haveman, 1977; Masters, 1975) have recently estimated that between 35 and 60 percent of the gap between black and white incomes is attributable to market discrimination. However, a significant percentage of the discrepancy is accounted for by sexism and the deficiencies of the American economy. Millions of women currently find themselves family heads; yet because of traditional discrimination practices many are unprepared to enter high-paying occupations, while many who are prepared for good or better positions are excluded or passed over because of sexism. Eliminating sexist barriers to the professions and to better-paying jobs will help women, but unless emphasis is focused on improving the pay of traditionally female occupations, such as teaching, nursing, clerical, and secretarial jobs, progress will be very slow and inevitably incomplete.

The other factor, besides discrimination, that accounts for the discrepancies between black and white income is the nation's long-standing economic woes. The high unemployment rate, especially for blacks, simply denies adequate opportunities to millions of Americans. Additionally, millions work at jobs that pay an extremely low wage. For example, in 1980, 25 million people worked full-time year-round and earned below $12,499; 31 million earned below $14,999 (U.S. Bureau of the Census, 1981, 23). Thus, millions of Americans have a great deal of difficulty in earning a decent living—and because of racism and sexism, minorities and women are most likely to get trapped in these low-wage jobs or be unable to find work. Until general economic conditions are substantially improved, regardless of the civil rights laws, millions of minorities and women will be left out of the job market or relegated to poverty-wage jobs.

FAIR EMPLOYMENT IMPLEMENTATION: POLICY, ADMINISTRATION, AND ENFORCEMENT VARIABLES

An analysis of fair employment laws, their administration, and their enforcement reveals important reasons why progress has been limited.

Clarity of Policy

In many ways the most fundamental fair employment issue that must be addressed is, What does nondiscrimination mean? Does it mean that employers will not overtly discriminate against minorities or does it mean more? While clearly the law does require more than an end to overt discrimination, the full dimension of the obligation of nondiscrimination has not been finally settled. This failure, understandable in some respects, has greatly impeded progress.

Throughout the twenty-year struggle to overcome racial discrimination in the job market a major question has been whether employers were required to make up for past discrimination by compensatory or affirmative action techniques. With the *Weber* decision in 1979 (discussed earlier) this question may have been settled as far as most private employers are concerned. However, while affirmative action plans are legal for federal and state agencies, for federal contractors, and as compensatory tools, they are still quite controversial. Many conservative members of Congress are opposed to affirmative action plans of any kind. With a Republican-dominated Senate, they may be successful in banning or greatly reducing the use of such plans. Additionally, there is still considerable resistance to affirmative action plans on the part of many contractors and government agencies, and the Reagan administration is very sympathetic to their complaints. Thus, in a very fundamental sense, the question of what constitutes nondiscrimination is still open to interpretation.

Precision of Standards

Not being able to define nondiscrimination definitively contributes to another problem. There is no easily identifiable quantitative standard by which to measure compliance or even progress. If an employer has no black employees, does it indicate discrimination? If a similar company has 12 percent black employees but they are all in low-income jobs, does it mean that the employer discriminates? There are no simple answers to these questions because the issues are complex. There are many reasons why an employer may have a greater or lesser percentage of black or female employees, and many of them (such as supply and demand) may be independent of employer behavior. Not having clear, universally accepted quantitative standards by which to measure in many cases compliance and progress, we often must fall back on the income and occupation figures discussed above, even though these figures only provide an approximation of progress and fail to target those areas where more legal attention is required.

Although there is no uniform, ultimate definition of discrimination, standards have been developed or negotiated in some cases. In many instances EEOC and OFCCP have developed standards for particular companies or industries. For example, in the early 1970s the OFCCP developed specific ratios of minorities that contractors doing construction work under federal contracts were required to hire. The hiring goals were based on the minority representation in the local work force. The contractors were given a specific period in which racial parity had to be achieved. Of course, this type of standard produced considerable short-term progress.

In working with private employers, the EEOC has often negotiated specific hiring and promotion policies for industries and their unions. In many of these cases the industry had requested EEOC assistance in developing a standard or asked EEOC to endorse the goals of a voluntary plan. In the *Weber* case, for example, the EEOC endorsed Kaiser Aluminum's decision to set aside 50 percent of the slots in a training program for black employees. The EEOC has helped many other companies and unions develop goals and timetables.

Monitoring

To a very large extent, the impact of a law is significantly determined by the quality of its enforcement. There will always be some voluntary compliance, but without enforcement noncompliance will generally be high. This is true, of course, of laws ranging from regulation of traffic, drugs, and littering to felony theft. As noted above, the quality of federal enforcement of fair employment laws has generally been rather poor.

Franklin Roosevelt's Executive Order 8802, prohibiting job discrimination by defense contractors, was never really enforced. Truman's Executive Order 9980 requiring fair employment throughout the federal sector suffered a similar fate. Presidents Kennedy and Johnson's Executive Orders prohibiting discrimination in jobs financed by federal contracts have been erratically enforced. In some cases the orders have been enforced with vigor (such as the city plans), but in most cases the OFCCP has relied on voluntary compliance. In more recent years, OFCCP has improved its monitoring and enforcement efforts, but its efforts are rather unsystematic, and under the Reagan administration without much support.

The EEOC's monitoring activities have improved over the years, but during the first twelve to thirteen years of its existence its enforcement powers were limited and its approach basically self-defeating. Until recently EEOC used a case approach, rather than industry-wide plans. EEOC was inadequately staffed, and its personnel was too poorly trained to handle its case load. As the case load built up, and delays became worse, confidence in the Commission eroded. Even when EEOC could get to the case, its enforcement powers were so weak that it often could not resolve even overt cases of discrimination.

During the Carter administration the EEOC's monitoring powers were enhanced, and its approach broadened. These were positive changes that significantly improved its ability to ensure fair employment practices. EEOC was also given jurisdiction over discrimination within the federal government because OPM adopted such a conservative approach that it was only concerned with the most overt forms of racial discrimination. Thus, the reorganization of 1978 creating a "Super-EEOC," EEOC's internal reorganization, its new leadership, and its new policies were a step in the right direction. But recent evidence indicates that these advances have been reversed by the Reagan administration. President Reagan's first nominee for the head of EEOC was vigorously opposed by civil rights groups, and after months of controversy the nomination was withdrawn. Reagan's second choice was acceptable to most civil rights groups, but none thought the choice a good one. During its months without leadership the EEOC has coasted along, doing its job with much less vigor than it did under the Carter administration. Most observers expect the EEOC to take a cautious, conservative approach as long as Reagan is at the helm.

Federal Involvement

Federal involvement is certainly the key factor in the progress minorities have made in employment and income status over the last twenty years. But, as noted throughout, the government's role in this area of civil rights has often been somewhat passive. Rather than aggressively seek out discrimination and set standards for its elimination, OFCCP, EEOC, and other government agencies have most often waited for complaints to be filed by plaintiffs.

Both OFCCP and EEOC have adopted a more active role in recent years, and the empirical evidence indicates that this more active role has produced more progress. The Reagan administration's clear intent is to shift the emphasis back to a passive role. The consequences of this alteration for continued gains are obvious.

Enforcement Agency Presence and Commitment

In the area of civil rights, executive orders and statutes generally created enforcement agencies. The commitment to fair employment, however, varied in enforcement agency responsibility over time. Roosevelt's Fair Employment Practices Commission had little real authority and accomplished very little. As noted above, EEOC's enforcement powers were initially very modest but have been significantly expanded. Also, during much of its history EEOC adopted a basically passive enforcement strategy and failed to adequately investigate and monitor the cases it did handle.

OFCCP's authority was always significant, but not until 1975 did OFCCP expand its efforts to obtain compliance. OPM deliberately adopted very modest goals and accomplished so little that its authority was finally transferred to the newly reorganized and enhanced EEOC.

Commitment of Enforcer's Superiors

Obviously, more progress can be achieved if those obligated to enforce the law can count on the support of their superiors. In the case of federal fair employment laws, the superiors are Congress and the executive. During the Kennedy, Johnson, and Carter administrations, the agencies could count on executive backing. Presidents Nixon and Ford were less supportive, sometimes even hostile to fair employment goals.

During the 1980 primaries, Ronald Reagan expressed reservations about affirmative action and criticized what he believed to be the "overregulation" of business to achieve employment goals. Reagan's commitment to civil rights goals of any type is questionable. He has long been a critic of the 1960s civil rights programs; even while expressing support for minorities he has always found some reason for withholding support from specific legislation.

Reagan's actions as president have thus far confirmed the worst fears of minorities and women. Reagan's aides have put forth a number of revised guidelines that reduce the government's role in promoting equal employment. In late August 1981, Reagan's Secretary of Labor Raymond

Donovan issued new guidelines for OFCCP that would limit its jurisdiction to government contractors with 250 or more employees and a federal contract of one million dollars or more. Previously OFCCP's jurisdiction included any federal contractor with 50 or more employees and contracts worth $50,000 or more. Additionally, contractors with more than 250 but fewer than 500 employees will be allowed to prepare an abbreviated affirmative action program. The standards by which contractors' hiring performance is judged will also be altered to set a less rigorous standard for hiring minorities and females (*Congressional Quarterly*, 1981, 1749). Donovan admitted that these new guidelines would exempt almost 75 percent of all federal contractors from affirmative action requirements.

On August 12, 1981, Vice-President Bush announced that the administration intends to review the civil rights guidelines that have been used to protect women from sexual harassment on the job and from discrimination in college athletics. On August 20, William Reynolds, head of the Justice Department's Civil Rights Division, announced that in the area of employment he would restrict remedies to the aggrieved party, rather than impose remedies to benefit an entire class of persons (*Congressional Quarterly*, 1981, 1750).

Congress' support for fair employment has always been rather erratic and basically modest. If Congress' commitment to fair employment had been really strong, there were alternative approaches that would have produced a great deal more progress. For example, Congress could have created a cabinet-level department charged with responsibility for equal employment and broadly empowered it to achieve that goal. The creation of a Department of Equal Opportunity has often been urged.

Congress also had the option of establishing an independent agency empowered to enforce fair employment standards. For example, in 1975 the U.S. Commission on Civil Rights (651–654) recommended that Congress establish a National Employment Rights Board (NERB). The Commission urged that the NERB be broadly empowered to design employment programs for minorities and women, and that it have the authority to formulate and initiate enforcement procedures. For example, the Commission recommended that NERB have the power to issue cease and desist orders, that it be commissioned to bring suit in federal court, that it be authorized to debar federal contractors and subcontractors, to terminate federal grants, to decertify labor unions and revoke federal licenses, and that it have investigative and subpoena powers (Lamb, 1980, 89).

The authority of such a board would have been somewhat greater than the combined power of EEOC and OFCCP as they are presently constituted; and, of course, the enforcement effort would have been better coordinated. There is little doubt that such a board would have been more effective. But Congress could only agree to pursue a modest and fragmented course; thus, it is not surprising that only limited progress has been achieved.

Congressional support for the equal employment laws became even more questionable in 1981 when the Republicans became the dominant party in the Senate. The new chair of the Labor and Human Resources Committee is Sen. Orrin G. Hatch (R.–Utah). Hatch's attitude toward affirmative action is summed up by the following excerpt from a speech he gave during the 1980 elections.

> I believe affirmative action is an assault upon America, conceived in lies and fostered with an irresponsibility so extreme as to verge on the malign. If the government officials and politicians who presided over its genesis had injected heroin into the bloodstream of the nation, they could not have done more potential damage to our children and our children's children. [*Congressional Quarterly*, 1981, 1749]

In February 1981, Hatch introduced a proposed constitutional amendment that would bar the use of quotas, timetables, goals, or preferential treatment to overcome discrimination against minorities or women.

Administrative Coordination

The coordination of federal enforcement efforts has always left a great deal to be desired. Legislation and executive orders of the 1960s created separate agencies with separate fair employment responsibilities. The EEOC also has the obligation of coordinating its efforts with those states that have fair employment statutes and enforcement agencies. Coordination between the agencies is virtually nonexistent. This has meant that some types of discrimination were attacked with considerable vigor, while other types were virtually ignored. The lack of a uniform approach frustrated any attempts at a consistent standard of compliance behavior, created large enforcement gaps, and created conditions which allowed some employers to claim that they were being held to high standards while other employers escaped scrutiny altogether.

Attitude of Beneficiaries

More progress occurs in any civil rights area when the potential beneficiaries are organized and determined to obtain their rights. Black activity, collectively and individually, in behalf of fair employment has varied over the last twenty years. Between 1965 and 1976 blacks filed thousands of complaints with the EEOC, only to become disillusioned when a year or more went by without an investigation. Discouragement deepened when EEOC finally investigated some cases and failed to successfully resolve situations involving even obvious cases of bias. The word spread that filing an EEOC complaint was futile. With its new powers and procedures EEOC was becoming more credible, but the Reagan administration may reverse this.

Minority groups have also found it difficult to monitor the success rates of OFCCP, the Justice Department, and the OPM. The first two agencies have rather broad jurisdictions, and assessing their impact is difficult because of the lack of clear data and standards by which to measure progress. Periods of increased enforcement or publicity about successful suits generally stimulate more minorities to take actions on their own behalf.

Cost–Benefit Analysis

Considered in the narrowest sense, the costs–benefits of fair employment implementation have tended to favor noncompliance rather than compliance. In terms of costs, few employers have had to fear that they would be seriously fined, lose valuable contracts, or suffer public condemnation because of their failure to comply. Overt resistance might, and did on occasion, produce some costs, but simply dragging one's feet rarely did. If employers, or companies, wanted to, in other words, many could avoid the issue for very long periods. Other companies handled fair employment by hiring minorities for entry-level jobs, but rarely hired or promoted them to executive positions. In turn, there were few efforts on the part of federal agencies to reward compliance. Compliers could not count on more contracts, grants-in-aid, or other tangible rewards.

The nation's slack economy often imposed another cost on compliance. With the slow expansion of jobs, minorities and women often could not be hired or promoted without bypassing white males—often white males with more skills and seniority. This situation encouraged white males to resist fair employment laws, on occasion causing them to file discrimination complaints or suits, and in general reduced the consolidation of the working class and unions on the issue.

CONCLUSIONS

In summary, the incomplete progress toward employment equality is explained in part by the following obstacles.

1. The policy goal has never been decidedly defined, and the controversy over the goal is far from over. This also means that there is no clear quantitative standard by which to measure progress.
2. Over the past fifteen years, monitoring and enforcement of nondiscrimination standards have mostly been passive and limited. While improvements have taken place, monitoring is limited by the lack of a clear policy goal.
3. The commitment of federal agencies to fair employment goals has varied by agency and over time. EEOC and OFCCP have always been supportive of the broad policy goals, but until recently neither

adopted effective enforcement strategies. The OPM commitment was very narrow and limited.
4. Presidents Kennedy, Johnson, and Carter supported fair employment goals, but Presidents Nixon and Ford were never enthusiastic supporters. Reagan is following the tradition of recent Republican presidents.
5. The activities of the various enforcement agencies have never been well coordinated.
6. Minorities have varied in the intensity with which they have sought compliance with the law. In the mid-1960s they were more active, but enthusiasm cooled as it became clear that compliance could not be easily achieved.
7. For the most part, the cost—benefit ratio of fair employment laws has favored noncompliance.

Progress toward equal employment and income equality for black Americans has been real but limited. The most overt forms of racial discrimination have generally been ended, and many blacks have been able to move into occupations that were once reserved primarily for whites, mostly white males. Black Americans who have made the most progress have been young, educated, and often in two-parent families. Young, poorly educated blacks, older blacks, and black female heads of families have made the least progress.

In fact, the number of black female-headed families has increased very rapidly in the last fifteen years, and the heads of these families have had such difficulty in obtaining well-paying jobs that many have been reduced to poverty. When looking at data for blacks, the great increase in these families cancels out the gains of other blacks, causing mean income figures to suggest that blacks are almost as far behind whites as they were two decades ago. But the analysis above shows that the impact of fair employment legislation on black Americans has varied by group and has been affected by several factors other than discrimination.

Two of the most important additional factors that limit progress are sexism and the nation's economic ills. Past sexism prevented many women from gaining the qualifications necessary for well-paying jobs and present sexism continues to erect barriers. The nation's continuing high rates of unemployment and subemployment also deny opportunities to millions of Americans, a disproportionate percentage of whom are minorities and women.

One last major factor that impedes progress has been the government's rather modest enforcement efforts. While government enforcement improved during the late 1970s, enforcement efforts are not now and never were designed to achieve the maximum change in the least amount of time. Basically, the enforcement efforts were designed only to produce the incremental changes that have occurred so far. Clearly, the Reagan administration intends to further limit the impact of the equal employment laws.

REFERENCES

Bullock, Charles S. III (1975). "Expanding Black Economic Rights." In Harrell R. Rodgers, Jr. (ed.), *Racism and Inequality: The Policy Alternatives*. San Francisco: W. H. Freeman, pp. 75–123.
Congressional Quarterly Weekly Report (1981). "Affirmative Action Assailed in Congress: Administration" 39, no. 37 (September): 1749–1753.
Derryck, Dennis A. (1972). *The Construction Industry: A Black Perspective*. Washington, D.C.: Joint Center for Political Studies.
Fullilove v. Klutznick, 100 S. Ct. 2758 (1980).
Garfinkel, Irving, and Robert H. Haveman (1977). *Earning Capacity, Poverty and Inequality*. New York: Academic Press.
Griggs v. Duke Power Co., 401 U.S. 424 (1971).
Lamb, Charles M. (1980). "Presidential Leadership, Governmental Reorganization, and Equal Employment Opportunity." In Charles Bulmer and John C. Carmichael, Jr. (eds.), *Employment and Labor-Relations Policy*. Lexington, Mass.: Lexington Books.
Masters, Stanley H. (1975). *Black–White Income Differentials: Empirical Studies and Policy Implications*. New York: Academic Press.
McCrone, Donald J., and Richard J. Hardy (1978). "Civil Rights Policies and the Achievement of Racial Economic Equality." *American Journal of Political Science* 22, no. 1: 1–7.
Regents of the University of California v. Bakke, 438 U.S. 265 (1978).
Rodgers, Harrell R., Jr., and Charles S. Bullock III (1972). *Law and Social Change: Civil Rights Laws and Their Consequences*. New York: McGraw-Hill.
Rosenbloom, David H. (1980). "The Federal Affirmative-Action Policy." In David Nachmias (ed.), *The Practice of Policy Evaluation*. New York: St. Martin's Press.
Rosenthal, Albert J. (1973). "Employment Discrimination and the Law." *Annals of American Academy of Political and Social Sciences* 407 (May): 91–101.
United States v. Local 189, United Paperworkers, 397 U.S. 919 (1970).
United Steelworkers v. Weber, 99 S. Ct. 2728 (1979).
U.S. Bureau of the Census (1980). "Money Income and Poverty Status of Families and Persons in the United States: 1979 (Advance Report)." Series P-60, no. 116. Washington, D.C.: U.S. Government Printing Office.
U.S. Bureau of the Census (1981). "Money Income and Poverty Status of Families and Persons in the United States: 1980 (Advance Report)." Series P-60, no. 127. Washington, D.C.: U.S. Government Printing Office.
U.S. Civil Service Commission (1970). *Employment and Payrolls*. Washington, D.C.: U.S. Government Printing Office.
U.S. Civil Service Commission (1976). *Employment and Payrolls*. Washington, D.C.: U.S. Government Printing Office.
U.S. Commission on Civil Rights (1970). *Federal Civil Rights Enforcement Effort*. Washington, D.C.: U.S. Government Printing Office.
U.S. Commission on Civil Rights (1971). *One Year Later*. Washington, D.C.: U.S. Government Printing Office.
U.S. Commission on Civil Rights (1973). *The Federal Civil Rights Enforcement Effort—A Reassessment*. Washington, D.C.: U.S. Government Printing Office.

U.S. Commission on Civil Rights (1975). *To Eliminate Employment Discrimination: A Sequel*. Washington, D.C.: U.S. Government Printing Office.
U.S. Commission on Civil Rights (1977). *The Federal Civil Rights Enforcement Effort—1977*. Washington, D.C.: U.S. Government Printing Office.
U.S. Commission on Civil Rights (1980). *The State of Civil Rights: 1979*. Washington, D.C.: U.S. Government Printing Office.

Chapter 5

Racial Desegregation in Higher Education

Q. Whitfield Ayres

In 1969, while controversies raged over efforts to achieve racially unitary schools in the South, the federal government tackled the same problem in public institutions of higher education. Some of the concepts and approaches are the same for both levels, but desegregation of higher education raises fundamentally different issues which have split the black community and created intense opposition to the government's requirements. This chapter examines the evolution of federal desegregation policy in higher education, explores the extent of policy success achieved during the 1970s, and identifies important factors and issues that help to explain variation in (1) policy success between elementary–secondary education and higher education, (2) federal government activity in promoting desegregation of higher education, and (3) state responses to federal government requirements.

The problem, as defined by federal authorities, is the existence of "racially identifiable" or "dual" systems of higher education in nineteen states, located mainly in the southeast but extending as far north as Ohio and Pennsylvania and as far west as Missouri and Arkansas. These states previously had colleges or universities intended exclusively for blacks, who were forbidden by state law from entering white institutions. Those legal restrictions fell gradually over a thirty-year period before 1969, as the federal courts ordered one state after another to open all public colleges and universities to students without regard to race—an effort that received national attention when black students were ordered admitted to the Universities of Alabama and Mississippi. But, as was the case in elementary and secondary education, "freedom of choice" did not eliminate racially identifiable schools. Thirty-seven publicly supported, traditionally black colleges have survived as the legacies of de jure segregation; all but three remain over one-half black in student enrollment, and all but five had student bodies that were over three-fourths black in 1978 (Office for Civil Rights, 1980).

Predominantly black public colleges and universities have other characteristics that distinguish them from predominantly white institutions of higher education. Many place a strong emphasis on black culture by including the study of black history, art, and music. Admissions standards are frequently low, sometimes even nonexistent, by the usual measures, for these institutions see an important part of their mission as accepting students who have weak educational backgrounds. For example, on the Scholastic Aptitude Test (SAT), where combined verbal and mathematics scores can range from 400 to 1600, in the fall of 1978 the average combined score for entering freshmen at North Carolina's five public black campuses ranged from 588 to 707, compared with 810 to 1060 for the eleven public white campuses (University of North Carolina, 1979). Mostly because of low admissions standards, graduates of black colleges generally have higher failure rates than students from white institutions on licensing examinations for teaching, nursing, law, and other postcollege standardized tests (Johnson and Basgall, 1980; Stith, 1977). Faculty members at traditionally black colleges are less likely to have a Ph.D., or other terminal degree, than those at white institutions (University of North Carolina, 1979). These characteristics, along with predominantly black enrollments, distinguish many traditionally black institutions of higher education from their white counterparts.

Traditionally black colleges and universities have played a major role in the education of black Americans. Many black leaders graduated from black colleges, including civil rights activists Martin Luther King, Jr. (Morehouse College) and Jesse Jackson (North Carolina Agricultural and Technical State University), politicians Maynard Jackson (Morehouse College and North Carolina Central University) and Andrew Young (Howard University), and Supreme Court Justice Thurgood Marshall (Lincoln and Howard Universities). In 1976 over two-thirds of all blacks receiving bachelor degrees earned them from traditionally black institutions (Middleton, 1979). Black colleges and universities continue to be a vital component in the education of black Americans.

FEDERAL POLICY

As with all policy areas, desegregation policy for higher education should be thought of as evolving or developing rather than "made." Because so much desegregation policy derives from the interpretation of general constitutional requirements or vague statutes, the policy requirements of the 1980s might be very different from those for the 1970s, even though Congress had passed no new legislation in the area. With ambiguous statutes, the actual policy emerges and evolves through the implementation process. Federal higher education policy has been shaped by a combination of court orders and statute-inspired negotiations among federal administrators, interest group leaders, elected officials, and university personnel. This section discusses that evolving policy, explores the major policy goals, and identifies the means most commonly promoted for reaching those goals.

Legal Basis

Federal higher education desegregation policy rests on two legal foundations. The first is the equal protection clause of the Fourteenth Amendment to the Constitution. Since the Supreme Court's *Brown v. Board of Education* decision in 1954, federal courts have interpreted that clause as requiring the desegregation of elementary and secondary schools, based on the reasoning that racially separate schools are inherently unequal. The same logic has been applied to publicly supported institutions of higher education.

In 1968, for example, a federal judge in Tennessee wrote:

> [T]he Court is convinced that there is an affirmative duty imposed upon the State by the Fourteenth Amendment to the Constitution of the United States to dismantle the dual system of higher education which presently exists in Tennessee. [*Sanders v. Ellington*, 1968, 922]

In 1971, a federal judge in Virginia used the Fourteenth Amendment to block expansion of a two-year branch of the College of William and Mary into a four-year school because the branch was located only seven miles from traditionally black Virginia State College near Petersburg, and would therefore perpetuate the dual system (*Norris v. State Council of Higher Education*, 1971). In 1977, the judge in the Tennessee case noted above ordered the merger of traditionally black Tennessee State University and traditionally white University of Tennessee at Nashville on Fourteenth Amendment grounds (*Geier v. Blanton*, 1977). The University of Tennessee branch at Nashville, located less than three miles from Tennessee State, had been started as an evening college catering to part-time adult students, but it had grown into a degree-granting institution competing for students with the older Tennessee State.

A second legal foundation for federal desegregation policy in higher education is Title VI of the Civil Rights Act of 1964. Section 601 of the familiar statute states:

> No person in the United States shall, on the ground of race, color, or national origin, be excluded from participation in, be denied the benefits of, or be subjected to discrimination under any program or activity receiving Federal financial assistance.

The responsibility for interpreting this general principle in higher education has fallen to the Office for Civil Rights (OCR), originally established in the Department of Health, Education, and Welfare, and now located in the Department of Education.[1]

OCR has interpreted the persistence of public colleges and universities with a particular racial identity as evidence of discrimination forbidden by Title VI, even when no overt discrimination against individuals could be identified. In a 1970 statement of OCR's interpretation, the agency's director wrote:

> Responsible federal agencies have emphasized repeatedly that the persistence of racially identifiable institutions supports the conclusion that [a state] is not in compliance with the requirements of the law.
>
> Educational institutions which have previously been legally segregated have an affirmative duty to adopt measures to overcome the effect of past segregation. To fulfill the purposes and the intent of the Civil Rights Act of 1964, it is not sufficient that an institution maintain a nondiscriminatory admissions policy if the student population continues to reflect the formerly de jure racial identification of that institution. [Panetta, 1970][2]

Throughout the evolution of federal desegregation policy for higher education, Title VI has remained the major legal basis for OCR requirements.[3]

Policy Goals and Means

Desegregation policy in higher education based on the Fourteenth Amendment and Title VI of the Civil Rights Act of 1964 has two overriding policy goals. The first is the elimination of dual systems of higher education, or the racial desegregation of students, faculties, administrations, and governing boards at traditionally black and traditionally white colleges and universities. OCR has consistently emphasized that institutions of higher education must not "continue to reflect the formerly de jure racial identification of that institution" (Panetta, 1970), that a state must "accomplish full disestablishment of the dual system within a specified period" (Holmes, 1974), and that it should "fulfill its affirmative obligation to eliminate the dual system of postsecondary education" (Holmes, 1975).

The second policy goal is the improvement of traditionally black colleges and universities. To some extent this second goal is a means for reaching the first, since upgraded black institutions might attract more white students and therefore be less racially identifiable. But some blacks view enhancement as a discrete goal, justified on the basis of overcoming past discrimination, and one that OCR should pursue more vigorously than the elimination of racial identifiability (Friedlein, 1979).

The federal government has promoted numerous other changes in addition to these policy goals. For example, OCR has encouraged states to ensure proportionality in the numbers of black and white high school graduates who continue their education in publicly supported institutions of higher education. Therefore, if 40 percent of a state's white high school graduates attend state-supported junior or senior colleges, then so should 40 percent of the black high school graduates. The logic extends to each educational level, so that if 30 percent of white college graduates enter graduate or professional school, then 30 percent of black college graduates should also continue (Office for Civil Rights, 1978, 6662). The ultimate purpose here is to bring black citizens into the mainstream of American society by providing not only the same educational opportunities but also the same educational results available for whites.

Initially federal officials provided little if any specific guidance for reaching their policy goals. Judges and OCR administrators indicated that, since the states had originally created segregated systems of higher education, it was the states' responsibility to figure out how to dismantle them. But by the mid-1970s, federal officials had suggested, and then later required, adoption of certain means designed to eliminate dual systems and enhance traditionally black institutions.

One method designed to eliminate racial identifiability is the merger of nearby predominantly black and predominantly white campuses, a step required thus far only by federal courts in Nashville, and never by OCR. Among the means promoted by OCR are: (1) recruitment programs and scholarships to induce students to enroll on campuses where their race is in the minority; (2) affirmative action plans to recruit black faculty members to teach on traditionally white campuses and vice versa; and (3) compensatory funding for upgrading traditionally black institutions.[4] OCR has also required states with dual systems to define a unique, nonracially oriented mission for each traditionally black campus, and to institute attractive new programs at those institutions consistent with that mission. An additional requirement at proximate black and white campuses has been the elimination of "educationally unnecessary program duplication." By closing down high-demand programs like teacher education and business administration at one campus, and moving the programs with their faculties to the campus dominated by the other race, OCR hopes that students will follow the program rather than transfer to another institution or change majors.

Presumably these means will, if pursued decisively by the states, decrease racial identifiability and strengthen black institutions. The success of various states at reaching these policy goals during the 1970s is the subject of the following section.

SUCCESS IN DESEGREGATING HIGHER EDUCATION

Policy success in desegregating higher education is a matter of degree; we cannot conclude that federal policy has completely "succeeded" or "failed" at eliminating racial identifiability in higher education or at enhancing black institutions. Changes have occurred in most publicly supported colleges and universities in the desired direction during the 1970s, but few observers would argue that the institutions are no longer racially identifiable or that traditionally black colleges and universities enjoy a reputation of equality with their white counterparts.

The most common measure used by federal officials to evaluate racial identifiability is the black percentage among enrolled students. Table 5-1 compares the racial composition of the student bodies of publicly supported traditionally black senior institutions in nineteen states between fall 1970, which roughly corresponds to the initiation of OCR enforcement efforts in higher education, and fall 1978, the latest available data. The table ranks the states with public, traditionally black, senior institutions from the greatest to the least change in racial identifiability.

Three points are evident from table 5-1. First, in seventeen of the nineteen states, traditionally black campuses had a lower percentage of

TABLE 5-1 Racial Composition of Formerly All-Black Campuses Ranked by State

Rank	State	No. of Public Traditionally Black Campuses	% Black Fall 1970[a]	% Black Fall 1978	Change 1970–1978
1	Kentucky	1	83.8%	64.4%	−18.4%
2	Texas	2	97.9	80.5	−17.4
3	Oklahoma[b]	1	95.2	81.9	−13.3
4	Arkansas[b]	1	98.1	85.7	−12.4
5	Alabama	2	92.1	82.1	−10.0
6	West Virginia	2	30.5	21.0	−9.5
7	Georgia[b]	3	98.9	90.1	−8.8
8	Missouri	1	45.0	36.3	−8.7
9	Tennessee[c]	1	99.4	91.7	−7.7
10	North Carolina[b]	5	97.8	90.7	−7.1
11	Ohio	1	91.6	85.2	−6.4
12	Florida[b]	1	98.1	93.0	−5.1
13	Mississippi	3	99.9	95.2	−4.7
14	Virginia[b]	2	98.1	93.9	−4.2
15	Maryland	4	87.8	84.9	−2.9
16	Louisiana	3	99.0	96.4	−2.6
17	South Carolina	1	99.6	97.4	−2.2
18	Pennsylvania[b]	2	88.5	91.9	+3.4
19	Delaware	1	65.0	72.3	+7.3

[a] OCR data are not as complete for fall 1970 as they are for fall 1978. Where an institution's enrollments by race are missing for fall 1970, this table uses the figures for fall 1972 rather than eliminating the campus entirely. Fall 1972 data are used for 4 of the 37 traditionally black campuses included here: one in Maryland, one in Pennsylvania, and two in West Virginia. This procedure slightly underestimates the change in racial composition for those states.

[b] States under Office for Civil Rights scrutiny from 1970 to 1978

[c] State under federal court scrutiny from 1970 to 1978

SOURCES: Office for Civil Rights (1972); Office for Civil Rights (1974); Office for Civil Rights (1980).

black enrollment in 1978 than in 1970. Second, despite that change, the vast majority of publicly supported traditionally black campuses remain racially identifiable by any definition. Only Bluefield State and West Virginia State in West Virginia, and Lincoln University in Missouri, have student bodies that are not predominantly black, and all but five campuses have student enrollments that are over 75 percent black. Third, the change in student enrollments is apparently not a result of direct federal involvement. The seven states with which OCR negotiated from 1970 to 1978,[5] and Tennessee, which was under federal court scrutiny throughout the period, registered average declines in black percentages at traditionally black institutions of 6.9 percent, compared with exactly the same average decline for those states *not* under federal pressure. The reasons for this finding are examined below.

The findings are similar for the racial composition of student enrollments at publicly supported traditionally white senior institutions: there was progress toward "policy success"—substantial in some instances—but without eliminating completely the racial identifiability of the student bodies. Table 5-2 ranks the nineteen states according to the degree of change in black enrollments at each state's traditionally white senior institutions.

Table 5-2 should be read with particular care for several reasons. In the first place, states with low percentages of blacks in the population tend to have less change in the percentage of blacks enrolled on traditionally white campuses. West Virginia places last in this list because its black population of only 3.9 percent is so small that there was little likelihood of a substantial increase in black enrollment at traditionally white institutions. Next, the early data for 17 of the 256 campuses included in the table come from fall 1972 because of missing data for fall 1970. Table 5-2 therefore underestimates the change over this period and shows the greatest effect for Florida, where three of eight campuses are affected, and West Virginia, where data for all eight campuses are from 1972. Moreover, states in which black enrollment at traditionally white campuses increased substantially during the 1960s had less potential for change during the 1970s. Finally, states with a high proportion of black to white campuses face more difficulty in attracting blacks to white institutions. North Carolina, with five black and eleven white public campuses, has more trouble in enrolling blacks at white institutions than does South Carolina, which also has eleven white public campuses but only one black public institution. All four factors affect the ranking of states in table 5-2.

Nevertheless, table 5-2 discloses three important points about policy success at desegregating traditionally white campuses. First, substantial progress in increasing black enrollment at traditionally white institutions

TABLE 5-2 Racial Composition of Formerly All-White Campuses Ranked by State

Rank	State	% Black Fall 1970[a]	% Black Fall 1978	% Black Population (1970)	Change 1970–1978
1	Georgia[b]	3.1	10.5	25.9	+7.4
2	Alabama	3.3	10.0	26.2	+6.7
3	Louisiana	5.0	11.5	29.8	+6.5
4	Mississippi	3.5	9.8	36.8	+6.3
5	Maryland	3.9	10.1	17.8	+6.2
6	South Carolina	2.8	9.0	30.5	+6.2
7	Arkansas[b]	4.6	10.4	18.3	+5.8
8	Tennessee[c]	4.1	9.7	15.8	+5.6
9	North Carolina[b]	2.4	6.6	22.2	+4.2
10	Ohio	2.8	7.0	9.1	+4.2
11	Virginia[b]	2.0	5.2	18.5	+3.2
12	Florida[b]	2.9	6.0	20.6	+3.1
13	Kentucky	3.1	5.1	7.2	+2.0
14	Pennsylvania[b]	4.1	6.1	8.6	+2.0
15	Missouri	2.6	4.5	10.3	+1.9
16	Oklahoma[b]	3.8	5.0	6.7	+1.2
17	Texas	4.3	5.3	12.5	+1.0
18	Delaware	2.3	3.1	14.3	+0.8
19	West Virginia	2.3	2.8	3.9	+0.5

[a] Where an institution's enrollments by race are missing for fall 1970, this table follows the same procedure as table 5-1 and uses figures for fall 1972 rather than eliminating the campus entirely. Fall 1972 data are used here for 17 of the 256 traditionally white campuses included: one in each of four states—Maryland, Mississippi, North Carolina, and Oklahoma—two in Georgia, three in Florida, and all eight in West Virginia. Therefore the change shown is a slight underestimation for these states and has the greatest effect on the figures for Florida and West Virginia. Where an institution was either founded or taken over by a state during this period, enrollment figures are included for 1978 but not 1970.
[b] States under scrutiny of Office for Civil Rights from 1970 to 1978
[c] State under federal court scrutiny from 1970 to 1978
SOURCES: Office for Civil Rights (1972); Office for Civil Rights (1974); Office for Civil Rights (1980).

was achieved during this period. For example, the mean percentage black enrollment at Georgia's traditionally white schools more than tripled, and the actual number of blacks enrolled at traditionally black campuses more than quintupled, from 1,791 in 1970 to 9,556 in 1978. Phrased another way, of all blacks enrolled in Georgia's senior public institutions, 78 percent attended traditionally black campuses in 1970, but only 35 percent did so by 1978. Eleven of the nineteen states on this list more than tripled the number of black students attending traditionally white campuses between 1970 and 1978.

Second, most traditionally white campuses would probably still be considered "racially identifiable." The determination is not as clear for white as it is for black campuses, and OCR has never defined the extent of desegregation that would eliminate racial identifiability at white schools, but presumably that determination would be related in some way to a state's black population. Table 5-2 indicates that in none of these states was the percentage of black enrollment on white campuses in 1978 as high as the percentage of blacks in the state's population. States having the lowest percentage of blacks in the population—West Virginia, Oklahoma, Kentucky, and Ohio—come the closest at matching the two percentages.

Third, as with enrollment change on black campuses, increased enrollment of blacks on white campuses is apparently not directly related to federal government involvement. Those states with active federal scrutiny during the 1970s had an average increase of 4.1 percentage points compared to an increase of 3.8 points for states lacking federal pressure. For those states with black populations greater than 15 percent—the states with the greatest potential for growth in black enrollment at white institutions—the average increase was 4.9 percentage points for states with federal scrutiny compared to 6.4 percentage points for states lacking federal pressure.

Assessing policy success at improving education offered at traditionally black institutions is far more difficult than determining the extent of racial identifiability. During the 1970s all states under OCR scrutiny took steps to upgrade black campuses, ranging from supplemental budget allocations to overcome past funding deficiencies, to sabbatical leaves to allow faculty members to complete doctoral degrees, to the allocation of new academic programs (Commonwealth of Virginia, 1978; State of Arkansas, 1977; State University System of Florida, 1978; University of North Carolina, 1978; University System of Georgia, 1977). The difficulty of reliably measuring enhancement is a major stumbling block in assessing policy success, for the real object of measurement is the educational reputation of an institution, a difficult task that usually involves extensive polling. A second problem arises in trying to link federal involvement to institutional changes. For example, in the 1960s before OCR activity in higher education, North Carolina moved to equalize faculty salaries among black and white institutions of similar scope and to provide compensatory funding at traditionally black campuses, with special focus on improving library facilities (State of North Carolina, 1974, 80–83). Disentangling OCR-induced changes in the 1970s from those that would have occurred anyway is an almost impossible task.

This disentangling problem, which also arises in analyzing changes in racial enrollments, is featured in further discussion below. Because evaluating enhancement suffers from an additional problem with measurement, the remainder of this chapter will focus primarily on the extent of policy success in achieving the ultimate goal of federal policy, the elimination of racial identifiability. Progress has occurred, but complete success remains distant, especially for traditionally black colleges and universities.

VARIATION IN POLICY SUCCESS

The previous section established that although states differed in the degree of success at eliminating racially identifiable institutions of higher education, states under federal government pressure were apparently no more successful than other states. This finding suggests that the variables identified in chapter 1 are not directly related to success in this policy area. Moreover, it is difficult to tie a variable, such as "superior support for an agency," directly to a change in the racial composition of a state's public colleges and universities in a manner that will satisfy even the most minimal standards of scientific inquiry.

This does not mean, however, that the variables in chapter 1 are unimportant for the implementation process in desegregating higher education. Many of those factors directly affect two important intervening variables: the level of *government activity* and the *state response*. To the extent that government activity and state response influence policy success at reducing racial identifiability in higher education, the variables identified in the first chapter do apply.

Figure 5-1 diagrams the implementation process in desegregating higher education and highlights the relationship among several sets of factors. Several aspects of the national political environment, such as support for agency action from superiors, directly affected federal government

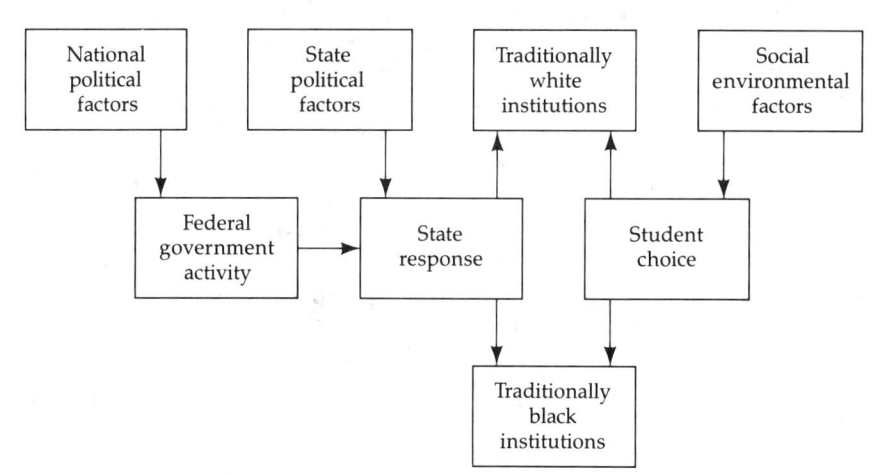

Figure 5-1 The Implementation Process for Desegregating Higher Education

activity in this area during the 1970s. Other variables describe characteristics of that activity, such as clarity of policy goals, which in turn affected state responses. Aspects of the state political environment—the number of traditionally black institutions is one example—also influenced state responses and help to explain why some states were so much more cooperative than others when faced with the same government requirements. State responses in turn create changes in both black and white colleges and universities, and these changes provide one indication of policy success. The ultimate measure of policy success, elimination of racial identifiability, is not directly affected by decisions of state officials but rather is largely determined by student choice. That choice may be influenced by institutional changes—indeed, that is the hope of OCR officials—but student choice also depends on social and environmental factors, such as students' racial attitudes, which are less amenable to control by either federal or state officials.

Figure 5-1 makes evident an important point about desegregating higher education: the federal government could be extremely active, and the states most cooperative, *yet policy success in eliminating racially identifiable campuses could still remain elusive because student choice is affected by so many factors that are not easily manipulated by federal or state officials.* This seemingly obvious point is often overlooked by commentators on higher education desegregation, much of whose rhetoric contains the underlying assumption that if the federal government were only more vigorous, and if state officials were only less recalcitrant, policy success would be achieved.

Figure 5-1 also offers an explanation of why states lacking federal pressure could achieve as much if not more success in eliminating racially identifiable campuses than states under federal scrutiny. One possible reason for this phenomenon is that officials in states not under federal pressure were aware of changes being ordered in states under federal scrutiny and were therefore making changes in anticipation of federal action. Another explanation, which is reflected in figure 5-1, asserts that student choices of higher education institutions are affected by a great variety of social and environmental influences, few of which can be manipulated by policymakers at any level of government. According to this argument, the forces that led increasing numbers of students to attend college on campuses dominated by another race were operating in all nineteen states, and those forces operated independently of federal involvement.

The first of three remaining parts of this chapter examines reasons for differing success at desegregation between the policy areas of higher education and elementary–secondary education. The second part identifies factors that affect government activity within the area of higher education desegregation, activity that has varied substantially both over time and among states. The third part addresses reasons for varying state responses to federal requirements for desegregating higher education. The second and third parts focus on *government activity* and *state response*, rather than on *desegregation success*, because explaining variation in desegregation success in higher education would require identifying myriad social and environmental elements in students' choice of a college or university, a task beyond the scope of this effort (for a review of those factors, see Kohn, Manski, and Mundel, 1976).

Variation in Policy Success between Elementary–Secondary and Higher Education

Particularly in the South, elementary and secondary schools are less racially identifiable than colleges and universities. Substantial desegregation occurred during the 1970s in Southern elementary and high schools, yet most public institutions of higher education remain over 75 percent black or over 85 percent white (Office for Civil Rights, 1980). If we look at the proportion of blacks attending school with whites, this also shows more desegregation in elementary and secondary schools than in higher education. For example, in 1972, over 98 percent of Delaware's black public school pupils attended with whites, but only 28.4 percent of the state's black college students attended Delaware's one predominantly white campus in 1978 (Office for Civil Rights, 1980). In North Carolina, 99.5 percent of the black elementary and secondary students were in schools with whites in 1972, compared to 29.2 percent of blacks in public higher education enrolled at predominantly white campuses in 1978. Comparable figures in Virginia show 99.4 percent of the black public school students in schools with whites, compared with 32.5 percent of blacks in public higher education.

At first glance these are curious findings, for many sources of desegregation resistance, such as white fears of eroding educational quality, are present at both levels, and presumably authorities associated with higher education would be more "enlightened" or willing to experiment with social change. But a closer examination reveals factors that hamper policy success in higher education.

One very important factor is the different *role of student choice* at the two educational levels. In elementary and secondary education, most students who attend public schools are assigned on the basis of geographical zones. Since attendance at some school is compulsory, a student's or family's only choices are to move to another public school district or to pay for attendance at a private school. Moreover, state-mandated curricula vary little from one school to another for the same grade level. The technical means for desegregating elementary and secondary education have long been available—students are assigned to school A rather than school B to create a racial balance. The major problems in desegregating elementary and high schools have been social and political, rather than technical.

The latitude allowed in student choice in higher education, naturally, is far broader. In higher education, attendance has traditionally not been free, compulsory, or based on geographical assignment. Students are able to choose any higher education institution to which they may be admitted and can afford, or they may forego college. In addition, colleges and universities differ far more than elementary and secondary schools in program emphases and educational strengths. Because of these characteristics, the technical means for desegregating higher education are not readily available without confronting a long-standing tradition of free student choice. To desegregate higher education, students must be induced to pay tuition and enroll as part of the minority race in institutions of widely varying educational emphases and quality. That poses a major technical, as well as political and social, challenge.

Another important factor in explaining variation in policy success between elementary–secondary and higher education is the *attitude of the policy's beneficiaries.* In this case, this is manifested by a sharp split among civil rights support groups. Black organizations generally are united behind efforts to desegregate elementary and secondary education, but they diverge on the question of whether traditionally black colleges and universities should continue to exist as racially identifiable institutions. The president of the NAACP Legal Defense and Education Fund (NAACP-LDF), a group that promotes thorough desegregation, argues that identifiably black campuses will inevitably be discriminated against in states where whites control economic and political power: "We have learned that black institutions just will not get the kind of funding and support that will make them competitive" (Chambers, 1979, 5B).

On the other hand, the National Association for Equal Opportunity in Higher Education, an organization of black college presidents, argues that OCR should concentrate on upgrading black institutions instead of vigorously seeking to eliminate racially identifiable colleges. According to this position, the black institutions' emphasis on black culture would never be available to the interested black student at traditionally white campuses, even through black studies programs. Traditionally black institutions, proponents argue, are examples of black accomplishment in which all blacks can take pride. Moreover, they provide educational opportunities for disadvantaged students in a compassionate, supportive environment, where students can feel a part of the social as well as academic life of an institution. In short, the argument asserts that, in a time of heightened ethnic consciousness, black institutions provide essential services that would be eliminated should they lose their racial identity (Friedlein, 1979, 1; 5B-6B).

Several fears lie behind this argument. Blacks associated with black campuses fear that desegregation will reduce educational opportunities for poorly prepared black students who, by traditional admissions standards, would not be accepted by most white colleges and universities. Blacks on black campuses fear that desegregation will lead to losing better-prepared blacks to white campuses. If white students do not quickly replace those blacks, state appropriations based on enrollment will fall. Last but not least, some black administrators and faculty members at black institutions fear for their jobs as a result of the desegregation experiences of elementary and secondary education, when many blacks were replaced by whites.

Opposition to federal desegregation requirements has been intense among some blacks. The transfer of the "educationally unnecessary" teacher education program from traditionally black Savannah State College to traditionally white Armstrong State College seven miles away, and the transfer of the business administration program from Armstrong State to Savannah State, sparked violent demonstrations on the black campus. A black newspaper columnist charged OCR with a "course of black genocide in higher education. They [OCR officials] think the destruction of black institutions is the salvation of black people" (Brown, 1979).

The wide leeway allowed for student selection in higher education based on the different characteristics and traditions of postsecondary education compared with elementary and secondary education, and disagreements in the black community, which had been united in support for efforts to desegregate elementary–secondary schools, help to explain why there has been less success in eliminating racial identifiability in colleges and universities.

Variation in Government Activity in Higher Education Desegregation

The amount and substance of government activity within the area of higher education desegregation has waxed and waned substantially, over time and among states. As indicated by the chronology of government actions presented in table 5-3, federal enforcement was characterized by surges of activity followed by periods of calm. The substance of federal requirements as well as the amount of activity has varied over time, with a pattern of moving from general exhortations that states must eliminate racial identifiability, to requirements specifying particular actions.

The first consideration is *support from superiors*, especially for OCR action; the greater the superior support, the more vigorous the government activity. Shortly after OCR began enforcing Title VI in higher education in 1969, the Nixon administration put the agency, in the words of

TABLE 5-3 Major Federal Actions in Desegregating Higher Education, 1964–1981

Year	Action	Agent
1964	Civil Rights Act of 1964 passed	Congress
1966	Office for Civil Rights (OCR) established	HEW
1969–1970	Letters requesting desegregation plans sent to Arkansas, Florida, Georgia, Louisiana, Maryland, Mississippi, North Carolina, Oklahoma, Pennsylvania, and Virginia	OCR
1970	Enforcement halted	Nixon administration
1973	OCR ordered to obtain desegregation plans from the 10 states contacted in 1969–1970	Federal court *Adams v. Richardson*
1974	Desegregation plans accepted from Arkansas, Florida, Georgia, Maryland, North Carolina, Oklahoma, Pennsylvania, and Virginia; Louisiana and Mississippi referred to Justice Department	OCR
1976	Maryland obtains injunction against OCR	Federal court *Mandel v. HEW*
1977	OCR ordered to revoke acceptance of existing desegregation plans from Arkansas, Florida, Georgia, North Carolina, Oklahoma, and Virginia, and obtain new plans under more stringent criteria	Federal court *Adams* case
	Predominantly white University of Tennessee at Nashville ordered to merge into predominantly black Tennessee State University	Federal court *Geier v. Blanton*
1978	Desegregation plans accepted from Arkansas, Florida, Georgia, Oklahoma, and Virginia	OCR
1979	Administrative proceedings started against North Carolina	OCR
1980	OCR ordered to obtain desegregation plans from Alabama, Delaware, Kentucky, Missouri, Ohio, South Carolina, Texas, and West Virginia	Federal court *Adams* case
1981	Desegregation plans accepted from Delaware, Missouri, South Carolina, West Virginia, and Texas (provisional acceptance); North Carolina case settled through consent decree	OCR
	Louisiana case settled through consent decree	Justice Dept.

one OCR official, "in a holding pattern" (Guthrie, 1976). At the time, the agency had only made initial on-site reviews of several racially identifiable campuses and had requested desegregation plans from ten states. As part of his Southern strategy, Nixon stopped this activity and fired OCR director Leon Panetta, who charged that "political pressures" had led to his removal (Panetta and Gall, 1971, 363). OCR effectively suspended action on Title VI enforcement in higher education for three years.

The importance of superior support for agency action can also be seen during the Reagan administration, when OCR adopted a much less aggressive stance in response to a more conservative president and his appointees. The agency settled a long-standing dispute with North Carolina and accepted state desegregation plans that were not always consonant with established desegregation criteria.

Any resumption of OCR activity during the Nixon administration, and its continuation during the Reagan years, resulted from the *attitudes of policy beneficiaries,* specifically *external pressure for action,* certainly one of the most powerful influences in explaining government activity in this policy area. The greater the external pressure for action, the more vigorous the government activity. One form of external pressure has been litigation brought by black plaintiffs against state officials. A second aspect has been suits by black organizations brought against OCR. Disgusted with the foot-dragging of the Nixon administration, the NAACP-LDF filed suit in federal district court in Washington, D.C., charging that OCR had found the desegregation plans of Arkansas, Georgia, Maryland, Pennsylvania, and Virginia unacceptable but had not formally commented or requested revisions. In addition, the suit charged that OCR had failed to receive plans from Florida, Louisiana, Mississippi, North Carolina, and Oklahoma but had taken no action in response. On February 16, 1973, Judge John Pratt ordered OCR to obtain acceptable desegregation plans from the ten states in 120 days or to begin enforcement proceedings leading to a cut-off of federal funds (*Adams v. Richardson,* 1973). That deadline was later extended for one year.

As table 5-3 makes clear, orders in the *Adams* case periodically stimulated and structured OCR activity. After OCR accepted desegregation plans from eight states in June 1974 and judged those plans to be in compliance with Title VI, the NAACP-LDF filed another motion arguing that the plans were unacceptable. In 1977, Judge Pratt agreed and ordered OCR to obtain new plans under more stringent criteria. In December 1980, responding to another NAACP-LDF motion, Judge Pratt ordered OCR to expand its efforts to seven other states that had not previously been required to submit plans. External pressure, particularly from the NAACP-LDF using the federal courts as an intermediary, has been a major force behind government action in higher education desegregation.

A third factor that has affected government action over time might be called *learning,* understanding, or experience. As more experience accrued, more direct linkages between government requirements and policy goals were evidenced. Both court and OCR requirements have become more specific as the authorities have become familiar with the unusual operations of state-supported higher education. In 1972, the Tennessee judge wrestled with the problem of how to desegregate public higher education when free student choice does not eliminate a dual system, but he was unable at that time to develop specific requirements. "What must be done now?" the judge wrote. "The answer is not simple, for, indeed, the law is not clear" (*Geier v. Dunn*, 1972, 576). Five years later he ordered the merger of Nashville's two state-supported institutions of higher education.

OCR officials, as well as federal judges, were not very knowledgeable about higher education in the agency's early years (Lepper, 1976). The tenure systems and collegial governance characteristic of higher education were foreign concepts to government officials used to the personnel relationships of the civil service and the hierarchical organization of federal bureaucracies. Even in 1980, after a decade of experience, a high-ranking OCR official said that the agency did not know the effect of eliminating "educational unnecessary program duplication" on student enrollments (Bryson, 1980). Even though requirements had become more specific with experience, OCR was still engaged in a trial-and-error implementation process where knowledge gleaned from one experiment would affect future requirements.

Two other variables, the *presence of an enforcement agency* and *personnel committed to civil rights*, appear to be less important for explaining the amount of government activity. OCR is clearly the responsible enforcement agency, and there is every reason to believe that its personnel are committed to their interpretation of civil rights. In this policy area, however, superior support and external pressure appear to be greater influences on government activity than the mere presence of an agency or the attitude of its personnel.

Support from superiors, external pressure for action, and agency experience all affect both the amount and the character of government activity over time. Government activity has also varied among the nineteen involved states, with OCR concentrating on a few states while virtually ignoring others with dual systems. In 1970, the agency focused on ten states *not* including Alabama, Delaware, Kentucky, Missouri, Ohio, South Carolina, Tennessee, Texas, or West Virginia—all of which contained racially identifiable public institutions of higher education. At least three factors help to explain inconsistencies in government activity among states.

The first is *administrative coordination* between OCR and the federal courts; the greater the attention given a state by federal courts, the lower the probability that the state will be selected for agency enforcement. Initially, OCR made a conscious decision to avoid states where federal courts were actively reviewing systems of higher education (Bryson, 1980). (OCR had followed a similar practice in elementary–secondary school desegregation.) Administrative coordination appears to be the dominant explanation of OCR avoidance of contact with Tennessee and Alabama in 1970. This division of states between the two federal authorities was reinforced by the *Adams* case, which directed OCR to pursue compliance vigorously in those states it had initially selected but did not require the agency to expand its enforcement efforts until 1981.

Political considerations are a second factor in explaining nonuniformity in OCR activity among states. Important here was the influence that particular politicians had with OCR's superiors. The greater the political influence of a state's leaders, the lower the probability that the state will be selected for agency enforcement. This factor is difficult to demonstrate conclusively, but a number of sources on different sides of the issue indicate that Republican Senator Strom Thurmond had a passive but important role in eliminating South Carolina from the initial set of states reviewed by OCR. In 1970, Thurmond was influential with the Nixon administration after having been an architect of Nixon's 1968 election victory. Apparently OCR ignored South Carolina to avoid antagonizing Thurmond, because to do so might have created conflicts with Congress and the White House. Republican Senator John Tower of Texas evidently played a role akin to Thurmond's and kept his state from being included in the initial enforcement group.[6]

An OCR decision to *concentrate resources on the most difficult cases* is a third factor in explaining government activity among states. States in which enforcement was expected to be more difficult or complex were more often designated for agency enforcement.[7] Seven of the ten original states targeted by OCR contain more than one traditionally black institution and therefore provided a greater desegregation challenge. An eighth state, Florida, while it maintains only one public black campus (Florida Agricultural and Mechanical University in Tallahassee), also supports a white campus (Florida State University) only five miles away.

Of the nine states *not* originally chosen by OCR, the absence of Alabama and Tennessee is accounted for by the division of labor between OCR and the courts, and South Carolina and Texas by political considerations. Of the five remaining excluded states, Missouri and West Virginia have one and two traditionally black campuses respectively, but these had majority white enrollments as early as 1970. The three remaining states each operated only one public black institution and therefore provided a less inviting target.

Administrative coordination between the federal courts and OCR, political considerations about politicians who might affect OCR's superior support, and an agency decision to concentrate resources on the most difficult enforcement targets all help to explain variation in government activity among states. The next section addresses variations in state responses to that government activity.

Variation in State Response

The response of states chosen for federal activity has fluctuated over time as a result of at least two factors. The first is *policy clarity*, or how an agency or court communicates policy goals. Periodic confusion about government policy has reduced the probability of a cooperative state response. Despite continual admonitions to eliminate racial identifiability, in 1976 the OCR Director stated that his agency had "no objection to institutions that were predominantly black in racial composition" (Holmes, 1976). Another OCR official indicated in 1980 that a traditionally black institution could comply with the demands of Title VI with a faculty that was only 25 to 30 percent nonblack (Bryson, 1980). Presumably a college would still be "racially identifiable" when blacks constitute a majority of both student enrollment and faculty. Confusion in stating goals can be traced back to the split in black support groups. OCR usually responds to NAACP-LDF preferences by pushing for desegregation, but on occasion it acquiesces to the demands of those who wish to maintain traditionally black institutions as racially identifiable schools.

Such inconsistency leads to confusion among the states regarding what goals are actually being promoted. Maryland's lieutenant governor complained:

> [W]e have been, from the beginning, anxious to do what we conceive Title VI to be all about. . . . But then began this incredible zig zag course, this pursuit of a moving target, sometimes an almost invisible target, where the Department simply wouldn't tell us what they wanted or wouldn't tell us in words that could be translated into a plan in the real world and their erratic changes of course and changes of pace, of speed, made it very difficult for the State. [Lee, 1976]

A second factor that has affected state response is the lack of *precise standards for measuring compliance* with desegregation goals. OCR and the courts were often unspecific in the early years of enforcement about what the states had to do to comply with policy goals. OCR began enforcement with a conscious attempt to avoid setting precise standards. As a former OCR director wrote in a 1969 memorandum, "It would seem prudent to place the burden for developing a plan on the State. If we make specific suggestions we are as a practical matter stuck with them, whether they 'work' or not" (Gerry, 1969). The result of such an approach was that OCR deemed all the plans initially received to be unacceptable because they lacked specificity. North Carolina's rejection letter included the statement, "Your State's submission does not provide us with a specific plan; rather it states a general 'Program' which could lead to the development of a specific plan" (Holmes, 1973). In 1974, more-specific requirements elicited plans that OCR judged to be acceptable.

With the exception of a 1973 requirement that "white students at predominantly black institutions ought to constitute 'one-third of their student bodies' " (Holmes, 1975), a standard that was later withdrawn, OCR has never identified ultimate desegregation standards. The agency did issue criteria in 1977 which included the specific requirement that states should increase the enrollment of blacks at traditionally white institutions by at least 150 percent over five years (Office for Civil Rights, 1978,

6662), a requirement that elicited a commitment from the five *Adams* states whose plans were accepted by the agency. But there are, at this writing, no precise standards by which OCR and the states can measure their ultimate compliance with Title VI.

OCR *monitors* progress on accepted plans annually. This, however, appears to be less important than clarity of policy goals and precise standards for measuring compliance for influencing state responses over time. Reaction to federal requirements has also varied among states at any one time. Four of the ten states originally targeted by OCR balked at the agency's enforcement efforts, and two others found agreement extremely difficult. Louisiana did not respond to the original 1970 OCR request to submit a plan to eliminate racial duality in higher education, so the Justice Department sued and the state countersued. In 1981, a panel of federal judges accepted a compromise agreement negotiated by the Reagan administration with the state. Mississippi's original plan was held unacceptable because it did not contain commitments regarding the state's community colleges. The Justice Department sued and that case is still pending. Maryland developed an acceptable plan in 1974, but state officials later charged OCR with harassment. The state sued in 1975 and won a restraining order against further OCR involvement. North Carolina decided in 1979 to face administrative hearings that could lead to the cut-off of federal funds rather than transfer programs to meet OCR's requirement to eliminate "educationally unnecessary program duplication." A negotiated settlement ended that confrontation in 1981. Georgia and Virginia engaged in intensive negotiations before their revised desegregation plans were accepted in 1978. On the other hand, of the original *Adams* states, Arkansas, Florida, and Oklahoma have thus far reached agreement with OCR with relatively less confrontation. Why are some states apparently so much more willing than others to cooperate with government requirements?

Several factors are important for explaining different state responses. One is the *elite attitudes* in a state. A clear indication of the importance of this factor occurred in Virginia, where the state was apparently on a collision course with OCR in the fall of 1977. But after a new governor was elected in November of that year, negotiations were reopened, and agency and state officials eventually agreed on a compromise plan for further desegregation (Holland, 1978). Elite attitudes also help to explain why Louisiana proved recalcitrant to early federal desegregation demands (Panetta and Gall, 1971, 323).

An assessment of costs versus benefits of compliance plays a role in shaping state reactions. In some states the costs of compliance are perceived to exceed the benefits of avoiding an expensive legal battle with the government. Three components of the cost–benefit calculus are outlined below.

The greater the *number of traditionally black public institutions*, the higher the cost of compliance. The three original *Adams* states that reached agreement with OCR most easily—Arkansas, Florida, and Oklahoma—each maintain only one public traditionally black campus. On the other hand, of the four original *Adams* states that chose adversary proceedings over continued negotiations with OCR, Louisiana and Mississippi each support three traditionally black institutions, Maryland supports four, and North Carolina supports five.

Many educators perceive the total size of a state's resources for higher education as fixed in any one year. Programs and dollars allocated to one institution come not from other state agencies but directly from other public colleges and universities. Indeed, Florida explicitly stated in a 1978 communication to OCR:

> A number of new programs have been established at Florida A&M University at a time when new programs at other institutions have been limited. . . . [T]he initiation of new programs at the State's other two older universities has been strongly curtailed during this period. Even the six new and developing universities have had, on the average, fewer programs approved than Florida A&M University. [State University System of Florida, 1978, 29]

If the proportion of a state's resources allocated for public higher education in any one year is fixed, white institutions in states with several black campuses will have to make greater sacrifices to meet OCR's enhancement criteria than will white colleges in states with only one black campus. Officials associated with new and developing traditionally white institutions view this burden as particularly heavy since their campuses are in the most intense competition for new programs with black campuses.

The number of traditionally black institutions also affects the amount of desegregation that must occur for the campuses to eliminate racial identifiability, because a higher proportion of black students are enrolled in black colleges in states with several black campuses. In Oklahoma, only 6 percent of blacks in public colleges and universities in 1978 attended the one black school at Langston; in North Carolina 70 percent of blacks enrolled in public higher education in 1978 attended the five black campuses. The greater change required of states with several black institutions raises the cost of compliance. In an ironic twist, the states that were more vigorous in providing educational opportunities for blacks during the days of de jure segregation are now the states for whom the cost of civil rights compliance is highest.

A second component of the cost calculus is the *perceived range of quality* among the various public colleges and universities in a state; the greater the perceived differences in quality, the higher the cost of compliance.[8] This is particularly true in states containing a leading research institution.

It is therefore no coincidence that, in the ten states originally targeted by OCR, the only two public universities that are members of the prestigious Association of American Universities, the University of North Carolina at Chapel Hill and the University of Virginia, are located in states that have found compliance with OCR requirements extremely difficult. Where state officials perceive great differences between leading white campuses and the black institutions in institutional quality as measured by admissions standards, faculty qualifications, available resources, and general reputation, then the leading campuses must make greater sacrifices to upgrade traditionally black institutions, raising the cost of compliance substantially.

OCR requirements to eliminate racial identifiability and enhance black campuses have added racial overtones to two long-simmering disputes in higher education, disputes reflected in the range of quality component of the cost calculus. The first conflict arises out of a tension between "flagship" research campuses and smaller institutions that hope to imitate the leading university by obtaining a broad range of attractive graduate and professional programs. For many years, some states concentrated their higher education resources, and especially their advanced academic programs, on one or two campuses in order to develop a nationally recognized center of educational excellence such as those in Berkeley, Ann Arbor, Madison, or Chapel Hill. Now, particularly where states have consolidated some or all of their publicly supported postsecondary institutions into one system, educators associated with the flagship institutions fear that, by spreading programs and appropriations among many public campuses, a leveling process will tarnish if not destroy the excellence of the major research institutions.

OCR requirements became entangled in this leveling dispute, which existed before the federal government's desegregation efforts, when the agency mandated that desegregation plans should

> commit the state to give priority consideration to placing any new undergraduate, graduate, or professional degree programs, courses of study, etc., which may be proposed, at traditionally black institutions, consistent with their missions. [Office for Civil Rights, 1978, 6661]

From the OCR perspective, past missions and program placement at traditionally black public colleges and universities were influenced by discriminatory conceptions of the proper role for those institutions. Therefore, to make up for past discrimination, states ought to define new, expanded, nonracially oriented missions for traditionally black campuses and support those new missions with attractive new programs. The compounding of this OCR requirement with the older leveling dispute is clearly evident in North Carolina, where one cannot overstate the determination of state officials to maintain Chapel Hill as a leading research institution. Any perceived threat to the excellence of that university, whether through lowered standards or program transfers, immediately raises costs to unacceptable levels in their eyes.

Another protracted dilemma that ties into the cost calculus is the role of disadvantaged students, of any race, in senior institutions of higher education. One argument asserts that a publicly supported institution has an obligation to educate any graduate of a state high school who wishes to attend. The opposing side holds that one of the major components of an institution's reputation is the educational preparation and academic capacity of the student body, and that any college or university striving for a strong academic reputation must be selective in student admissions.

OCR requirements added racial overtones to this historical dispute because of the wide range in the educational preparation of student bodies in some states' black and white campuses. In North Carolina, for example, the average combined SAT verbal and mathematics score for the student bodies at two public black campuses was about 600 in 1978, compared with 1100 at the Chapel Hill campus (University of North Carolina, 1979, 128). Educators associated with white campuses fear that the enrollment of many students who are poorly prepared, as judged by traditional admissions standards, will divert institutional resources toward remedial programs, lower scores on postcollege standardized tests and licensing exams, hinder recruitment of faculty, and generally harm the reputation of the institutions. Where the perceived range of quality among public senior institutions is great, the costs of eliminating racial identifiability are higher, and federal desegregation policy has met more resistance.

Assuming that all higher education institutions care about maintaining decision-making autonomy, a third element in analyzing cost–benefit considerations is the *perception of autonomy in valued decisions.* The perceived loss of autonomy is apparently affected by the style of agency enforcement.

In 1975 Maryland obtained an injunction against further OCR activity in the state's higher education system by charging the agency with capricious and arbitrary enforcement. OCR had claimed that "Maryland has repeatedly failed to act in a manner which would indicate that it is executing the [Desegregation] Plan promptly and vigorously." The agency identified a number of specific actions that would have to be completed within sixty days to avoid enforcement proceedings leading to termination of federal funds. Included in the actions was a requirement that the state "within 60 days obtain and allocate the funds necessary to overcome all deficiencies" in "financial handicaps, inadequate educational backgrounds, and unfair and discriminatory social conditions" (Dodds, 1975). Maryland officials countered that the state legislature, which would have to approve new appropriations, would not be in session during any of the sixty-day period. The state's reply cited a table contained in a status report to OCR that listed the racial composition of Maryland's higher education institutions and claimed:

> This table demonstrates—in absolute numbers and by percentages—a tangible and visible progress toward the 1980 targets. Four institutions reached the 1980 projected range in the 1974–1975 academic year, and most of the others are well on the way. . . . [T]he accompanying list of absurd demands can only be viewed as a unilateral repudiation by the Office for Civil Rights of the Plan itself and of OCR's approval of it a year ago. . . . The Maryland Council for Higher Education will continue to direct the program, but it will submit to no further bureaucratic harassment by your office. [*Mandel v. HEW*, 1976]

In addition to the style of agency enforcement, personal relationships between OCR administrators and state officials also affect the perceived degree of state autonomy. Where relationships are characterized by mutual respect, and where state officials view OCR officials as reasonable people of good will who will promote desegregation without harming higher education institutions, cooperation with OCR does not seem to involve a significant loss of autonomy. This appears to be the case with at least some Florida officials who deal with the agency (Groomes, 1980). On the other hand, some North Carolina officials believe that OCR would willingly destroy the excellence of higher education in the state in order to serve the agency's civil rights goals. The chairman of the University of North Carolina board of governors claimed that if the state were to follow OCR's 1977 criteria, "it would probably destroy the University of North Carolina system as we know it today" (Christensen, 1978). In addition, some North Carolina officials have little respect for the capabilities and particularly the higher education expertise of OCR administrators.

Another sore point that predates desegregation controversies lies behind the autonomy component of the cost calculus. For many years public colleges and universities fought off intrusion by state governments in the areas of admissions, hiring, and curriculum. Federal desegregation initiatives strike some university administrators as the same fight with a different antagonist. In their view, federal desegregation efforts involve the same old attempt by "politicians" and "bureaucrats" to help their constituents by influencing decisions that rightfully belong in the hands of educators.

This issue is well illustrated by the OCR criterion that requires a plan for eliminating racial duality to

> commit the state to advise OCR of proposed major changes in the mission or the character of any institution within the state system which may directly or indirectly affect the achievement of its desegregation goals prior to its formal adoption.

Such proposed changes include but are not limited to: the establishment or major expansion of new programs of study, of departments or institutions; the alteration of two year to four year institutions; the conversion of a private to a public institution, or the closing or merger of institutions or campuses. [Office for Civil Rights, 1978, 6661]

This criterion, particularly the reference to new programs or departments, raises the defenses of higher education officials concerned about preserving decision-making autonomy. Reactions of different states to this criterion can be explained in part by differing perceptions of the degree of autonomy sacrificed by making the commitment.

The two major benefits of compliance are the continuation of federal funding and the avoidance of court battles with their expense and negative publicity. From a state perspective these are substantial benefits, so substantial that some states are reluctant to challenge OCR even when higher education officials resist agency requirements. Virginia's governor requested $250,000 from the state legislature in 1978 for a legal contingency fund, at a time when negotiations for an acceptable desegregation plan were making little progress, but he received only minor support (Holland, 1978). State politicians clearly wished to avoid another race-related battle with the federal government like those waged over efforts to desegregate elementary and secondary education, which had consumed so much time and money during the 1960s.

From the perspective of state officials, the threat of losing federal funds provides substantial leverage for OCR, even though no state has yet been denied federal higher education dollars. The loss of federal funds for scholarships and research grants would be devastating for any state's higher education program. Some higher education officials fear that even a well-publicized disagreement with OCR harms a state's research universities by discouraging leading scholars from accepting appointments at a school which might be placed off-limits for federal grants (Sanders, 1975). Since all states see substantial benefits in complying with OCR requirements, differences in their responses to OCR are better explained by elite attitudes and varying costs of compliance.

CONCLUSION

Desegregating higher education involves complex and difficult questions, many of which did not arise in efforts to desegregate elementary and secondary schools. The wide latitude historically accorded student choice in higher education, and the intense opposition of some blacks to thorough desegregation of traditionally black institutions, have inhibited desegregation efforts in postsecondary education. The vast majority of previously segregated public colleges and universities have achieved some progress toward desegregation during the 1970s, and such change has occurred in states with and without federal scrutiny. Still, racial identifiability stubbornly persists in higher education. That persistence cannot simply be attributed to government inactivity or state intransigence, for many factors beyond the ready control of public decision makers affect a student's choice of a college or university. Consequently, in the absence of a marked restriction of student choice or institutional closings, some racial identifiability is likely to continue for years, especially on traditionally black campuses.

Because of the importance of relatively uncontrollable social and environmental factors that affect student choice of an institution, state-to-state variation in "policy success" at desegregating higher education cannot be adequately explained by variables discussed in chapter 1. Both the degree of and changes in racial identifiability between West Virginia's and Virginia's public colleges, for example, are more attributable to differences in the percentage of blacks in the states' populations than to other more controllable factors. The variables do, however, help to explain alterations in federal government activity and differences in state reactions. The amount and substance of government activity to desegregate higher education has, over time, been shaped by support from superiors, attitudes of policy beneficiaries, and learning or experience in the policy area. The focus of agency activity among states has been influenced by administrative coordination between the courts and the Office for Civil Rights, by political considerations to preserve superior support, and by an effort to focus resources on the most difficult cases first. The presence of an enforcement agency and personnel committed to civil rights appear to be less important for explaining fluctuations in government activity. State responses over time have been influenced by policy clarity and the precision of standards for measuring compliance. At any one time, responses of different states to the same government requirements have been molded by elite attitudes and by a cost calculus involving the number of traditionally black campuses in the state, the perceived range of quality among publicly supported higher education institutions, and perceived levels of self-determination. Agency monitoring of state compliance appears to be less important than elite attitudes and the cost calculus for explaining differences in state responses.

Desegregation of higher education may be an example of the increasing complexity of civil rights issues in which the "right" and the "wrong" sides are not as easily identified as they were in the civil rights disputes of the 1960s. Federal efforts to desegregate higher education raise legitimate issues for debate, issues that cannot be simply dismissed as racism in disguise for whites, or as economic self-protection for blacks associated with traditionally black institutions. Among these issues are the role of federal officials in higher education decision making, the tension between demands for equity and the desire to maintain and promote excellence in higher education, and the future of traditionally black colleges and universities as racially identifiable institutions. Failure to resolve these very fundamental dilemmas will mean continued complications in implementing civil rights policy in higher education.

NOTES

1. For the history and organizational development of the Office for Civil Rights, see Orfield, 1969, 328–342; and Rabkin, 1980.
2. OCR did not at first use the traditional means of the *Federal Register* to communicate legal requirements to the states, but instead sent letters to state governors or education officials. The agency followed this procedure because of time constraints and the need to adapt requirements to distinctive characteristics of higher education in each state. While letters to different states varied in some particulars, general policy interpretations were the same.
3. OCR has also used Executive Order 11246, which prohibits discrimination in employment, as the basis for affirmative action plans for faculty members and administrators. In 1978 that responsibility was shifted to the Labor Department's Office of Federal Contract Compliance Programs (Rabkin, 1980, 437).
4. These suggestions and requirements are taken from letters sent to states between 1970 and 1977 (Holmes, 1973, 1974, 1975), and from the set of desegregation criteria that OCR issued in 1977 (Office for Civil Rights, 1978).
5. Maryland, which won an injunction against OCR in 1975 forbidding further enforcement, is not included in this group of seven states. From 1970 to 1973, OCR was inactive in enforcing desegregation in higher education, and the first state desegregation plans were not approved until June of 1974. Therefore Maryland had only one year of actual enforcement of a desegregation plan before it obtained the injunction.
6. Other implementation studies also reveal the importance of this factor. In 1966 the Economic Development Administration selected Oakland to be the site for an ambitious jobs program, in part because the city had a Republican mayor who could not appeal over the heads of the administrators to Democratic President Johnson (Pressman and Wildavsky, 1973, 14–15).
7. This factor is also not unique to implementation of desegregation in higher education. It is common in other administrative efforts, notably antitrust enforcement. The opposite pattern was followed by OCR in public schools, however, where desegregation plans were initially sought from districts which had few blacks and therefore were expected to be less resistant.

8. Much of the information about perceptions of state officials, on which the second and third components of the cost calculus are based, is gleaned from formal interviews in Florida (Flory, 1980; Groomes, 1980), Georgia (Ashmore, 1980; Hall, 1980), and North Carolina (Robinson, 1975; Sanders, 1975; Thompson, 1976), and from numerous informal discussions with University of North Carolina officials from 1975 to 1979.

REFERENCES

Adams v. Richardson, 356 F. Supp. 92 (D.D.C.) (1973).
Ashmore, Henry L. (1980). Interview with the president of Armstrong State College, Savannah, Ga., June 12, 1980.
Brown, Tony (1979). Quoted in Ken Friedlein, "Slow Fade to White—Worry on Black Campuses: Can Identity Survive Integration?" Charlotte *Observer*, September 9, 1979.
Bryson, Louis (1980). Interview with director of Higher Education Division, Atlanta Regional Office of Office for Civil Rights, July 23, 1980.
Chambers, Julius (1979). Quoted in Ken Friedlein, "Slow Fade to White—Worry on Black Campuses: Can Identity Survive Integration?" Charlotte *Observer*, September 9, 1979.
Christensen, Rob (1978). "UNC Decries Proposal From HEW." Raleigh *News and Observer*, February 2, 1978.
Civil Rights Act of 1964. 42 U.S.C. 2000d.
Commonwealth of Virginia (1978). *The Virginia Plan for Equal Opportunity in State-Supported Institutions of Higher Education* (Rev. 1978). Richmond: Council of Higher Education.
Dodds, Dewey (1975). Letter from director of Philadelphia Regional Office of Office for Civil Rights to Maryland Governor Marvin Mandel, August 7, 1975.
Flory, Daisy (1980). Interview with the dean of the faculties, Florida State University, Tallahassee, June 24, 1980.
Friedlein, Ken (1979). "Slow Fade to White—Worry on Black Campuses: Can Identity Survive Integration?" Charlotte *Observer*, September 9, 1979.
Geier v. Blanton, 427 F. Supp. 644 (M.D. Tenn.) (1977).
Geier v. Dunn, 337 F. Supp. 573 (M.D. Tenn.) (1972).
Gerry, Martin (1969). Memorandum to Office for Civil Rights Director Leon Panetta, November 1969. Quoted in *Mandel v. U.S. Department of Health, Education, and Welfare* (1976), 411 F. Supp. 542 at 551 (D.D.C.).
Groomes, Freddie (1980). Interview with assistant to the president, Florida State University, Tallahassee, June 24, 1980.
Guthrie, Claire (1976). Interview with Office for Civil Rights official, June 23, 1976.
Hall, Clyde S. (1980). Interview with acting president of Savannah State College, Savannah, Ga., June 12, 1980.
Holland, Robert G. (1978). "Virginia Looks At Compromise On Desegregation." Raleigh *News and Observer*, March 26, 1978.
Holmes, Peter (1973). Letter from the Office for Civil Rights Director to William Friday, president of University of North Carolina, November 10, 1973.
Holmes, Peter (1974). Letter from the Office for Civil Rights Director to William Friday, president of University of North Carolina, April 24, 1974.

Holmes, Peter (1975). Letter from the Office for Civil Rights Director to North Carolina Governor James Holshouser, July 31, 1975.
Holmes, Peter (1976). Quoted in *Mandel v. U.S. Department of Health, Education, and Welfare*, 411 F. Supp. 542 at 552 (D.D.C.).
Johnson, Sherry, and Monte Basgall (1980). "Black Nursing Schools' Scores Drop." Raleigh *News and Observer*, September 10, 1980.
Kohn, M.; C. Manski; and D. Mundel (1976). "An Empirical Investigation of Factors Which Influence College-Going Behavior." *Annals of Economic and Social Measurement* 5: 391–419.
Lee, Blair III (1976). Quoted in *Mandel v. U.S. Department of Health, Education, and Welfare*, 411 F. Supp. 542 at 551 (D.D.C.).
Lepper, Mary (1976). Interview with former director of Higher Education Division, Office for Civil Rights, April 7, 1976.
Mandel, Marvin (1976). Letter from Maryland Governor to Dewey Dodds, director of Philadelphia Regional Office of the Office for Civil Rights, August 13, 1975.
Mandel v. U.S. Department of Health, Education, and Welfare, 411 F. Supp. 542 (D.D.C.) (1976).
Middleton, Lorenzo (1979). "Enrollment of Blacks Doubled Since 1970." *Chronicle of Higher Education*, January 29, 1979.
Middleton, Lorenzo (1980). "Louisiana Proposes Compromise on Higher Education Desegregation." *Chronicle of Higher Education*, June 23, 1980.
Norris v. State Council of Higher Education, 327 F. Supp. 1368 (E.D. Va.), aff'd, 404 U.S. 907 (1971).
Office for Civil Rights (1972). *Racial and Ethnic Enrollment Data from Institutions of Higher Education, Fall 1970*. Washington, D.C.: U.S. Government Printing Office.
Office for Civil Rights (1974). *Racial and Ethnic Enrollment Data from Institutions of Higher Education, Fall 1972*. Washington, D.C.: U.S. Government Printing Office.
Office for Civil Rights (1978). "Revised Criteria Specifying the Ingredients of Acceptable Plans to Desegregate State Systems of Public Higher Education." *Federal Register* 43, no. 32 (February 15, 1978): 6658–6664.
Office for Civil Rights (1980). *Racial, Ethnic, and Sex Enrollment Data from Institutions of Higher Education, Fall 1978*. Washington, D.C.: U.S. Government Printing Office.
Orfield, Gary (1969). *The Reconstruction of Southern Education: The Schools and the 1964 Civil Rights Act*. New York: Wiley.
Panetta, Leon (1970). Letter from the Office for Civil Rights Director to North Carolina Governor Robert Scott, February 16, 1970.
Panetta, Leon E., and Peter Gall (1971). *Bring Us Together*. Philadelphia: Lippincott.
Pressman, Jeffrey, and Aaron Wildavsky (1973). *Implementation*. Berkeley: University of California Press.
Rabkin, Jeremy (1980). "Office for Civil Rights." In James Q. Wilson (ed.), *The Politics of Regulation*. New York: Basic Books.
Robinson, Richard (1975). Interview with the assistant to the president, University of North Carolina, October 20, 1975.
Sanders, John L. (1975). Interview with the former vice-president for planning, University of North Carolina, November 20, 1975.
Sanders v. Ellington, 288 F. Supp. 937 (M.D. Tenn.) (1968).
State of Arkansas (1977). *Arkansas College and University Plan for Compliance with Title VI of the Civil Rights Act of 1964* (Rev. 1977). Little Rock: Department of Higher Education.

State of North Carolina (1974). *The Revised North Carolina State Plan for the Further Elimination of Racial Duality in the Public Post-Secondary Education Systems.* Raleigh: Governor's Office.

State University System of Florida (1978). *Revised Plan for Equalizing Educational Opportunity in Public Higher Education in Florida.* Tallahassee.

Stith, Pat (1977). "One Third of Black College Grads Fail Test." Raleigh *News and Observer,* June 26, 1977.

Thompson, Cleon (1976). Interview with the vice-president for student affairs, University of North Carolina, May 7, 1976.

University of North Carolina (1978). *The Revised North Carolina Plan for the Further Elimination of Racial Duality in Public Higher Education Systems, Phase II, 1978–1983.* Chapel Hill: Board of Governors.

University of North Carolina (1979). *Statistical Abstract of Higher Education in North Carolina, 1978–1979.* Chapel Hill: Board of Governors.

University System of Georgia (1977). *A Plan for the Further Desegregation of the University System of Georgia.* Atlanta: Board of Regents.

Chapter 6

Equal Housing Opportunity

Charles M. Lamb

Housing discrimination against minorities has always existed in the United States (Bracey, 1971; Taeuber and Taeuber, 1965; Vose, 1959). Additionally, despite incremental progress in fair housing,[1] discrimination remains widespread in many American suburbs and white areas of cities, although there has been a growing percentage of minority suburbanites in recent years (Clark, 1979; Lake, 1979). Discrimination in housing has at least three fundamental characteristics. It persists because the question of fair housing is highly controversial (Hamilton, 1970; Wolfinger and Greenstein, 1968). It is fueled by whites' beliefs that they significantly benefit from continued discrimination and segregation (Bullock and Rodgers, 1975, 5–6; Downs, 1981, 50–52). And discrimination leads to a number of intolerable living conditions being forced upon ghetto and other urban minorities who cannot escape to better living environs (Harrington, 1981; Hill, 1974; Lamb, 1981a, 386–395).

Of all fields of civil rights implementation examined in this book, probably least success has been made toward achieving equal housing opportunity. Fair housing is therefore the last major frontier in civil rights issues addressed herein—the area in which progress is slowest and the possibility of genuine change is most remote (Orfield, 1981; Rodgers and Bullock, 1972, chap. 6; Lamb, 1981a). In explaining why this is true, this chapter analyzes four principal factors to account for the failure to achieve fair housing in America: (1) historical traditions of housing discrimination and segregation, and their continuation because of practices that are

---

I would like to thank Charles S. Bullock III, Michael N. Danielson, Glenda G. Sloane, Stephen L. Wasby, and anonymous reviewers for their comments on an early draft of this chapter.

still widely used; (2) the lack of wide-ranging federal statutes, judicial decisions, and presidential decrees that unequivocally require an end to housing discrimination in all its forms; (3) general federal policies that have perpetuated housing discrimination and segregation; and (4) specific inadequacies in the federal fair housing implementation process. Each of these factors is examined, with particular emphasis on federal fair housing implementation, in light of the variables introduced in chapter 1.

As a preface to examining these topics, however, it should be stressed that one of the main political obstacles to promoting fair housing has been the ambivalence and even opposition of many minority leaders and organizations. Minority politicians in some segregated areas have not supported fair housing; indeed, they have perceived fair housing, and especially efforts to open the suburbs for minorities, as a direct and grave threat to their political base. Although this is understandable, the fact that minority politicians often do not push for housing desegregation makes equal housing opportunity far more difficult to accomplish.

HOUSING DISCRIMINATION AND SEGREGATION: HISTORICAL DEVELOPMENTS AND CONTINUING TRENDS

Racial discrimination has consistently been a trait of the American housing market and continues largely unabated. Discriminatory practices, in turn, inevitably lead to housing segregation and a dual housing market. Elaborating on these ideas, the focus here is on the development and continuation of housing discrimination against blacks and then on resulting segregation. Yet it should be remembered that housing discrimination has also been practiced against other racial and ethnic groups and women (Hershberg et al., 1979; U.S. Com. on Civil Rights, 1975a, 1–13).

Until the twentieth century, housing discrimination per se against blacks was usually unnecessary because their economic status rarely permitted them to indulge in the "luxury" of homeownership or mobility in renting desirable housing. Some blacks did purchase farmland in which whites had little or no interest, but these farms were commonly characterized by shanty-style housing. Most other blacks lived in substandard housing on white-owned farms, or in the servants' quarters of wealthy households or alley dwellings in the cities, without the remotest chance of ever owning a home or property (Bracey, 1971, 1–3; Wood, 1979, 369–370).

During this century, housing discrimination in the modern sense of the term became very pronounced and grew primarily out of black migratory patterns from the South after World Wars I and II (Hauser, 1965, 851–852; Roof, 1979, 2–4; Taeuber and Taeuber, 1965, 11–12). This migration of blacks may be principally explained in political and economic terms. Many blacks naturally wanted to leave behind them the cradle-to-grave legacy of slavery and Southern political subservience. The major economic consideration was that from the early 1920s to the 1950s, the United States witnessed unprecedented economic growth, especially in the Northeast and the Midwest, both of which attracted large numbers of Southern blacks (Forman, 1970, 18). This migratory shift had a profound and lasting influence on the distribution of the black population in particular regions, urban areas, and central cities (Hauser, 1965, 851–852).[2] As a consequence of the black influx to large metropolitan centers, housing discrimination for the first time pervaded many areas east of the Mississippi River and outside the South. The resulting ghetto living environment was thus a twentieth-century development which all but the most economically fortunate blacks have had to face and endure.

But what do we mean by housing discrimination in the modern sense of the term? In particular, what are the main discriminatory techniques used in the 1980s? One common way to keep minorities out of white neighborhoods in the cities and the suburbs is through *exclusionary zoning laws* (Danielson, 1976, chap. 5; Note, 1971). These laws, which have been upheld as legal in many courts, require minimum lot sizes, minimum square footage in the size of houses, and high-quality building materials that make such property too expensive for many minorities. Zoning codes also may prohibit the building of federally subsidized housing, privately developed multifamily units, or the use of prefabricated houses and mobile homes. The exclusion of these types of lower-cost housing naturally decreases the likelihood of minority families moving into a community. Where exclusionary zoning is employed, the intent may clearly be to discriminate, although the publicly stated reason is to avoid the higher taxes and costs that minorities are thought to bring. Yet it should be stressed, on the other hand, that zoning laws in general are not "bad." On the contrary, they are essential to control urban and suburban growth in an orderly manner. Exclusionary zoning is negative, however, when deliberately used to keep out those who could otherwise move into a community and wish to do so but are denied that right because of their race or ethnicity.

A second current discriminatory technique, which is illegal, is called racial *steering* (Lamb, 1982, 1146–1161; Note, 1976). Here, minorities seeking to rent or purchase housing are shown property by real estate agents only in minority, racially changing, or deteriorating neighborhoods.[3] One explanation for steering is that many real estate brokers, bankers, and white homeowners believe that even incremental housing desegregation eventually leads to minority-dominated neighborhoods and declining property values (Helper, 1969; Note, 1976). Although this belief is a myth unless a large number of minorities move into a neighborhood within a short period of time (Ladd, 1962; Laurenti, 1960), steering remains an obvious form of discrimination that continues to be widely used (U.S. Senate, 1979, 165).

Blockbusting is another discriminatory practice which, although illegal, still occasionally occurs (Lamb, 1982, 1141–1146). Blockbusting typically takes place in lower- and moderate-income white areas where minorities can afford to purchase homes.[4] The concept refers to a situation in which a real estate agent sells a house to a minority family and then typically passes the word around the neighborhood that a minority household is moving in. Soon thereafter, realtors encourage other whites in the area to sell their property before "neighborhood change" sets in and their property values precipitously decline. When a minority family is able to penetrate the invisible wall of housing segregation, realtors may thus use blockbusting to turn a community into one that is soon mostly minority, and to make large profits. In the classic form of blockbusting, the realtor approaches a homeowner in a targeted neighborhood, informs him that minorities are moving in, spins tales of rising crime rates, declining property values, and deteriorating public schools, and makes assorted other prophecies of impending doom. Unfortunately, as in the case of steering, the federal courts have done little to prohibit blockbusting except in its most blatant forms.[5]

Redlining is an additional form of housing discrimination which, in particular, extends the effects of past discrimination. Redlining refers to a cluster of practices engaged in by banks and mortgage companies. For example, they may refuse to make loans for housing in minority areas of cities, require stricter lending terms for low-income housing which is most likely to be occupied by minorities, and reject applications for loans on houses over a certain age. Although federal law is intended to curtail redlining (Lamb, 1982, 1129), it nevertheless continues and compounds the many severe problems that minorities already experience in the urban setting. As an illustration, homeowners in redlined areas have extreme difficulty selling their homes. If they rent out their property, the character of the neighborhood is altered since tenants have little incentive to keep property attractive and well maintained. These changes in the neighborhood then discourage other potential homeowners from buying in the area. Even if the housing is marketable, strict mortgage terms promote rates of default. The result is that property increasingly becomes converted for commercial or industrial use, and, once redlining sets in, community decline accelerates.

One revealing 1979 study which extensively documents the extent of housing discrimination in America, and especially steering, was sponsored by the Department of Housing and Urban Development (HUD) in forty major metropolitan areas. That study showed that, despite federal statutes, court decisions, and presidential decrees making housing discrimination illegal, blacks were discriminated against in 27 percent of all instances in which they sought to rent housing. The comparable figure for discrimination in the selling of homes to blacks was 15 percent. Further, it was discovered that when blacks contacted four different real estate agents, there was a 72 percent chance of encountering discrimination in rentals and a 48 percent chance in sales. The study found, too, that steering "is probably the single most widely practiced form of racial discrimination in the sales market," but the extent to which steering occurs is *not* included in the above figures on discrimination (U.S. Department of HUD, 1979; U.S. Senate, 1979, 165). Perhaps most significantly, the data on steering indicated "that equal treatment was accorded to whites and blacks in only 30 percent of [the cases] in the rental market and in only 10 percent in the sales market" (U.S. Senate, 1979, 166). In other words, as of the late 1970s, 70 percent of all whites and blacks in forty large American cities were steered into "their own neighborhoods" where rental property was being sought, and in 90 percent of all cases where the aim was to purchase housing! This is not, needless to say, equal opportunity in housing—not by a far cry.

A brief examination of one direct effect of discrimination, namely, housing segregation or racial residential polarization, is in order. Because of discrimination and poverty, black ghetto residents are forced into the position of being the most residentially isolated large minority group in America. While there are exceptions, trends in population movement since the 1920s have reinforced segregation. As more minorities moved to cities after World Wars I and II, white flight accelerated, and surrounding segregated white suburbs sprang up like mushrooms (Danielson, 1976, chap. 2). Therefore, most data on housing patterns through the late 1970s clearly show that increasing segregation by race has been a basic metropolitan trend (Farley, Bianchi, and Colasanto, 1979; Farley and Taeuber, 1968; Kain and Quigley, 1972; Sorensen, Taeuber, and Hollingsworth, 1975). From 1960 to 1970, for example, the population in the nation's thirty-four largest cities decreased by 1.9 million whites, whereas the black city population rose by 2.8 million. In contrast, these cities' suburbs gained 12.5 million whites but only 0.8 million blacks (U.S. Com. on Civil Rights, 1974, 4). The 1980 census figures suggest that this trend has slowed, but not strikingly (Weaver, 1982, 82).

Although overt discriminatory practices in housing are not as common in the 1980s as they were in prior decades, studies document the fact that discriminatory attitudes and accompanying policies still lead to segregated housing. One especially insightful examination of American housing segregation in the late 1970s was conducted by Farley and his colleagues (1978). It verified that resistance by whites to housing desegregation accounted for continued racial separation much more than either the idea that the economic status of blacks might prohibit them from moving into desegregated neighborhoods or the notion that blacks prefer to live together in their own communities. They concluded:

> White resistance to mixed neighborhoods is very evident. Even in the situation of minimum integration—one black and 14 white families—one-quarter of the whites claimed they would be uncomfortable. As the proportion of blacks rose, so too did discomfort among whites. In a neighborhood which was half black, 72% of the whites said they would be uncomfortable.
>
> We asked those white respondents who reported being uncomfortable in a neighborhood whether they would actually try to move out. . . . This proportion was quite low for the neighborhood which contains one black family— only 7% of the whites would try to leave—but increases rapidly. Forty percent say they would move away from the neighborhood which is one-third black and 64% would leave the majority black area. [Farley et al., 1978, 333, 336]

We get a far clearer impression of the magnitude of housing segregation in the United States from table 6-1, which depicts levels of residential segregation of minorities between 1940 and 1970 in forty-five cities. Among other things, in 1970 housing segregation was very high in such Southern cities as Atlanta, Birmingham, Charlotte, Dallas, Houston, Jacksonville, Little Rock, Memphis, Miami, Mobile, Nashville, Richmond, and Tampa. However, other regions had cities with highly polarized residential patterns, including Baltimore, Buffalo, Chicago, Cleveland, Dayton, Indianapolis, Kansas City, Philadelphia, Pittsburgh, St. Louis, Toledo, and Wichita. Housing segregation is therefore by no means solely a Southern phenomenon; it is a nationwide problem which requires a nationwide solution. Additionally, table 6-1 verifies the fact that relatively few cities have become significantly more desegregated over time. The main exceptions are Cambridge, Camden, East Orange, East St. Louis, New Haven, San Francisco, Seattle, Wilmington, and Yonkers. Yet, overall, incremental increases in racial segregation were obviously far more common between 1940 and 1970, and segregation was much more often practiced against blacks than other minorities in cities such as Berkeley, Cambridge, Denver, Los Angeles, Minneapolis, Oklahoma City, Portland, Sacramento, St. Paul, San Diego, San Francisco, Seattle, and Tulsa.

LAWS FORBIDDING HOUSING DISCRIMINATION

Federal law prohibiting unfair housing practices generally falls into four basic categories: constitutional protections, statutory protections, judicial decisions, and executive orders. (Administrative agency regulations have the effect of law but are not addressed until the last section on the implementation process.) Table 6-2 depicts the chronological evolution of these major legal standards. It shows that some discriminatory housing prac-

TABLE 6-1 Indexes of Residential Segregation of Whites and Nonwhites, 1940 to 1970, and Whites and Blacks, 1970

	Indexes of Residential Segregation				
	White v. Black	White v. Nonwhite			
City	1970	1970	1960	1950	1940
Atlanta, GA	91.9	91.5	93.6	91.5	87.4
Baltimore, MD	89.4	88.3	89.6	91.3	90.1
Berkeley, CA	75.4	62.9	69.4	80.3	81.2
Birmingham, AL	91.8	91.5	92.8	88.7	86.4
Buffalo, NY	87.3	84.2	86.5	89.5	87.9
Cambridge, MA	63.4	52.6	65.5	75.6	74.3
Camden, NJ	68.3	67.4	76.5	89.6	87.6
Charlotte, NC	93.7	92.7	94.3	92.8	90.1
Chicago, IL	93.0	88.8	92.6	92.1	95.0
Cleveland, OH	90.1	89.0	91.3	91.5	92.0
Dallas, TX	95.9	92.7	94.6	88.4	80.2
Dayton, OH	91.1	90.1	91.3	93.3	91.5
Denver, CO	88.9	77.6	85.5	88.9	87.9
East Orange, NJ	61.4	60.8	71.2	83.7	85.3
East St. Louis, IL	76.9	76.8	92.0	94.2	93.8
Houston, TX	92.7	90.0	93.7	91.5	84.5
Indianapolis, IN	89.6	88.3	91.6	91.4	90.4
Jacksonville, FL	94.3	92.5	96.9	94.9	94.3
Kansas City, KS	87.0	84.7	91.5	92.0	90.5
Kansas City, MO	90.5	88.0	90.8	91.3	88.0
Little Rock, AR	90.6	89.7	89.4	84.5	78.2
Los Angeles, CA	90.5	78.4	81.8	84.6	84.2
Memphis, TN	92.4	91.8	92.0	86.4	79.9
Miami, FL	92.0	89.4	97.9	97.8	97.9
Minneapolis, MN	80.4	67.9	79.3	86.0	88.0
Mobile, AL	91.5	91.0	91.9	89.4	86.6
Nashville, TN	90.3	89.0	91.7	88.7	86.5
New Haven, CT	71.5	69.1	70.9	79.9	80.0
Oklahoma City, OK	95.6	81.8	87.1	88.6	84.3
Philadelphia, PA	84.4	83.2	87.1	89.0	88.0
Pittsburgh, PA	85.9	83.9	84.6	84.0	82.0
Portland, OR	86.2	69.0	76.7	84.3	83.8
Richmond, VA	91.4	90.8	94.8	92.2	92.7
Sacramento, CA	71.1	56.3	63.9	77.6	77.8
St. Louis, MO	90.1	89.3	90.5	92.9	92.6
St. Paul, MN	87.1	76.8	87.3	90.0	88.6
San Diego, CA	85.6	71.6	81.3	83.6	84.4
San Francisco, CA	75.0	55.5	69.3	79.8	82.9
Seattle, WA	82.2	69.2	79.7	83.3	82.2
Tampa, FL	92.0	90.7	94.5	92.5	90.2
Toledo, OH	89.1	86.7	91.8	91.5	91.0
Tulsa, OK	94.5	76.4	86.3	91.2	84.6
Wichita, KS	93.0	85.0	91.9	93.3	92.0
Wilmington, DE	70.5	69.8	79.8	86.2	83.0
Yonkers, NY	73.1	68.0	78.1	81.7	82.0

SOURCE: Sorensen, Taeuber, and Hollingsworth, 1975, 128–130. The original table contains data for 109 American cities.

TABLE 6-2 Major Federal Legal Standards Forbidding Housing Discrimination

Year	Legal Provision	Requirement
1866	Civil Rights Act of 1866	All U.S. citizens have equal rights to inherit, purchase, lease, sell, hold, or convey real and personal property.
1868	Fourteenth Amendment	No state shall deprive any person of life, liberty, or property, without due process of law; nor deny any person the equal protection of the laws.
1917	*Buchanan v. Warley*	Local zoning ordinances which explicitly forbid housing for blacks in white neighborhoods are unconstitutional.
1948	*Shelley v. Kraemer*	Private restrictive covenants are unconstitutional.
1962	Executive Order 11063	All federal agencies with housing-related activities must take all action necessary and appropriate to eliminate housing discrimination based on race, color, religion, and national origin.
1964	Civil Rights Act of 1964, Title VI	There shall be no discrimination on grounds of race, color, or national origin in any federal or federally assisted programs.
1968	Civil Rights Act of 1968, Title VIII	National policy is for fair housing regardless of color, race, sex, religion, and national origin.
1968	*Jones v. Alfred H. Mayer Co.*	The Civil Rights Act of 1866 prohibits racial discrimination in all housing, public and private.
1976	*Hills v. Gautreaux*	The Constitution requires that low-cost public housing be spread throughout larger metropolitan areas and not be solely concentrated in areas that are already predominantly minority.

tices have in fact been illegal for over a century but were nevertheless long ignored by judicial and political officials for fighting housing discrimination. In other words, the table demonstrates that fair housing law which has been *enforced* is a twentieth-century development. Indeed, with the exception of Supreme Court decisions in 1917 and 1948, fair housing law is of recent vintage, essentially awakening in the 1960s from a deep sleep.

Two of the oldest provisions of fair housing law involve the relevant sections of the Fourteenth Amendment (the Constitution, of course, being the highest form of law), and the Civil Rights Act of 1866. The Fourteenth Amendment provides that "[n]o State . . . shall . . . deprive any person of life, liberty, or *property*, without due process of law; nor deny any person within its jurisdiction the equal protection of the laws." For decades, the due process and equal protection clauses were rarely construed to support the concept of fair housing (not until the *Buchanan* and *Shelley* decisions discussed below). Additionally, the Civil Rights Act of 1866 explicitly requires that "all citizens of the United States . . . [have] the same right, in every state and Territory, as enjoyed by white citizens thereof to inherit, purchase, lease, sell, hold, or convey real and personal property." This statutory provision, however, was similarly not enforced for over a century. It was not until the Supreme Court's decision in *Jones v. Alfred H. Mayer Company* (1968) that the actual intent of the 1866 act was officially recognized. In *Jones*, the Court held for the first time that the 1866 act was specifically designed to prohibit discrimination against blacks in the sale, leasing, and rental of *all* housing, public and private.

Prior to *Jones*, attempts by the Supreme Court to eliminate housing discrimination were reflected in two major decisions. In *Buchanan v. Warley* (1917), the Court announced that local zoning ordinances expressly forbidding housing opportunities for blacks in white neighborhoods were unconstitutional under the equal protection and due process clauses of the Fourteenth Amendment. *Buchanan* stimulated the development by private interests of an alternative to antiblack zoning ordinances—namely, private restrictive covenants through which white purchasers of housing agreed not to sell or lease their property to members of certain racial, religious, and ethnic groups. These private agreements were upheld and enforced by state courts. Because such "state action" is illegal (Lamb, 1981b, 16-18), in *Shelley v. Kraemer* (1948), the Supreme Court ruled that restrictive covenants were unconstitutional under the equal protection clause.

Since *Buchanan*, *Shelley*, and *Jones*, the Supreme Court, under Warren E. Burger's chief justiceship since 1969, has decided against the housing discrimination claims of minorities several times (Lamb and Lustig, 1979). For instance, in *James v. Valtierra* (1971) and *City of Eastlake v. Forest City Enterprises, Inc.* (1976), the Burger Court upheld the constitutionality of municipal referenda, under the equal protection and due process clauses respectively, through which white voters refused to allow low-income federal housing to be constructed in their towns which could be used to house minorities. Also, in the case of *Village of Arlington Heights v. Metropolitan Housing Development Corp.* (1977), the Court required low- and moderate-income blacks challenging exclusionary zoning practices to prove that Arlington Heights, Illinois, specifically *intended* to exclude them from the town. Although the zoning law had an exclusionary *effect* of keeping minorities out, the Court said that a discriminatory *purpose* had to be proven, which is virtually impossible to do.

Therefore, while historically the Supreme Court has taken steps to ensure equal opportunity in housing, it has not played a key role in this regard since 1969 because of the newest justices' conservative decisional tendencies. Indeed, since 1969, the Court has handed down only one noteworthy decision with the effect of combating housing discrimination. That case was *Hills v. Gautreaux* (1976). In *Gautreaux*, the Burger Court ruled that it was unconstitutional under the Fifth Amendment for HUD and the Chicago Housing Authority to concentrate federally assisted low-income public housing in minority areas of the city alone. Rather, low-cost public housing must additionally be provided in the surrounding suburbs, which of course are primarily white. From all appearances, however, *Gautreaux* has had a limited impact on polarized housing patterns nationwide.

As a result of conservative Burger Court rulings, civil rights lawyers have had to argue their cases based upon a few lower federal court fair housing decisions which have the effect of preventing such practices as racial steering and blockbusting (Lamb, 1982, 1141–1161). In the case of *Zuch v. Hussey* (1975), for example, a U.S. district court declared as illegal incidents of steering involving certain types of advice by real estate agents to white customers. The steering activities were couched in explicit racial terms and were buttressed by references to declining property values and high crime rates, and hints that white customers should avoid desegregated areas in which they had expressed an interest. The court defined unlawful steering as "the use of a word or phrase or action by a real estate broker or salesperson which is intended to influence the choice of a prospective buyer on a racial basis" (*Zuch v. Hussey*, 1975, 1047).[6] Further, the court declared that "any action by a real estate broker which in any way impedes, delays, or discourages on a racial basis a prospective home buyer from purchasing housing is unfair." In the area of blockbusting, consider the case of *United States v. Mitchell* (1971). There a federal district court held that, under Section 804(e) of the Fair Housing Act of 1968, which outlaws blockbusting, "Congress surely did not intend that in order to violate the Act a salesman must say, 'For my own profit, I would like to induce you to sell your house by telling you that Negroes are moving into your neighborhood' " (*U.S. v. Mitchell*, 1971, 479). Deciding against the real estate agents engaging in blockbusting in *Mitchell*, the court went so far as to indicate that mailed solicitations to sell houses in white neighborhoods may be illegal, even if they make no mention of major changes in the racial composition of a community.[7]

A different type of legal guarantee for fair housing was established in 1962. It was President Kennedy's Executive Order 11063, which requires that all federal departments and agencies, "insofar as their functions relate to the provision, rehabilitation, or operation of housing and related facilities, . . . take all action necessary and appropriate to prevent discrimination because of race, color, creed, or national origin." But Kennedy's executive order is narrow and contains some serious limitations, particularly since it does not cover discrimination by private lending institutions. Nevertheless, it demonstrated a good faith effort on the part of the White House toward achieving equal housing opportunity.

In addition to Supreme Court decisions and E.O. 11063, during the 1960s Congress passed two landmark statutory provisions to combat housing discrimination: Title VI of the Civil Rights Act of 1964 and Title VIII of the Civil Rights Act of 1968. Although several statutes passed during the 1970s contained provisions making different forms of housing discrimination illegal,[8] Title VI helped pave the way for later legislation. It provides that there shall be no discrimination based on race, color, or national origin in any federal or federally assisted program. This means that federal housing or housing-related programs, or state and local housing activities receiving federal funds, cannot contain discriminatory elements. Like E.O. 11063, however, Title VI does not extend to discrimination by lending institutions.

This oversight highlighted the need for a second and more comprehensive piece of federal legislation, Title VIII of the Civil Rights Act of 1968, commonly referred to as the Fair Housing Act of 1968 (Lamb, 1982). In sweeping language, this act declares fair housing to be official federal policy throughout the nation and prohibits discrimination on grounds of color, race, sex, religion, and national origin. Notably, Title VIII applies to those most responsible for housing discrimination and segregation—the real estate industry and financial lending institutions. It forbids a broad variety of discriminatory actions, including steering and blockbusting. By filling in some of the gaps left under E.O. 11063 and Title VI, Title VIII makes discrimination illegal for the vast majority of all housing in the United States (U.S. Com. on Civil Rights, 1975a, 37). Nevertheless, as will be explained later, Title VIII has its shortcomings, and congressional attempts in 1979 and 1980 to strengthen the law failed.

THE FEDERAL GOVERNMENT AS AN ACCOMPLICE

The central themes of this chapter thus far have been that housing discrimination remains widespread, that it results in segregated residential living patterns, and that there are a number of legal provisions and court decisions that seek to prohibit it. Prior to examining the variables introduced in chapter 1, the role of the federal government in furthering housing segregation and discrimination is assessed.

Federal policies were a chief cause of American suburban growth during the 1940s and 1950s, but those policies did little to promote fair housing in outlying areas of the cities (Mitchell and Smith, 1979; Orfield, 1974, 785–790; Taeuber, 1975, 91–92). Indeed, both before and after World War II, various federal agencies actually contributed significantly to unfair housing by essentially endorsing policies which had long been employed by real estate and lending interests to discriminate against minorities (Orfield, 1974, 785). The federal government's role in housing then expanded substantially during the 1950s and 1960s, but fair housing remained a low priority. Therefore, "[b]ecause of the extensive nature of its involvement in housing and community development, the Federal Government . . . has . . . been most influential in creating and maintaining urban residential segregation" (U.S. Com. on Civil Rights, 1975a, 39). Former HUD Secretary Robert C. Weaver underscored this point in 1979, noting that during the 1950s and 1960s "the Federal Government acquiesced to discrimination and encouraged segregation in housing" (U.S. Senate, 1979, 92).

In particular, six critical federal policies have had a discriminatory or segregative impact on the American housing picture. These policies involve: (1) home mortgage insurance; (2) federal income tax write-offs; (3) federal subsidies to develop new highways; (4) location of federal facilities; (5) location of public housing; and (6) urban renewal.

Federal mortgage guarantees have assisted millions of Americans to buy homes (Danielson, 1976, 203). The creation of the mortgage programs of the Federal Housing Administration (FHA) were especially important in this development. FHA mortgage insurance caused considerable changes in the financing of homes by insuring payment on mortgages that met its quality standards. However, a very high proportion of FHA-supported homes were purposefully located in the suburbs to house whites. The FHA encouraged segregation through its guidelines, which for fifteen years "warned of the infiltration of 'inharmonious racial groups' into neighborhoods occupied by families of a different race. FHA actively promoted the use of a model racially restrictive covenant by builders and owners whose properties would receive FHA insurance" (U.S. Com. on Civil Rights, 1975a, 39-40). Hence, only 2 percent of all FHA-insured loans were awarded to blacks from the mid-1940s through 1960. Programs of the Veterans Administration (VA) also provide veterans with low-interest loans for purchasing homes. These programs have had a similar segregative impact, although not because of specific guidelines as in the case of the FHA, but because of the discriminatory way in which the VA has implemented its general housing policies (U.S. Com. on Civil Rights, 1975a, 40). Subsequent changes in FHA and VA policies and their implementation have had little effect on segregation which is firmly entrenched (U.S. Com. on Civil Rights, 1979, 107-130). Therefore, "increasing the supply of housing for minorities is possible, but mostly under conditions of continued or increased segregation" (Mitchell and Smith, 1979, 175).

Federal tax policies also have contributed to economic inequities among races and to housing segregation (Falk and Franklin, 1976, 94; Mitchell and Smith, 1979, 173; Rubinowitz, 1974, 94). These policies bestow property tax and mortgage interest write-offs for those who can afford to purchase high-quality housing, thus exacerbating the exodus of middle- and upper-income people to suburbs and abandoning low-income minorities in the central cities. During the mid-1970s, economist Henry Aaron estimated that these tax breaks amounted to some $10 billion per year (Starr, 1977, 7). Using data from the 1960s and 1970s, Downs had earlier argued that such tax deductions clearly constitute subsidies (unusual benefits) to middle- and upper-class suburbanites.

> The United States Treasury estimates that this subsidy equaled about $5.7 billion in 1971 alone—more than *double* all other housing subsidies combined. In 1966, owner-occupant families with incomes over $100,000 received an average benefit of $1,144 from this subsidy—or 18 times as much as the $64 average benefit received by owner occupants with medium incomes, and 381 times as much as that received by the poorest owner-occupant households. [Downs, 1973, 57]

Housing tax breaks discriminate against low- and moderate-income persons and against renters. Since minorities are much less likely to own homes than whites, they naturally are deprived of these tax benefits.[9]

Third, white suburbs could not have become widespread without federal highway subsidies. Congress earmarked billions of dollars in the 1970s for highways between cities and the suburbs. These new highway systems obviously make it convenient for persons earning their livings in the cities to escape to surrounding areas to live, with the accompanying loss of tax revenues for downtown areas. Little attention was paid by many officials of the Department of Transportation during the 1960s to whether the expansion of these highway systems accelerated residential segregation by the growth of suburbs, to the effect that new highways had on the minority neighborhoods through which they passed, or to whether the highways were designed and located to separate white and minority city areas (U.S. Com. on Civil Rights, 1974, 44–46).

Compounding these factors, the federal government has often relocated federal job sites in white suburbs and away from minority city areas. In the words of Danielson, "[i]n its role as the nation's largest employer, the federal government . . . fueled the exodus to the suburbs" (1976, 202). For instance, between 1963 and 1968 over 17,000 federal jobs were moved from predominantly black Washington, D.C., to the predominantly white suburbs of Virginia and Maryland, and rarely were local suburban officials pressured by the federal government to open up their suburbs for minorities (Danielson, 1976, 202). These job relocation policies are directly linked to increased housing segregation. The absence of moderately priced suburban housing, coupled with other practices that control suburban growth, has meant that city minority residents could not move to new federal employment sites, and at times they have had to forfeit job opportunities with federal agencies. Moreover, since minorities often cannot find affordable suburban accommodations and must continue to live in the cities, weak or nonexistent public transportation systems make commuting to work difficult, time-consuming, costly, or even impossible.

Site selection in federal public housing programs has also contributed to segregation.[10] The federal government for years allowed local housing authorities (LHAs) to practice a "separate but equal" policy, which they chose to do in many instances. According to the Commission on Civil Rights, "Under the separate but equal policy, LHAs assessed the need for low-rent housing separately for minorities and whites and provided housing according to relative needs on a segregated basis." Additionally, only persons who could afford a minimum rent qualified to participate in the public housing program. Thus, minorities were discriminated against because they constitute a large percentage of the unemployed and persons with the lowest incomes. These practices continued through 1970, despite laws and court decisions suggesting that they were unconstitutional (U.S. Com. on Civil Rights, 1975a, 46–47). Moreover, even during the 1970s there was little mixed occupancy, and separate locations for white and minority public housing were created. Two different waiting lists were used to maintain segregated housing patterns, and much public housing was used to house the white elderly instead of indigent minority families (Mitchell and Smith, 1979, 174; U.S. Com. on Civil Rights, 1975a, 47–48). Generally speaking, the federal government did little to prohibit these practices. Indeed, as the earlier discussion of *Hills v. Gautreaux* suggests, during the 1970s HUD permitted cities to perpetuate segregation by allowing them to place most or all public housing in neighborhoods that were already overwhelmingly minority, rather than promoting the dispersal of minorities throughout larger metropolitan areas.

Finally, federal urban renewal programs disrupted the lives of many minority families, while maintaining housing segregation.[11] The basic purposes of urban renewal were to begin slum clearance and to rehabilitate existing housing in decaying neighborhoods. However, as Orfield has explained, "urban renewal was [frequently] devastating."

> Financially strapped central cities often forgot the social goals of the program in a futile rush to escape the vicious cycle of urban deterioration and escalating costs. To get the projects moving, local officials often certified that replacement housing was available for poor blacks when there was none. Federal officials who knew they were lying accepted their assurance and provided funds. [1974, 788]

Federal policies in recent years have contributed less to residential segregation, but efforts are continually underway to maintain the status quo. While housing discrimination is illegal, many lending institutions and real estate companies still perpetuate a dual polarized housing market. Unfortunately, the federal government has been basically passive about eliminating practices that have a segregative or discriminatory effect (Lamb, 1981a; Mitchell and Smith, 1979).

IMPLEMENTATION PROCESS AND POLITICS

The remainder of this chapter analyzes fair housing implementation in terms of the variables introduced in chapter 1.[12] By focusing on these variables, one is able to assess in a systematic manner the ways in which the political system has or has not succeeded in dealing with the problems of housing segregation and discrimination. Reports of the United States Commission on Civil Rights are primarily relied on as a benchmark for determining success and failure of fair housing policies over time.

Clarity of Policy

As explained earlier, the two key federal statutory provisions prohibiting housing discrimination are Title VI of the 1964 Civil Rights Act and, more importantly, Title VIII of the Civil Rights Act of 1968. Yet it must be emphasized that both these statutes contain vague provisions and fail to state precisely what national policy is regarding equal housing opportunity or how it shall be implemented.

Title VI is couched in such sweeping language that it has seldom been used to fight discrimination in the housing market. Title VI provides that "[n]o person in the United States shall, on the ground of race, color, or national origin, be excluded from participation in, be denied the benefits of, or be subjected to discrimination under any program or activity receiving Federal financial assistance." Perhaps because of a lack of clarity and specificity in Title VI, three years after its passage HUD had not terminated any funds to recipients of federal housing monies or even convened any hearings concerning the law's implementation (Comment, 1968, 994). By 1971 there was still "little activity by HUD" in implementing Title VI (U.S. Com. on Civil Rights, 1971a, 349). By 1975 HUD was conducting Title VI compliance reviews, but only where a formal complaint had been filed (U.S. Com. on Civil Rights, 1975b, 329). Such passiveness by HUD can partially be blamed on Title VI's overly broad language.

Title VIII states more explicitly than Title VI that unfair housing practices are unlawful. At the outset, Title VIII contains the unambiguous declaration that "[i]t is the policy of the United States to provide, within constitutional limitations, for fair housing throughout the United States." Title VIII goes on to prohibit discrimination on the basis of race, color, religion, sex, or national origin in the sale, rental, or financing of housing. The only circumstances under which Title VIII is inapplicable involve persons who own fewer than four dwellings that are sold or rented without the use of a broker and without being advertised as not available to the above protected classes, and, second, a housing facility for up to four families in which the owner also resides.

Despite the clarity of its introductory policy statement, Title VIII contains a number of vague provisions which impede successful implementation (Lamb, 1982, 1127–1141). There is no clear definition of what constitutes "fair housing" or an "unfair housing practice" under the law. There are no guidelines explaining how federal agencies should go about affirmatively promoting fair housing. In many instances, HUD has issued no regulations to clarify what its officials think Congress intended concerning how implementation should be carried out. And Title VIII is nebulous concerning whether racial redlining and discrimination in property insurance are outlawed, the type of relief that courts can provide in Title VIII litigation, and whether money damages can be awarded to those subjected to discrimination (U.S. Senate, 1979, 94, 97–98, 100). Generally speaking, HUD has issued relatively few regulations to clarify what it thinks Congress intended by Title VIII.[13]

Beyond the question of policy clarity, Title VIII is weak in that, even if a community blatantly engages in exclusionary practices, the law permits HUD to investigate only if a formal housing discrimination complaint is filed. Under Title VIII, third parties not directly affected by discrimination cannot file a complaint with HUD, which effectively prevents civil rights groups from mobilizing their resources to help fight housing discrimination against individuals. Nor can HUD initiate lawsuits or request a court injunction to halt discriminatory practices (U.S. Com. on Civil Rights, 1979, 230). Instead, the agency must refer cases involving a pattern or practice of discrimination to the Department of Justice for possible lawsuits.[14]

Complaint Resolution, Processing, and Monitoring

HUD is given very limited powers under Title VIII to resolve complaints. Ultimately, the agency must rely on "conference, conciliation, and persuasion" to resolve fair housing disputes. In other words, HUD must attempt to induce the parties to a complaint to sit down and settle it with HUD assistance. If an alleged violator of Title VIII refuses to participate in the complaint resolution process, there is little that HUD can do. Therefore, in the policy implementation process, the powers of conference, conciliation, and persuasion must be backed up with a credible form of legal coercion to be effective. Intransigence is so great in civil rights generally, and in fair housing in particular, that complete reliance on conciliation is a totally ineffective means of handling complaints. If either party to a housing discrimination complaint decides to be uncompromising, conciliation becomes a waste of time.

The number of formal housing discrimination complaints indicates, however, only the tip of the proverbial iceberg concerning the extent to which unlawful housing practices actually occur. Many victims never file formal complaints with HUD and other federal housing-related agencies. Regardless of this fact, it is still instructive to examine how HUD processes the complaints it does receive under Title VI and Title VIII.

HUD maintains separate offices for processing Title VI and Title VIII complaints (U.S. Com. on Civil Rights, 1979, 26–40). Some of the basic traits of HUD's Title VI complaint processing for fiscal years 1974 through 1977 are shown in table 6-3. The number of Title VI complaints filed with HUD was relatively high in 1974 and 1975 but declined significantly thereafter. Yet the most revealing aspect of the table is the ratio of findings of noncompliance to complaints filed. During the last year of the Ford administration, the rate of noncompliance findings was only 11 percent (1 of 9), as compared to 25 percent (1 of 4) during the first year of the Carter administration. These data suggest that President Carter and his HUD appointees implemented Title VI more strictly than did the Ford administration, though more complaints were filed during the Ford years.

The Title VI data in table 6-3 may also be meaningfully compared with the Title VIII data on complaint processing shown in table 6-4. A comparison of the data indicates that HUD consistently received at least ten times as many Title VIII complaints as Title VI complaints annually. Table 6-4 further portrays the large backlog of Title VIII complaints carried over from preceding years, thereby making the total workload for HUD exceedingly burdensome. During these years, HUD was only able to conciliate successfully anywhere from 1 to 11 percent of all its Title VIII workload annually, although HUD did "close" or dispose of a much higher percentage of complaints. The data suggest the great magnitude of Title VIII complaint processing problems at HUD. These problems are reflected in the large number of Title VIII complaints filed, ineffectiveness in avoiding a heavy backlog of complaints annually, and a low level of success in conciliating fair housing disputes.

TABLE 6-3 HUD Title VI Complaint Processing

	\multicolumn{4}{c}{Fiscal Year}
	1974	1975	1976[a]	1977
Number of complaints filed	235	265	142	87
Number of findings of noncompliance	48	42	16	6
Ratio of findings of noncompliance to complaints filed	1/5	1/6	1/9	1/4

[a]Includes the transition quarter.
SOURCE: U.S. Commission on Civil Rights, 1979, 37.

Equal Housing Opportunity 165

TABLE 6-4 HUD Title VIII Complaint Processing

	1973	1974	1975	1976[a]	1977
Number of complaints received	2,763	2,602	3,167	4,121	3,391
Number of complaints carried over from previous year	1,293	1,680	1,092	1,684	1,018[b]
Total workload	4,056	4,282	4,259	5,805	4,409
Number of complaints closed	2,376	3,190	2,575	4,801[b]	2,982
Number of attempted conciliations	363	610	651	1,170	530
Number of successful conciliations	207	351	355	670	277

[a] Includes the transition quarter.
[b] Due to an adjustment made when HUD data processing was automated, the sum of these two numbers exceeds HUD's 1976 fiscal workload by 14.
SOURCE: U.S. Commission on Civil Rights, 1979, 29.

One major distinction between table 6-3 and table 6-4 derives from the differences in Title VI and Title VIII. Under Title VI, HUD can reach a finding of noncompliance and then delay or terminate funding to recipients of agency monies. But under Title VIII, all HUD is empowered to do is conciliate the differences between those who are allegedly discriminated against and those who allegedly discriminated. Given this fact, it is worth reemphasizing that between 1973 and 1977, HUD was never able to conciliate grievances successfully in more than 11 percent of its total workload. This indicates that the 1979 and 1980 congressional efforts were clearly needed to strengthen HUD enforcement powers to bypass conciliation and to permit HUD to initiate lawsuits in federal district court and to request court injunctions to halt temporarily discriminatory practices.

Tables 6-3 and 6-4 additionally suggest passive implementation by HUD; that is, the agency acted only when formal complaints were filed. This approach is too slow and has too limited an impact in combating discrimination. For relatively rapid change in civil rights, federal agencies must regularly monitor the degree to which civil rights laws are being complied with and apply stringent sanctions uniformly when there is noncompliance (Bullock and Rodgers, 1976; Rodgers and Bullock, 1976).

Regarding fair housing, this requires the monitoring of builders, lenders, realtors, and even entire cities and their suburbs so that illegal attempts to exclude minorities can be detected. Precise agency standards must be established to prohibit such discrimination, and regular follow-up compliance reviews are essential. Yet thus far, no federal agency has fully met its duties to monitor fair housing enforcement with precise standards. Before such monitoring can take place, an agency must possess data which permit a finding of housing discrimination. When such data are available, an agency must issue regulations establishing quantifiable compliance standards. To date, many federal agencies have not even required those that they regulate to collect adequate data on fair housing—and even when they have, quantifiable standards for detecting discrimination either have not been issued as regulations, or the regulations are so nebulous as to be of marginal value.

For instance, consider HUD, which is statutorily named as the lead agency in implementing Title VIII. As of 1970, HUD had gathered no racial and ethnic data that would be essential for determining whether discrimination existed in its programs (U.S. Com. on Civil Rights, 1971a, 150; 349). However, in 1971 HUD collected some data which conclusively demonstrated that substantial segregation was present in HUD programs and that regular compliance reviews were "desperately needed" (U.S. Com. on Civil Rights, 1971b, 44). By 1974, HUD was collecting data for more of its programs, but these data were rarely used by HUD field representatives actually involved in enforcing equal housing opportunity. Additionally, HUD had not gathered data on the racial and ethnic composition of most single-family-dwelling neighborhoods where HUD housing was being built. It was therefore impossible to determine whether communities receiving HUD funds were still practicing discrimination (U.S. Com. on Civil Rights, 1975b, 116–119). Since the mid-1970s, however, HUD has improved its data collection and usage (U.S. Com. on Civil Rights, 1979, chap. 1).

On-site compliance reviews are another key component of a successful monitoring system. Yet five years after the passage of Title VIII, HUD had not conducted any compliance reviews and stated that even when it began using such reviews, it would do so only where there were obvious indications of discrimination (U.S. Com. on Civil Rights, 1973, 34). Even in the late 1970s, HUD had not conducted on-site inspections frequently enough to meet its equal housing opportunity responsibilities. For example, HUD area offices are responsible for monitoring affirmative fair housing marketing plans. But in the country's major regions, little monitoring was occurring in 1979, and in instances where monitoring had detected practices that required a full compliance review, such reviews had not been forthcoming in too many instances. Only sixty-three compliance reviews were conducted for the entire year of 1977, representing less than 0.3 percent of all HUD-approved affirmative fair housing marketing plans (U.S. Com. on Civil Rights, 1979, 23). This is clear evidence of a passive role in civil rights monitoring which must be corrected by HUD.

Enforcement Agencies

All federal agencies have the responsibility of promoting fair housing in their programs according to the 1968 Fair Housing Act, Title VI of the 1964 Civil Rights Act, and E.O. 11063. For our purposes, however, only seven of these enforcement agencies require attention: the Federal Housing Administration (FHA), the Veterans Administration (VA), the Federal Reserve System (FRS), the Federal Deposit Insurance Corporation (FDIC), the Comptroller of the Currency (COC), the Federal Home Loan Bank Board (FHLBB), and, most importantly, the Department of Housing and Urban Development (HUD).

At the outset, one must stress that simply because enforcement agencies are in place does not mean that they will successfully execute their civil rights duties, and one trait that these seven agencies share is that they consider fair housing to be a low priority when compared to their central programs. Therefore, equal housing opportunity receives short shrift when it conflicts with building housing, making loans, distributing assistance, or undertaking other housing-related activities. The failure of the federal financial regulatory agencies to fulfill their assignment to execute fair housing laws is reflected in the fact that the National Committee Against Discrimination in Housing has pursued litigation against each agency over a period of years (U.S. Senate, 1979, 98).

The Federal Housing Administration was the main federal enforcement agency in the field of fair housing before the creation of HUD in 1965. (FHA, previously a part of the Housing and Home Finance Administration, was merged with HUD in that year.) However, FHA's implementation record has long been pathetic. Indeed, as explained earlier, FHA has actually contributed to housing discrimination throughout most of its history (U.S. Com. on Civil Rights, 1975a, 39–40). Even in the early 1980s, FHA had not completely changed its policies to become consonant with the country's fair housing laws. One of the most thorough studies ever conducted on the FHA found that, as of 1979, "FHA policies and practices with respect to equal opportunity persist in the historical pattern of lagging behind the state of the law" as outlined by the Fair Housing Act of 1968 (Rubinowitz and Trosman, 1979, 496).

Another agency with significant fair housing implementation responsibilities is the Veterans Administration. Among other things, the VA assists veterans in buying homes through low-interest loans. Yet enforcement by the VA has frequently been as weak as that of the FHA. The Commission on Civil Rights therefore found that "VA administrative policies with respect to segregation [have] closely paralleled those of FHA." Specifically, "FHA and VA housing for the most part has benefitted moderate- to middle-income families. Thus, many minorities have not been eligible for FHA mortgage insurance or VA loan guarantees simply on the basis of income" (U.S. Com. on Civil Rights, 1975a, 40). Only years after the Supreme Court's ruling in *Shelley v. Kraemer* (1948) did the FHA and the VA change their policies supporting housing segregation. Nor has either agency pushed aggressively for desegregation in recent years. Available data suggest that these agencies, particularly the VA, continued to discriminate against minorities in the 1970s.

Table 6-5 compares black, Hispanic, and white participation in the VA's direct loan program for 1976. From the data clearly emerges that fact that a huge majority (96.1 percent) of all VA direct loans were given to white applicants, although the percentage of white applicants eligible was much lower (U.S. Com. on Civil Rights, 1979, 120). More telling, whites received a larger average loan than did minorities, despite the fact that the average borrower's income for minorities was often higher than that of white loan recipients. Also, the average borrower's assets for minorities were vastly higher than the assets of whites. A much higher percentage of VA loans should have been given to minorities because their assets ($6,273 for blacks and $4,016 for Hispanics, as contrasted to only $2,573 for whites) show them to be a better credit risk. Finally, the average number of months for repayment was longer for whites than for minorities, again unnecessarily favoring white borrowers. The data in table 6-5 thus reveal discriminatory practices that, as of 1976, were still being openly practiced by the VA, and significant changes in this pattern had not emerged by the early 1980s. Again, the presence of an enforcement agency may be necessary, but not sufficient in itself, to ensure meaningful progress in civil rights implementation.

The equal housing opportunity programs of the federal financial regulatory agencies (the FRS, the FDIC, the COC, and the FHLBB) can be examined together since they all perform related functions. These four agencies regulate the mortgage lending practices of virtually all banks and savings and loan institutions, but their fair housing programs have largely failed. In the mid-1970s, the FHLBB was the only one of the four issuing regulations simply reaffirming the fact that discrimination based on race, national origin, and color was illegal, and it was the only agency discouraging sex discrimination in housing. On the other hand, each of

TABLE 6-5 Black, Hispanic, and White Participation in 1976 VA Direct Loan Programs

Group[a]	Number of Direct Loans	Percent of Total Direct Loans[b]	Average Down Payment	Average Loan Size	Average Veteran Income	Average Borrower's Income	Average Borrower's Assets	Average Number of Months for Repayment
Black	45	1.8%	$3,594	$18,230	$9,032	$ 9,942	$6,273	280
Hispanic	24	1.0	2,885	16,969	9,577	10,004	4,016	270
White	2,364	96.1	1,276	19,709	9,219	9,319	2,573	290

[a]VA also collects data for American Indian/Alaskan Native and Asian/Pacific Islander veterans. These data are not included in this exhibit. The Commission believes that, due to the small size of the direct loan program, valid conclusions could not be drawn concerning these groups' participation in VA programs.

[b]In calendar year 1976, VA made 2,460 direct loans.

SOURCE: U.S. Commission on Civil Rights, 1979, 121.

the agencies had not required Title VIII affirmative action programs of their regulatees (U.S. Com. on Civil Rights, 1975b, 334–335). Yet, as the 1980s approached, all four agencies had improved their fair housing programs in some ways. For example, these agencies had proposed or issued regulations reminding lenders that they must stop certain discriminatory practices, and they had required the collection of racial and ethnic data on mortgage application forms. This does not mean, however, that the four agencies are completely meeting their fair housing duties. As of 1979 these agencies had weak monitoring systems to determine if their regulatees were still discriminating, and they were taking little corrective action where Title VIII was being violated (U.S. Com. on Civil Rights, 1979, 76, 232). These failures suggest that all four agencies still have not met either the letter or the spirit of Title VIII.

HUD has been the major federal agency responsible for enforcing fair housing since its creation in 1965. HUD's Office of Fair Housing and Equal Opportunity is assigned the job of ensuring equal opportunity in all HUD programs. Generally, HUD has more closely approximated its fair housing responsibilities than have the six agencies discussed above, but it has still only partially met its designated legal role. For instance, in 1975 HUD was still taking an ad hoc approach to combating discrimination by relying on individual complaints to indicate where discrimination was occurring, rather than actively conducting compliance reviews in cities and towns known to discriminate. HUD had also failed to diminish significantly its large number of backlogged fair housing complaints, had passed few cases of discrimination on to the Justice Department for lawsuits, had poorly monitored compliance agreements, and had rarely imposed sanctions (such as fund termination) for those who discriminated (U.S. Com. on Civil Rights, 1975b, 329–331).

HUD resolved some of these deficiencies, but on the eve of the 1980s others remained. HUD's complaint processing mechanism was still ad hoc, oriented toward individual complaints. Communities which had entered into voluntary compliance agreements with HUD were not being regularly monitored. The enforcement of Title VIII was just one of a number of responsibilities of the Assistant Secretary for Fair Housing and Equal Opportunity, and thus Title VIII still did not receive the emphasis that it should at HUD. Nor, as of 1979, had HUD even issued comprehensive guidelines clearly defining what constitutes housing discrimination under the Fair Housing Act (U.S. Com. on Civil Rights, 1979, 229–232).

Equally as critical as these shortcomings, the size and use of HUD's budget has not been conducive to successful implementation of the agency's Title VIII enforcement duties. Table 6-6 demonstrates this point. At first blush, it appears that congressional appropriations have increased significantly for HUD's Title VIII effort—from $8.5 million in 1974 to $18.8

TABLE 6-6 HUD Budget for the Administration of Title VIII (in Millions of Dollars)

Fiscal Year	Expenditures for Fair Housing and Equal Opportunity	Expenditures for Title VIII Administration	Title VIII Expenditures as Percent of Fair Housing and Equal Opportunity Expenditures	Title VIII Expenditures in Constant (1969) Prices[b]
1974	$ 8.5	$4.3[a]	50.9	$3.0
1975	10.9	4.7[a]	43.1	3.0
1976	10.6	5.2[a]	49.1	3.1
1977	12.8	5.1[a]	39.8	2.8
1978	15.5[a]	5.8[a]	37.4	3.0
1979	18.8[a]	7.8[a]	41.5	3.8

[a] Estimate
[b] Derived from price deflectors supplied by the Office of Management and Budget.
SOURCE: U.S. Commission on Civil Rights, 1979, 18.

million in 1979. However, in constant dollars, there was virtually no increase between 1974 and 1978, although there was an estimated $800,000 increase between 1974 and 1979. HUD's Title VIII enforcement budget is also very small when contrasted to civil rights enforcement budgets in other areas of discrimination. The projection for HUD's enforcement program for 1979 to 1980 was $17.4 million as compared, for instance, to $301.1 million for fighting employment discrimination (U.S. Com. on Civil Rights, 1979, 18). While equal job opportunity is obviously important, its budget should not be seventeen times that set aside for fair housing. Finally, since 1975 the majority of funds appropriated to HUD for enforcing Title VIII have actually been diverted to overseeing civil rights compliance in the contracts that HUD approves. Thus, the percentage of what was intended to be spent on Title VIII enforcement was in fact a mere 50.9 percent of the total sum in 1974 and gradually diminished to only 37.4 percent in 1978. That figure rose slightly to 41.5 percent in 1979.

Commitment of Enforcement Personnel

Determining the extent to which federal enforcement personnel are committed to their implementation duties is essentially a subjective question, but there are some conclusions regarding this question with which few would disagree. Take the Veterans Administration, for example. The VA has a notorious reputation of contributing to housing discrimination. Throughout VA's history, one of its highest goals has been to provide loans for the families of white veterans, with equal opportunity being a low priority. Thus, three years after the passage of the Fair Housing Act of 1968 and the Supreme Court's decision in *Jones v. Alfred H. Mayer Co.* (1968), the VA still had only conducted compliance reviews where a formal complaint had been made. Where discrimination was found to be practiced by builders, VA merely required the builder to provide housing for the complainant, not housing for others similarly situated. By 1971, VA had conducted no surveys to determine the degree to which minorities occupied housing in VA subdivisions (U.S. Com. on Civil Rights, 1971a, 164). This obviously demonstrates a lack of commitment by VA officials in the early 1970s.

Later studies by the Commission on Civil Rights found only slight indications of a greater commitment. In 1973 the Commission found that its 1971 recommendations to the VA for eliminating discrimination in its housing programs were "still at the planning stage" (U.S. Com. on Civil Rights, 1973, 44). In 1975, VA still had not required lenders with which it dealt to promise nondiscrimination (U.S. Com. on Civil Rights, 1975b, 338–339). By 1979, VA still did not regularly monitor whether the real estate industry was complying with promises not to discriminate against minority and female veterans (U.S. Com. on Civil Rights, 1979, 107). It seems unlikely that one could find a better illustration of a greater lack of commitment on the part of fair housing personnel in any other federal agency. However, the related equal opportunity activities of the FHA, the FRS, the FDIC, and the COC may come reasonably close.

Commitment of the Enforcer's Superiors

The commitment of a president and his high-level appointees ordinarily has a significant impact on how, and the extent to which, fair housing programs are implemented (Lamb, 1978c, 841–844). For example, President Johnson assumed a strong leadership role in fair housing by placing pressure on Congress for four years until it finally passed the Fair Housing Act of 1968 (Lamb, 1982, 1116–1127). In contrast, the Nixon–Ford era demonstrates the effects that unsympathetic conservative administrations may have on fair housing implementation.

President Nixon's support for equal housing opportunity was minimal. At times Nixon gave lip service to the idea of fair housing, but his actual policies were completely alien to that basic concept. He refused to take actions to eliminate the use of exclusionary housing practices. Instead of acknowledging that such practices are usually designed to exclude minorities from white areas, Nixon disguised the issue in economic terms. He would not "impose economic integration" on communities that objected to the building of federally subsidized low- or moderate-income housing. Nor would he allow then HUD Secretary George Romney to promote programs in white suburbs that could be used to house minorities (Danielson, 1976, 205–236).

President Ford's administration also was characterized by little concern for fair housing. Consider, for instance, the equal housing opportunity activities of HUD during the Ford years. HUD regulations were ineffective and of limited success in supplying low-income housing to minorities. In fact, HUD officials candidly acknowledged that they were not carefully monitoring the application of the civil rights requirements of the Housing and Community Development Act of 1974 (Lamb, 1978a, 642–643). This act was passed to provide new housing opportunities for minorities and the poor outside inner cities. However, since Ford, like Nixon, opposed "economic integration," HUD regulations fell short of the congressionally established goal of dispersing minorities and the poor throughout larger metropolitan areas. In addition, Ford's 1976 budgetary proposals to Congress so ignored housing for low-income families that the Commission on Civil Rights strongly criticized the administration's position (1975a, 33). Ford, like Nixon, was clearly more concerned about gaining the political support of middle- and upper-class white suburban voters than in implementing national fair housing laws. In fact, Ford stated publicly that the idea of open housing did not describe his administration's policies (Lamb, 1978a, 646).

The Carter administration was more successful at achieving equal housing opportunity. Among other things, new regulations were issued by the FRS to outlaw redlining in the granting of home mortgages, and HUD leaders were somewhat more outspoken on the need to eliminate housing discrimination (Lamb, 1978a, 651–653). President Carter also announced that he supported 1979 and 1980 congressional attempts to strengthen HUD's fair housing enforcement powers (U.S. Senate, 1979, 4). These and other indicators separate Carter from Nixon and Ford as a supportive superior. Yet, although enforcement improved during the Carter years, the administration could have been far more supportive than it was in actuality.

This is far more true, however, of the Reagan administration which, from the beginning, placed pressure on HUD to develop "a compromise on proposals for tougher fair housing laws" ("Who Are These People," 1981, 22). In a speech to the 1981 NAACP Convention, Reagan received "the coolest reception of his presidency" ("Reagan," 1981, 6), and the president's position on the housing welfare of blacks surely had an effect on his reception. Despite rhetoric to the contrary, Reagan's negligence regarding civil rights made it "a major domestic issue—and a political embarrassment—for the first time in more than a decade" (Wines, 1982, 536). Among other things, President Reagan instructed the Justice Department to slow down prosecution in fair housing litigation, and his administration officials asserted that the "heavy-handed enforcement of laws against discrimination is now unneeded" (Wines, 1982, 537). This led one Department of Justice attorney to describe the Reagan administration as having a "blind ideology—an airtight, rightist view of the world. They're reactionary. It's that simple." Under the leadership of Reagan's Attorney General, William French Smith, the Justice Department failed to file a *single* housing discrimination suit in federal court in 1981, and had filed only two such cases as of January 1983 (Kurtz, 1983, 13). Although as of the writing of this book, the final verdict is still out, it is entirely possible that President Reagan will be remembered in history as a superior even less sympathetic to equal housing opportunity than either President Nixon or President Ford.

Program Beneficiaries

Of course, the major beneficiaries of attempts to eliminate housing discrimination and segregation are minorities. But, in addition, other groups accrue advantages from the fulfillment of fair housing goals and especially from the building of low- and moderate-income housing in the suburbs. Developers and landowners benefit economically when they are allowed to build low- and moderate-income housing throughout suburban areas. The higher density the housing, the more money builders and landowners make. Business and unions benefit when their members are able to live near where they work. Otherwise, workers—mainly minorities—may find it difficult to get to their job sites, and labor shortages or high rates of absenteeism may develop. Similarly, low-paid public employees (police officers, fire fighters, and teachers) in the suburbs benefit from the building of low- and moderate-income housing in the community where they work. Nor should one overlook the benefits that would accrue to young persons who grew up in a suburban community but who would otherwise be unable to continue living there because of escalating prices. To some extent, one would expect the parents of newly married couples to support some low- and moderate-income housing so that their children could remain in the area, even if some of the housing is used by minorities. The same is true of the elderly who may have lived in a neighborhood all their lives, want to remain there, but can no longer afford to keep up their suburban lifestyle. Whites living within the jurisdiction of the city also benefit from more minorities being dispersed in suburbs because they no longer have to bear the heavy burden of paying for the majority of public services for the poor (Danielson, 1976, 123–124; Rubinowitz, 1974, 3).

Some individuals, in seeking the benefits of equal housing opportunity, have at times made their political weight felt. This is particularly true with respect to civil rights activists who have protested unfair housing practices to bring discrimination to the public's attention. Individual activists have also filed lawsuits and have taken other efforts to jar governmental officials out of their complacency. Yet there is only so much that individuals can accomplish in the field of fair housing. When "victory" at the individual level finally occurs, it is often too late since these persons have been denied the housing they preferred and have had to move elsewhere.

Obviously, therefore, forms of collective action have a more affirmative effect on equal housing opportunity than individuals acting on their own. The civil rights groups which have been most active in fair housing include the National Committee Against Discrimination in Housing and the Suburban Action Institute. They have received some assistance from more general-purpose civil rights groups such as the NAACP, the Southern Christian Leadership Conference, the Leadership Conference on Civil Rights, and the Center for National Policy Review. By documenting injustices and statutory violations, monitoring programs, and initiating litigation aimed at clarifying the law, these civil rights groups keep the national fair housing mandate in view. However, the extent of their impact can never match the potential consequences of effective fair housing enforcement by a committed president and his bureaucracy. Rather, such groups are most influential in devoting their limited resources to selected lawsuits that have the prospect for major change in housing discrimination.

Coordination of Enforcement Agencies

The overlapping implementation responsibilities in civil rights of different federal agencies have long been an impediment to successful civil rights enforcement in some areas (Lamb, 1978b, 857–860; Orfield, 1979, 1981). In the early 1980s, significant strides had been taken to solve coordination problems in equal employment opportunity (Lamb, 1979, 1980). Yet these problems remain as significant obstacles to successful civil rights implementation in equal housing opportunity, although some progress has been initiated.

The Fair Housing Act of 1968 requires HUD to coordinate the activities of all federal agencies with fair housing duties (Lamb, 1982, 1131–1132). However, by 1971 HUD had taken few steps to fulfill this responsibility (U.S. Com. on Civil Rights, 1971a, 148–149). HUD's long-awaited coordination activities were ultimately initiated when it and the General Services Administration (GSA) agreed to work together to ensure that low- and moderate-income housing for minorities would be available before GSA would locate a federal facility in an area. HUD also convinced the four federal financial regulatory agencies to distribute questionnaires to all the institutions that they regulate, soliciting data on their lending practices involving minorities (U.S. Com. on Civil Rights, 1973, 36–37). In 1975, however, the HUD–GSA agreement was not working, since there had been few efforts to determine whether communities where federal facilities were being placed were actually discriminating (U.S. Com. on Civil Rights, 1975a, 121–122).

On another front, HUD reached another agreement with the Department of Justice providing that the agencies would exchange information regarding housing discrimination throughout the country. HUD was still referring few cases of housing discrimination to the Justice Department for prosecution, however, and the Justice Department was filing lawsuits in no more that 10 percent of all HUD referrals (U.S. Com. on Civil Rights, 1975a, 127–129).

Weak coordination between HUD and other federal agencies with fair housing duties led to a 1979 report by the Commission on Civil Rights detailing HUD's successes and failures. The Commission found that HUD had succeeded in creating the Federal Equal Housing Opportunity Council. Yet the Council was a low HUD priority and was doing a poor job in coordinating fair housing implementation. The Council's key project has been an Interagency Fair Housing Agreement to ensure that minority federal employees are not discriminated against, but of the fifty-two Council member agencies, only eight had entered into the agreement. Also, the Commission discovered that "[t]he Council [had] not attempted to seek interagency solutions to the problems of exclusionary zoning, discrimination by the real estate industry, or the need for interagency sharing of compliance information." Due to ineffective coordination, "there [was] no mechanism to prevent duplicative reviews and investigations, to ensure that participants in one Federal program who violate Title VIII are not allowed to continue that violation in other Federal programs, and to enable HUD to be aware of all possible Federal sanctions when it attempts to conciliate resolution of a Title VI violation" (1979, 216). As of 1979, then, little coordination had occurred. Redundancy of effort, inconsistent compliance standards, and infrequent sharing of civil rights data among other agencies continued to be problems impeding progress toward successful civil rights implementation.

Cost–Benefit Calculus

Those who have practiced housing discrimination have seldom experienced any substantial direct costs, and thus the benefits of noncompliance have been significantly greater than the costs. The benefits of noncompliance continue to outweigh the disadvantages because federal agencies with fair housing enforcement responsibilities rarely utilize sanctions that would make the costs of housing discrimination surpass its advantages.

For example, in 1971 HUD had never terminated any federal funding because of discrimination (U.S. Com. on Civil Rights, 1971b, 42). While one might assume that HUD would be the agency most likely to decide in favor of Title VI complaints in housing discrimination disputes, findings by HUD against alleged violators have not been common. As another illustration, one might expect that HUD would refer to the Department of Justice a reasonably large percentage of Title VIII complaints when it has indications that there is discrimination. Yet even where discrimination is obvious, most HUD regulatees do not change their practices, because adverse steps are rarely taken by HUD and the Justice Department. By 1970, HUD had referred only 33 out of some 1,500 Title VIII complaints to the Justice Department, which in turn filed only 22 lawsuits (U.S. Com. on Civil Rights, 1971b, 146). As of 1979, the Justice Department was filing fewer than 30 Title VIII suits per year (although this was far more than were filed during the first two years of the Reagan administration; see Kurtz, 1983, 13), and on the average only three of those 30 were referred to the Department of Justice by HUD (U.S. Com. on Civil Rights, 1979, 31). In short, the Justice Department fails to initiate litigation against most of those engaging in housing discrimination, and severe administrative sanctions by HUD are unlikely to be forthcoming (Orfield, 1981, 30). Nor can one expect voluntary compliance, or for many white communities to accept federal inducements in the form of additional funds to build subsidized housing for minorities. Thus, under current conditions, there is little hope that federal fair housing laws will be strictly implemented.

Federal Involvement

The federal government seldom became actively involved in fighting for fair housing until President Johnson essentially pushed a reluctant Congress into passing the Fair Housing Act of 1968 (Lamb, 1982, 1116–1127). Certainly there has never been any supplanting of local or state authority with respect to fair housing as there has been in voting rights (Hamilton, 1973, chap. 10; Rodgers and Bullock, 1972, chap. 2). Hence, the major recourse for those discriminated against prior to 1968 was time-consuming and costly private litigation.

Although federal involvement to bring about fair housing reached high tide in 1968 with the Fair Housing Act and the Supreme Court's decision in *Jones v. Alfred H. Mayer Co.*, the election of Richard Nixon threw a damper on the developing progress. Without presidential leadership, federal involvement becomes passive (Lamb, 1978c, 841–844), and the leadership provided by both Presidents Nixon and Ford, as explained earlier, was minimal in fair housing (Lamb, 1978a, 637–649). Even HUD openly admitted at the end of eight years of Republican White House control that "[a]lthough the Federal Fair Housing Law, Title VIII of the 1968 Civil Rights Act, has been in effect for nearly a decade, residential segregation and overt discrimination in housing continue" (1977, 1).

The Carter administration, as also noted earlier, became more actively involved in fair housing implementation. Unlike Nixon and Ford, Carter's appointees at HUD cautioned some cities and suburbs that federal funds would be delayed or terminated if low- and moderate-income housing was not spread throughout urban areas and suburban communities (Lamb, 1978a, 655). President Carter also endorsed the 1979 and 1980 congressional efforts to strengthen HUD's enforcement powers under Title VIII (U.S. Senate, 1979, 4). However, the enforcement effort under Carter did not move quickly enough to fulfill the promise of fair housing, and federal involvement was further reduced significantly during President Reagan's first two years in the White House (Kurtz, 1983).

CONCLUSION

While progress has been made in the past decade, particularly for upper- and middle-income minorities, housing segregation and discrimination continue throughout much of the United States primarily because of practices by real estate interests, financial lending institutions, local governments, and white homeowners. Since the question of fair housing is a very controversial one, and since whites believe that they gain from housing segregation, discrimination continues even though it is contrary to the Fourteenth Amendment, the Civil Rights Act of 1866, Title VI of the Civil Rights Act of 1964, Title VIII of the Civil Rights Act of 1968, and several federal court decisions. Exclusionary zoning laws, racial steering, and other techniques are still used by many suburbs and exclusive white areas of cities to keep minorities out. Although many minority leaders oppose dispersal from the central cities because it threatens their power base, minorities must be given an equal opportunity to escape unbearable ghetto or inner-city living conditions.

Successful policy implementation in the field of equal housing opportunity has been limited for several reasons, but principally because Title VIII, the most vital fair housing weapon in the federal arsenal, is a vague and weak piece of legislation and because presidents have been reluctant, to varying degrees, to push for housing desegregation. Of the federal agencies responsible for eliminating housing discrimination, only HUD has come reasonably close to its designated role—and clearly not close enough. Administrative coordination for fighting discrimination in housing has been extremely weak, and the benefits of continued discrimination still far outweigh the costs. In the final analysis, federal agencies must be heavily relied upon to bring about effective resolutions to the herculean tasks of eliminating housing discrimination and segregation, with strong support from the White House. If the liberal faith in the efficacy of federal governmental action to alleviate festering racial problems is still valid, Title VIII must also be amended by Congress to give HUD and the Department of Justice far greater enforcement powers, and the federal courts must broadly interpret such a law. Only then will this nation make meaningful progress toward the goal of achieving equal housing opportunity for all Americans, especially for low- and moderate-income minorities.

NOTES

1. It should be noted that the terms *equal housing opportunity* and *fair housing* are used synonymously in this chapter.
2. Nor did the migrations of blacks out of the South seem to decline significantly through 1970. See Forman, 1970, 19.
3. For an example of a steering case in the courts, see the discussion in the section on laws forbidding discrimination in housing.
4. In this chapter, economic groups in America are generally referred to as either low-income, moderate-income, middle-income, or high-income. Of course, minorities are primarily concentrated in the low- and moderate-income categories. Between 1950 and 1976, "blacks and other races received incomes amounting to less than two-thirds of white families." The median income for white families in 1950 was $3,445, for example, while the median income for minority families was only 54 percent of that ($1,869). By the mid-1970s, the gap had been closed somewhat (see McCrone and Hardy, 1978). For instance, in 1976, the median income of whites had significantly risen to $15,537, while the median income for minorities had grown to 63 percent of that at $9,821 (U.S. Com. on Civil Rights, 1978, 48–49). In 1975, however, 28 percent of all black families were living at the poverty level, while the poverty levels for Native Americans, Mexican-Americans, and Puerto Ricans were 26, 24, and 32 percent respectively (U.S. Com. on Civil Rights, 1978, 62).
5. For an illustration of a blockbusting case, see the discussion in the section on laws that forbid housing discrimination later in this chapter.
6. See also *United States v. Real Estate One, Inc.* (1977).
7. For details on these and other steering and blockbusting cases, see Lamb, 1982, 1141–1161.
8. See, for example, the Housing and Community Development Act of 1974, the Equal Credit Opportunity Act of 1974, and the Home Mortgage Disclosure Act of 1975.
9. For the years 1960, 1970, and 1976, the proportion of homeownership by minority groups was as follows: Native Americans/Alaskan Natives, 41, 45, and 46 percent; blacks, 37, 42, and 42 percent; Mexican-Americans, 52, 52, and 47 percent; Japanese-Americans, 31, 43, and 35 percent; Chinese-Americans, 36, 42, and 39 percent; Filipino-Americans, 34, 35, and 41 percent; Puerto Ricans, 22, 33, and 32 percent. The highest percentages for minority homeownership were 52 percent for Mexican-Americans in 1960 and 1970. However, even during those *highest* of all years, Mexican-Americans were less than 90 percent as likely to own houses as were whites. In contrast, in 1960, Puerto Rican families were only 37 percent as likely to own homes as were white families (U.S. Com. on Civil Rights, 1978, 72).

10. For general discussions of the evolution of public housing programs over the years, see Hartman, 1975, chaps. 4–5; Keith, 1973; Taggart, 1970, chap. 3.
11. Many of the problems associated with urban renewal and revitalization are detailed in Rosenthal, 1980; Wilson, 1966. With regard to the displacement of blacks by urban renewal projects, see Mitchell and Smith, 1979, 174; 176.
12. See also Ball, Krane, and Lauth, 1982, chap. 1; Bullock and Lamb, 1982.
13. There are a number of provisions of Title VIII that have not been successfully addressed by HUD regulations. For example, as of the late 1970s, HUD had not issued regulations to guide other federal agencies pursuant to its responsibility as the lead agency in enforcing Title VIII, or regulations pertaining to discrimination in the sale or rental of housing, discrimination in the financing of housing, and discrimination by brokerage services (U.S. Com. on Civil Rights, 1979, 26). Even where HUD regulations have been forthcoming, they have too frequently lacked the clarity and specificity needed to enforce Title VIII fully.
14. The statutory reliance on the Justice Department permits too much discretion concerning whether legal action will be pursued by the federal government. In many instances, the Justice Department has decided not to ask for an injunction or to file a lawsuit, even though HUD has discovered and informed the Department of Justice of a pattern or practice of discrimination in violation of Title VIII. Indeed, Orfield concluded in 1979 that for several years the Department of Justice "[had] initiated no important litigation against suburban housing exclusion" (1979, 13). Since fair housing implementation is often dependent on a viable threat of litigation by the Justice Department, that is one key reason why Title VIII has had a limited impact on practices of housing discrimination and segregation.

REFERENCES

Ball, Howard; Dale Krane; and Thomas P. Lauth (1982). *Compromised Compliance: Implementation of the 1965 Voting Rights Act*. Westport, Conn.: Greenwood.
Bracey, John H. (1971). *Rise of the Ghetto*. Belmont, Calif.: Wadsworth.
Buchanan v. Warley, 245 U.S. 60 (1917).
Bullock, Charles S. III, and Charles M. Lamb (1982). "Toward a Theory of Civil Rights Implementation." *Policy Perspectives* 2: 376-393.
Bullock, Charles S. III, and Harrell R. Rodgers, Jr. (1975). *Racial Equality in America: In Search of an Unfulfilled Goal*. Pacific Palisades, Calif.: Goodyear.
Bullock, Charles S. III, and Harrell R. Rodgers, Jr. (1976). "Coercion to Compliance: Southern School Districts and School Desegregation Guidelines." *Journal of Politics* 38: 987-1011.
City of Eastlake v. Forest City Enterprises, 426 U.S. 668 (1976).

Clark, Thomas A. (1979). *Blacks in Suburbs: A National Perspective.* New Brunswick: Rutgers University Center for Urban Policy Research.
Comment (1968). "Title VI of the Civil Rights Act of 1964—Implementation and Impact." *George Washington Law Review* 36: 824–1022.
Danielson, Michael N. (1976). *The Politics of Exclusion.* New York: Columbia University Press.
Downs, Anthony (1973). *Opening Up the Suburbs: An Urban Strategy for America.* New Haven: Yale University Press.
Downs, Anthony (1981). *Neighborhoods and Urban Development.* Washington, D.C.: Brookings Institution.
Falk, David, and Herbert M. Franklin (1976). *Equal Housing Opportunity: The Unfinished Agenda.* Washington, D.C.: Potomac Institute.
Farley, Reynolds; Suzanne Bianchi; and Diane Colasanto (1979). "Barriers to the Racial Integration of Neighborhoods: The Detroit Case." *Annals of the American Academy of Political and Social Science* 441: 97–113.
Farley, Reynolds; Howard Schuman; Suzanne Bianchi; Diane Colasanto; and Shirley Hatchett (1978). " 'Chocolate City, Vanilla Suburbs': Will the Trend toward Racially Separate Communities Continue?" *Social Science Research* 7: 319–344.
Farley, Reynolds, and Karl E. Taeuber (1968). "Population Trends and Residential Segregation Since 1960." *Science* 159: 953–956.
Forman, Robert E. (1970). *Black Ghettos, White Ghettos, and Slums.* Englewood Cliffs, N.J.: Prentice-Hall.
Hamilton, Charles V. (1973). *The Bench and the Ballot: Southern Federal Judges and Black Voters.* New York: Oxford University Press.
Hamilton, Howard D. (1970). "Direct Legislation: Some Implications of Open Housing Referenda." *American Political Science Review* 64: 124–137.
Harrington, Michael (1981). *The Other America: Poverty in the United States.* Baltimore: Penguin.
Hartman, Chester W. (1975). *Housing and Social Policy.* Englewood Cliffs, N.J.: Prentice-Hall.
Hauser, Philip M. (1965). "Demographic Factors in the Integration of the Negro." *Daedalus* 94: 847–877.
Helper, Rose (1969). *Racial Policies and Practices of Real Estate Brokers.* Minneapolis: University of Minnesota Press.
Hershberg, Theodore; Alan N. Burstein; Eugene P. Ericksen; Stephanie Greenberg; and William L. Yancy (1979). "The Tale of Three Cities: Blacks and Immigrants in Philadelphia: 1850–1880, 1930, 1970." *Annals of the American Academy of Political and Social Science* 441: 55–81.
Hill, Richard Child (1974). "Separate and Unequal: Governmental Inequity in the Metropolis." *American Political Science Review* 68: 1557–1568.
Hills v. Gautreaux, 425 U.S. 284 (1976).
James v. Valtierra, 402 U.S. 137 (1971).
Jones v. Alfred H. Mayer Company, 392 U.S. 409 (1968).
Kain, John F., and John M. Quigley (1972). "Housing Market Discrimination, Homeownership, and Savings Behavior." *American Economic Review* 62: 263–277.
Keith, Nathaniel S. (1973). *Politics and the Housing Crisis Since 1930.* New York: Universe.
Kurtz, Howard (1983). "HUD's Approach to Housing Bias Stresses Cooperation over Litigation." *Washington Post* (Jan. 4, 1983): 13.
Ladd, William M. (1962). "Effect of Integration on Property Values." *American Economic Review* 52: 801–808.

Lake, Robert W. (1979). "Racial Transition and Black Homeownership in American Suburbs." *Annals of the American Academy of Political and Social Science* 441: 142–156.
Lamb, Charles M. (1978a). "Presidential Fair Housing Policies: Political and Legal Trends." *Cumberland Law Review* 8: 619–660.
Lamb, Charles M. (1978b). "Administrative Coordination in Civil Rights Enforcement: A Regional Approach." *Vanderbilt Law Review* 31: 855–886.
Lamb, Charles M. (1978c). " 'New Federalism' and Civil Rights." *University of Toledo Law Review* 9: 816–845.
Lamb, Charles M. (1979). "Equal Employment Opportunity and the Carter Administration: An Analysis of Reform Options." *Policy Studies Journal* 8: 377-383.
Lamb, Charles M. (1980). "Presidential Leadership, Governmental Reorganization, and Equal Employment Opportunity." In Charles Bulmer and John C. Carmichael (eds.), *Employment and Labor-Relations Policy*. Lexington, Mass.: Lexington Books, chap. 6.
Lamb, Charles M. (1981a). "Housing Discrimination and Segregation in America: Problematical Dimensions and the Federal Legal Response." *Catholic University Law Review* 30: 363–430.
Lamb, Charles M. (1981b). "Legal Foundations of Civil Rights and Pluralism in America." *Annals of the American Academy of Political and Social Science* 454: 13–25.
Lamb, Charles M. (1982). "Congress, the Courts, and Civil Rights: The Fair Housing Act of 1968 Revisited." *Villanova Law Review* 28: 1115–1162.
Lamb, Charles M., and Mitchell S. Lustig (1979). "The Burger Court, Exclusionary Zoning, and the Activist-Restraint Debate." *University of Pittsburgh Law Review* 40: 169–226.
Laurenti, Luigi (1960). *Property Values and Race*. Berkeley: University of California Press.
McCrone, Donald J., and Richard J. Hardy (1978). "Civil Rights Policies and Achievement of Racial Economic Equality, 1948–1975." *American Journal of Political Science* 22: 1–17.
Mitchell, Robert E., and Richard A. Smith (1979). "Race and Housing: A Review and Comments on the Content and Effects of Federal Policy." *Annals of the American Academy of Political and Social Science* 441: 168–185.
Note (1971). "Exclusionary Zoning and Equal Protection." *Harvard Law Review* 84: 1645–1669.
Note (1976). "Racial Steering: The Real Estate Broker and Title VIII." *Yale Law Journal* 85: 808–825.
Orfield, Gary (1974). "Federal Policy, Local Power, and Metropolitan Segregation." *Political Science Quarterly* 89: 777–802.
Orfield, Gary (1979). "Federal Agencies and Urban Segregation: Steps toward Coordinated Action." In *Racial Segregation: Two Policy Views*. New York: Ford Foundation.
Orfield, Gary (1981). *Toward a Strategy for Urban Integration*. New York: Ford Foundation.
"Reagan and His Speech Bomb" (1981). *Buffalo Evening News*, June 30, 1981, p. 6.
Rodgers, Harrell R., Jr., and Charles S. Bullock III (1972). *Law and Social Change: Civil Rights Laws and Their Consequences*. New York: McGraw-Hill.
Rodgers, Harrell R., Jr., and Charles S. Bullock III (1976). *Coercion to Compliance*. Lexington, Mass.: Lexington Books.

Roof, Wade Clark (1979). "Race and Residence: The Shifting Basis of American Race Relations." *Annals of the American Academy of Political and Social Science* 441: 1–12.
Rosenthal, Donald B. (ed.) (1980). *Urban Revitalization*. Beverly Hills, Calif.: Sage.
Rubinowitz, Leonard S. (1974). *Low-Income Housing: Suburban Strategies*. Cambridge, Mass.: Ballinger.
Rubinowitz, Leonard S., and Elizabeth Trosman (1979). "Affirmative Action and the American Dream: Implementing Fair Housing Policies in Federal Homeownership Programs." *Northwestern University Law Review* 74: 491–616.
Shelley v. Kraemer, 334 U.S. 1 (1948).
Sorensen, Annemette; Karl E. Taeuber; and Leslie J. Hollingsworth, Jr. (1975). "Indexes of Residential Segregation for 109 Cities in the United States, 1940–1970." *Sociological Focus* 8: 125–142.
Starr, Roger (1977). *America's Housing Challenge: What It Is and How to Meet It*. New York: Hill and Wang.
Taeuber, Karl E. (1975). "Racial Segregation: The Persisting Dilemma." *Annals of the American Academy of Political and Social Science* 422: 87–96.
Taeuber, Karl E., and Alma F. Taeuber (1965). *Negroes in Cities: Residential Segregation and Neighborhood Change*. Chicago: Aldine.
Taggart, Robert III (1970). *Low-Income Housing: A Critique of Federal Aid*. Baltimore: Johns Hopkins Press.
United States v. Mitchell, 335 F. Supp. 1004 (1971).
United States v. Real Estate One, Inc., 433 F. Supp. 1140 (1977).
U.S. Commission on Civil Rights (1971a). *Federal Civil Rights Enforcement Effort*. Washington, D.C.: U.S. Government Printing Office.
U.S. Commission on Civil Rights (1971b). *The Federal Civil Rights Enforcement Effort: One Year Later*. Washington, D.C.: U.S. Government Printing Office.
U.S. Commission on Civil Rights (1973). *The Federal Civil Rights Enforcement Effort—A Reassessment*. Washington, D.C.: U.S. Government Printing Office.
U.S. Commission on Civil Rights (1974). *Equal Opportunity in Suburbia*. Washington, D.C.: U.S. Government Printing Office.
U.S. Commission on Civil Rights (1975a). *Twenty Years After Brown: Equal Opportunity in Housing*. Washington, D.C.: U.S. Government Printing Office.
U.S. Commission on Civil Rights (1975b). *The Federal Civil Rights Enforcement Effort: To Provide . . . for Fair Housing*. Washington, D.C.: U.S. Government Printing Office.
U.S. Commission on Civil Rights (1978). *Social Indicators of Equality for Minorities and Women*. Washington, D.C.: U.S. Government Printing Office.
U.S. Commission on Civil Rights (1979). *The Federal Fair Housing Enforcement Effort*. Washington, D.C.: U.S. Government Printing Office.
U.S. Department of Housing and Urban Development (HUD) (1977). *The Federal Government: Fair Housing 1976*. Washington, D.C.: U.S. Government Printing Office.
U.S. Department of Housing and Urban Development (1979). *Measuring Racial Discrimination in American Housing Markets*. Washington, D.C.: U.S. Government Printing Office.
U.S. Senate (1979). *Fair Housing Amendments Act of 1979: Hearings Before the Subcommittee on the Constitution of the Committee on the Judiciary*, 96th Congress, 1st Session. Washington, D.C.: U.S. Government Printing Office.
Village of Arlington Heights v. Metropolitan Housing Development Corp., 492 U.S. 252 (1977).
Vose, Clement E. (1959). *Caucasians Only: The Supreme Court, the NAACP, and the Restrictive Covenant Cases*. Berkeley: University of California Press.

Weaver, Robert C. (1982). "The Impact of Ethnicity upon Urban America." In Lance Liebman (ed.), *Ethnic Relations in America*. Englewood Cliffs, N.J.: Prentice-Hall, chap. 3.

Wilson, James Q. (ed.) (1966). *Urban Renewal: The Record and the Controversy*. Cambridge: MIT Press.

Wines, Michael. (1982). "Administration Says It Merely Seeks a 'Better Way' to Enforce Civil Rights." *National Journal* 9: 536–541.

"Who Are These People—And What Do They Stand For?" (1981). *U.S. News and World Report* 90 (Jan. 19, 1981): 18–22.

Wolfinger, Raymond E., and Fred I. Greenstein (1968). "The Repeal of Fair Housing in California: An Analysis of Referendum Voting." *American Political Science Review* 62: 753–769.

Wood, Jack E. (1979). "Race and Housing." In Gertrude S. Fish (ed.), *The Story of Housing*. New York: Macmillan.

Zuch v. Hussey, 394 F. Supp. 1028 (1975).

Chapter 7

Conditions Associated with Policy Implementation
Charles S. Bullock III

The preceding chapters have chronicled a number of changes that were produced in response to civil rights policy requirements. Hundreds of school systems that were rigidly segregated before the *Brown* decision now have biracial student bodies and faculties. In the South where black voters once numbered in the hundreds of thousands, there are now millions and where once there were no black elected officials, today there are more than 2,000. Blacks now have wider options in job opportunities, choice of college or university, and selection of residence. Hispanics and others for whom English is not their first language are no longer cut off from important opportunities. Their children can receive a bilingual education and the adults may have access to voting materials printed in their native language.

The magnitude of the changes that have occurred since the 1950s may not seem all that impressive from one vantage point. That a citizen should be allowed to vote free of racial barriers seems so eminently fair, so reasonable, that it may be hard to comprehend the struggles involved in achieving this basic right, which is premised on the Fifteenth Amendment. Similarly, the right to a job based on skill and qualifications or to a home or a college education based on taste and resources may seem to be less than monumental objectives to those who have never been denied them for reasons of race or ethnicity.

The assaults on the first children to desegregate the schools of Little Rock, Boston, New Orleans, and some other cities, the murders of civil rights workers, and the terrorism aimed at those who sought to register to vote should remind us of the opposition which had to be overcome to secure the rights that are enjoyed today. The vehemence with which many whites once vowed that blacks or Hispanics would never be allowed to attend desegregated schools in their communities, to vote, or to obtain a good job may be used as a baseline for comparing the changes that have occurred.

Although changes many of our parents thought they would never see are now commonplace, the policies discussed in this book have rarely been fully implemented. There remain communities in which the right to vote is still impeded and where realtors steer white clients to homes in white neighborhoods and blacks to homes in black or transitional neighborhoods. In schools, approximately 18 percent of the nation's black students still attend schools that are all black, and in many schools inadequate instruction is provided to youngsters who have limited English-speaking abilities.

The primary focus of this chapter is cross-sectional. By comparing achievements across policy areas we hope to understand better which variables can distinguish between the relatively more and relatively less well-implemented policies. Before assessing the usefulness of the variables introduced in chapter 1, we need to determine the relative amount of implementation which has occurred in each civil rights policy area.

IMPLEMENTATION SUCCESS

In a field like civil rights, it is often difficult to measure precisely the extent to which policy has been implemented. The amount of civil rights one enjoys is inherently less quantifiable than one's standard of living. Thus, there are greater dangers in using quantitative data to assess the implementation of civil rights programs than when evaluating the success of economic programs.

Caution is appropriate when interpreting the available data. It is possible that, because of a variety of factors, a civil rights program might be succeeding even though there is little evidence of that in existing data. For example, civil rights policies that extend to minorities' opportunities for open housing and for attending previously all-white institutions of higher education were never intended to *force* minorities to enter predominantly white environments. Even if the racism which enforced segregation were eliminated, the choices of millions of individuals might still result in little biracial presence. Along the same lines, while authorities can redraw attendance zones to produce greater desegregation in a district's schools, most of a system's schools may soon become uniracial again if white parents move to other districts or place their children in private schools rather than accept desegregation. In short, a policy can be carried out by the officials responsible for its implementation but the results may not be visible in the data.

Another difficulty in rating implementation success results from variations in the amount and quality of the available data. Figures with which to evaluate the three public education programs and higher education segregation are collected by the federal government biennially. Estimates of voter registration and turnout by race are made after each congressional election by the U.S. Bureau of the Census. Figures on the racial composition of neighborhoods, blocks, or apartment projects are available only from the decennial census.

A third consideration complicating comparative assessments is uncertainty about what the upper limits of implementation are. Some schools will be entirely or almost entirely one race under any reasonable desegregation plan. Because so few minorities are trained as engineers or doctors, it is likely that engineering firms and hospitals will often have only white professionals even if the employers carry out affirmative action recruitment efforts. Differences in the economic resources of blacks and whites mean that expensive neighborhoods and colleges will have fewer blacks than will less expensive ones. Geographical distributions of ethnic groups further contribute to what might appear to be the effects of failure to implement civil rights policy. In states such as Wyoming and North Dakota which have few black residents, it will be difficult for employers to hire black workers. National figures do not always reflect these considerations.

For the reasons touched on above, it is unlikely that all differences between blacks and whites will be quickly obliterated. What then would constitute full implementation in the early 1980s? People disagree on the answer. Civil rights activists are far less likely to see current accomplishments as approaching the upper limits of what is attainable than are most government officials.

Keeping these shortcomings in mind, let us now look at a suggested clustering of programs in terms of implementation. The policy goals in voting rights and school desegregation have been the most extensively implemented. In an intermediate category, implementation has been somewhat less in equal employment and bilingual education. Implementation has been least complete in promoting higher education desegregation, fair housing, and the elimination of second-generation discrimination.

While these groupings are admittedly somewhat imprecise, let us briefly review the evidence that underlies the ranking. The substantial increase in the proportion of Southern blacks who are registered to vote and the narrowing of the difference between black–white registration and turnout rates are reported in tables 2-1 and 2-2. These figures indicate the impact of federal policy in overcoming racial obstacles to black participation. Even though racial disparities in participation persist, they are less than would be expected based on the economic differences between blacks and whites (Murray and Vedletz, 1977; Verba and Nie, 1972, 151–160). Increases in black turnout have produced a substantial rise in the number of black officeholders.

Remarkable changes have also been registered in school desegregation. The first three tables in chapter 3 report that the proportion of blacks in majority white schools has increased while the proportion who are racially isolated has dropped. The changes have been most striking in the South, where racial balance has been achieved among the schools of all but large systems. To some extent, the proportion of black students in majority white schools is artificially depressed since twelve of the fifty largest school districts are majority black.[1]

Change has also occurred in employment opportunities. However, as chapter 4 shows, blacks, Hispanics, and women remain underrepresented in the better-paying occupations while being overrepresented in the less lucrative ones where they have traditionally been concentrated. Only one-third of the jobs held by blacks and Hispanics are white-collar jobs, compared with the half of all jobs in the nation which fall into this broad category. Despite improvements in the types of jobs held by women and minorities, and the higher wages earned by those who hold the better jobs, women and minorities earn only three-fifths as much as white males. The good salaries enjoyed by women and minorities who are trained to compete in today's job market are offset by the growing numbers of unemployed among these groups. The net effect is that the income disparities between white males and other groups in society have not been reduced over the last fifteen years. Overall, conditions in the economic sphere give less evidence of equity than in voting and school desegregation.

Since the mid-1970s, bilingual education programs have grown in number and size. Literally hundreds of school districts which had ignored this need now have programs. However, the Department of Education (DOE) estimates that a large number of students are still not given the bilingual training the legislation calls for.

Desegregation of institutions of higher education has come slowly. The objective of eliminating racial identifiability which has sometimes been articulated by DOE has generally not been achieved. All of the traditionally white schools in the covered states remain overwhelmingly white. Except for Texas and some border states, the proportion of blacks at white institutions remains substantially below the proportion of blacks in the states' population. With the exception of two border states, traditionally black institutions remain predominantly black.

American residential patterns also continue to be segregated. Racial steering and redlining continue in many American communities. The fair housing policies stipulated by the courts and Congress have expanded the options of middle-income minority families. However, federal policy has done virtually nothing to promote stable biracial communities. While token desegregation is now found more often than in the past, much of what appears to be integrated housing in a census survey is in reality simply neighborhoods in transition. Frequently when large numbers of whites and blacks live in the same neighborhood, it is only for the brief interval between the time the first black family moves in and the time the last white one moves out.

Second-generation discrimination in the public schools is another area in which much remains to be done. Schools throughout the country give evidence of inequitable treatment of black faculty and students—and the inequities appear to be increasing.

In all aspects of civil rights there have been some changes; in none has full equality been achieved. Keeping in mind the relative nature of the classifications, we will use the following groupings for categorizing implementation success in the remainder of the chapter.

Greatest Implementation
  Voting
  School Desegregation
Moderate Implementation
  Employment
  Bilingual Education
Least Implementation
  Higher Education
  Housing
  Second-Generation Discrimination

Federal Involvement

The federal government has become actively involved in pursuing the objectives of the first four policy areas. Active involvement has been manifest in lawsuits brought by federal attorneys, fund cut-offs, and the targeting of districts for enforcement activities. In contrast, the federal government has taken a passive role vis-à-vis higher education and fair housing. Litigation has rarely been filed by government attorneys, no funds have been withheld, and in the sphere of fair housing there has been virtually no targeting of cities or neighborhoods for reviews or enforcement proceedings except when numerous complaints have been filed in a particular area.

Second-generation discrimination is the one policy area that may appear not to conform to the expected pattern. However, although efforts to curb postdesegregation abuses have not been notably successful, there is less evidence of discrimination in those districts in which federal authorities have taken an active rather than a passive stance.

In the policies in which there has been greater federal activity, implementation was more successful once the federal government shifted from passive to active enforcement. Before federal resources were committed to rooting out discrimination, increases in the numbers of blacks registered to vote, attending schools with whites in the South, and obtaining better jobs came as slowly as the sands slipping through an hourglass. To give but one example: Between 1956 and 1962 the proportion of the South's voting-age black population registered to vote rose from 25 to only 29 percent. An additional bit of evidence on the importance of federal activism is evident in school desegregation. After the Department of Health, Education, and Welfare (HEW) lost its power to deny funds to segregated school districts, the pace at which additional desegregation was achieved declined.

EXPLAINING VARIATIONS IN IMPLEMENTATION

Now that we have classified civil rights policies into three categories of implementation, we may reexamine the variables used throughout the book. The objective is to determine which variables are useful in explaining differences in the degree of implementation success. To the extent that we succeed, we will be reducing the laundry lists of variables that have been suggested (see Sabatier and Mazmanian, 1980; Van Horn and Van Meter, 1976).

Under what conditions will we conclude that a variable affects implementation? To be useful in helping us understand the conditions under which implementation proceeds or is derailed, the value which is incorporated in the variable should be most prevalent when implementation has been greatest and least frequent when implementation has been least. To be more concrete, if specificity of standards is related to implementation, then the most specific standards should exist for voting and school desegregation and the most imprecise should be found for housing, higher education, and second-generation discrimination. If we find that standards are equally specific for all seven policies, then this variable would not, taken by itself, be able to account for variations in the extent to which the different policies have been implemented. Nor is a variable useful if we find it more prevalent for policies marked by the least amount of success.

Table 7-1 compares the seven policies across the ten implementation variables. You may want to refer to this table as each variable is introduced.

The pattern supports the hypothesis that federal involvement determines the extent of implementation. The greatest changes have occurred when the federal government was an active ally of minorities. When minorities have had to pursue their rights by bringing private suits or filing complaints, conditions have changed less.

TABLE 7-1 Summary of Implementation Variables

	Federal Involvement	Clarity of Policy Goals	Specificity of Standards	Monitoring	Enforcement Agency
Greatest Implementation					
Voting	Active after 1960 act authorized Dept. of Justice (DOJ) suits. 1965 act allowed the replacement of local registrars.	Clarification provided by the 1965 Voting Rights Act.	1965 act contained specific trigger for identifying areas which are covered and indicated what constituted compliance. Ambiguous on some preclearance standards.	On-site monitoring has been relatively infrequent.	DOJ's Civil Rights Division.
School desegregation	Active federal involvement essential to eliminate dual schools.	Clear in the South after 1968; remains unclear for systems not guilty of de jure segregation.	Introduction of quantitative standards promoted desegregation in the South. These have not been developed for most Northern districts.	Present in HEW but not DOJ districts during 1960s. More desegregation occurred in the former. Infrequently done now.	Dept. of Education's (DOE) Office for Civil Rights (OCR) has primary responsibility; obstinate districts referred to DOJ for litigation.
Moderate Implementation					
Equal employment	Active after EEOC was authorized to file suits in 1972.	Unclear.	Missing from statute, but established as objectives in some court orders and negotiated settlements.	Inadequate in the past, due to small staff and poor training, but some improvements recently.	EEOC, OFCCP.

	Federal Involvement	Clarity of Policy Goals	Specificity of Standards	Monitoring	Enforcement Agency
Moderate Implementation					
Bilingual education	Major changes came after federal reviews of targeted districts.	*Lau* decision (1974) specified that schools must offer bilingual education, but it remains unclear what must be done in a bilingual education program.	Quantitative standards have been developed.	Monitoring which occurs is unrelated to implementation.	DOE's OCR.
Least Implementation					
Higher education	Largely passive.	Uncertain whether racial identifiability is acceptable.	None.	Infrequent.	DOE's OCR.
Fair housing	Still largely passive; HUD cannot bring suit but must refer cases to DOJ which rarely acts.	Vague. No definition of fair housing.	None.	Rarely carried out.	HUD is lead agency; others are involved.
Second-generation discrimination	Active involvement associated with less evidence of discrimination.	Multiple goals create uncertainty.	Precise quantitative standards have been established but are frequently waived.	Done in conjunction with Emergency School Aid applications. Some indication that it promotes implementation.	DOE's OCR.

(Table 7-1 continues)

TABLE 7-1 (continued)

	Agency Commitment	Support from Superiors	Program Beneficiaries	Administrative Coordination	Costs/Benefits
Greatest Implementation					
Voting	Has declined as DOJ has opted increasingly for voluntary compliance and has assigned lower priority to voting rights.	Strong from Congress, president and courts during 1960s. Since then, greater support in Congress than White House.	Active in monitoring elections and putting pressure on DOJ. Declined some in the 1970s.	Not a factor.	Favored compliance to the extent of allowing blacks to vote.
School desegregation	High commitment to agency goals during 1960s; subsequently declined.	Strong support from president, courts, and Congress prior to 1969. Increasing opposition since then, although courts remain more supportive than other branches.	Important in establishing new rights through litigation, but having little independent influence in local implementation.	Rare since 1970.	A number of variables may influence perceived costs, especially at the time of initial desegregation.
Moderate Implementation					
Equal employment	Mixed.	Weak support from Congress and Republican presidents; stronger from Democratic presidents.	Active in filing complaints.	Poor.	Generally favored noncompliance.
Bilingual education	This goal never enjoyed high priority.	Opposition from president and Congress in 1980s; previously indifferent.	Beneficiaries divided.	Not a factor.	No data available.

	Agency Commitment	Support from Superiors	Policy Beneficiaries	Administrative Coordination	Costs/Benefits
Least Implementation					
Higher education	Committed but less important than other variables.	Little support from Congress, White House, or the courts.	Suits against federal and state officials. Divided on issue of eliminating racial identifiability vs. maintaining black schools.	Poor; enforcement rigidly divided between OCR and the courts.	Important considerations: (1) number of black institutions; (2) range of quality among schools; (3) loss of autonomy; (4) potential loss of federal funds.
Fair housing	FHA and VA have a history of discrimination which was slow to change. Few resources devoted to fair housing by HUD. Low commitment.	Little support from Congress, White House, or the courts.	Some activity but lacking a major impact. Some division on opening suburbs and housing desegregation in inner cities.	Poor; HUD fails to function as lead agency. HUD agreements with other agencies have little effect.	Few costs assessed against noncompliers. Therefore benefits outweigh costs for realtors, white homeowners, and investors.
Second-generation discrimination	Commitment has dropped.	Largely indifferent since the early 1970s.	Supportive; forced OCR to address complaints.	Not a factor.	Some indications that districts behave so as to avoid unacceptable costs, although evidence is less clear for the variables considered than for school desegregation.

193

Clarity of Policy Goals

Policy objectives have been most clearly stipulated for voting and Southern desegregation. The 1965 Voting Rights Act culminated the process begun eight years earlier of banning local practices which discriminated against prospective black voters. The 1965 statute comprehensively barred tests and devices which had been used to exclude black voters. The absoluteness of the 1965 prohibitions eliminated uncertainty over what local voter registrars could legally do. In the past this uncertainty had necessitated numerous legal challenges in the courts. A decade later, when the Voting Rights Act was renewed, it was expanded to prescribe which types of bilingual voter aids were required.

An important clarification of what was required of Southern school districts came in 1968 with the new regulations issued by HEW and the *Green v. New Kent County School Board* decision. These policy statements eliminated confusion over what constituted desegregation. Thereafter, tokenism and freedom of choice (where only students who asked to transfer to another school were desegregated) were inadequate. Desegregation plans had to provide for the disestablishment of racially segregated dual school systems.

Objectives of other policies remain less clear. In the field of housing, federal authorities have not defined what constitutes fair housing. Ambiguity clouds the definition of higher education desegregation and equal employment. In these areas, as well as in bilingual education and second-generation discrimination, federal law has tolerated a variety of local interpretations of what constitutes compliance with antidiscrimination policy. This situation is similar to what occurred prior to 1968 in school desegregation. For example, acceptable bilingual programs may be designed to move a child quickly toward competence in English through the help of a teacher who has no fluency in the child's native language. At the other end of the continuum, a bilingual program may strive to maintain students' fluency in their home language and foster an appreciation of their heritage while simultaneously promoting English-speaking ability.

Equal employment is a second example of policy ambiguity, in that it is unclear whether employers must have some minority workers. And, if some are hired, federal policy does not indicate whether there must be minorities in all major job categories.

The "clarity of policy goals" variable helps to distinguish between the policies in which implementation has been greatest and the other five in which it has been less pronounced. While ambiguity may prevent maximum implementation, the changes in employment and bilingual education suggest that some progress can be achieved even when policy goals are imprecise.

Specificity of Standards

There are two dimensions along which specificity of standards will be evaluated here. One is the use of quantitative criteria for determining the acceptability of behavior or for selecting where to direct limited enforcement resources. When standards for legal compliance are established with mathematical precision, gaps between policy requirements and behavior become more obvious, which should promote implementation.

The second dimension is the use of intent or effect when evaluating whether an action is discriminatory. Focusing on the discriminatory effect of an action, since effect is more susceptible to objective measurement, should result in implementation being easier to achieve than would be the case when standards rest on a need to demonstrate that the defendants intended to discriminate.

Specific, quantitative standards have been established to some extent for all policies except higher education and housing. Precise standards were first established in 1965 when Congress created a quantitative "trigger" mechanism for determining which counties might have federal officials sent in to register blacks and monitor elections. There is also a quantitative standard for determining the acceptability of municipal annexations. Annexations that would reduce black political influence will be rejected by the Justice Department for those jurisdictions which must submit their proposed electoral changes to the Department for preclearance. In evaluating redistricting plans, the Justice Department requires that the proportion black in a heavily black district not be reduced.

Since 1968, whenever de jure segregation has been found, full desegregation has been the corrective. In 1971 the Supreme Court ruled that achieving approximately the same racial proportions throughout all of a district's schools was an appropriate objective (*Swann v. Charlotte-Mecklenburg Board of Education*, 1971). Two years earlier a lower federal court had established the acceptable variations for faculty racial composition (*Singleton v. Jackson Municipal Separate School District*, 1969).

Quantitative standards have been developed for the other two public school programs, although schools have not always been required to meet the standards. The precise standards used to test for the likelihood of second-generation discrimination are not always enforced, since schools may be able to provide nondiscriminatory explanations to account for the disproportionate numbers of black children in special education classes or for a disproportionately white faculty.

Numerical standards have been used in bilingual education to target districts for compliance reviews. The DOE has a formula for determining the thoroughness with which districts are serving children who have limited English-speaking ability. The districts with the worst scores are more likely to be reviewed by the Department's Office for Civil Rights (OCR).

Although a uniform set of specific standards has not been set for the employment of minorities and women, a number of employers are covered by precise guidelines. This coverage has come about through plans negotiated at the local level for federal contractors; voluntary hiring objectives set by employers, like the one litigated in *United Steelworkers v. Weber* (1979); and hiring goals and timetables for meeting those goals, which are imposed by judges or are developed by employers who have lost cases in which they were charged with employment discrimination. The presence of goals and timetables spurs employers on to hire a more racially, ethnically, and sexually balanced labor force.

Another facet of specificity of standards is the imprecision introduced by the use of "intent" test. When courts have interpreted the policy objective to be one of preventing intentional discrimination rather than of eliminating rules or practices that have the effect of discriminating, implementation has been more difficult. When courts have searched for intent to discriminate in voting (*Mobile v. Bolden*, 1980), school desegregation (*Dayton Board of Education v. Brinkman*, 1977),[2] or employment (*Washington v. Davis*, 1976), plaintiffs have lost and the alleged discriminatory acts have been allowed to stand. Since intent to discriminate is so subjective, it is very hard to prove that a defendant *intended* to cause the inequities which have resulted. Critics claimed that it was awareness of the difficulties in proving an intent to discriminate that provoked the Reagan administration's congressional allies to demand that intent become the standard for proof under the 1982 Voting Rights Act renewal. This effort failed when Congress overruled the *Mobile* case and decided that minorities need prove only that the effects of an election provision were discriminatory. Minority challenges would succeed when the effect was discriminatory, regardless of intent.

Specificity of standards is a useful variable for understanding implementation. Greatest implementation has occurred where precise standards are most common; it has been least extensive where quantitative standards are absent or the conclusions to which they point are frequently overruled. Focusing on the intent rather than the effect of policies introduces another type of imprecision.

Monitoring

The availability of specific standards is particularly useful when federal authorities monitor the behavior of those being regulated. The more precise the standards for determining what constitutes compliance and the clearer the policy goal, the more effective monitoring should be in identifying shortcomings in implementation.

Monitoring, in recent years, has been most widespread in bilingual education and second-generation discrimination. The 334 districts identified in the mid-1970s as likely to need bilingual education programs were required to file annual reports with the DOE for three years. These reports show the processes by which bilingual education is being implemented and the extent to which limited English-speaking students are being served.

Monitoring for second-generation discrimination was done only for districts seeking Emergency School Aid Act (ESAA) funds. All applicants must supply employment statistics by race and sex for job categories and similar statistics for five different special education programs. School districts which receive funding, as well as those denied funds because DOE believes them to be guilty of discrimination, must file reports with the Department. In addition, most school districts must file biennial statistical reports with DOE even if they do not apply for ESAA. These reports are less comprehensive than those required of ESAA applicants and are less likely to be reviewed by DOE.

HEW (which was responsible for education before the creation of DOE) conducted annual monitoring of Southern school districts until the early 1970s. These reviews turned up instances of noncompliance and were important in determining how the Department would use its enforcement resources. Data from these reports were used by HEW and Department of Justice personnel in proving the existence of segregation. For the last decade, HEW and DOE have done little monitoring of school desegregation, although occasionally federal judges (for example, Arthur Garrity in Boston) have required that desegregating districts periodically report on their progress.

Monitoring of employment practices has been confined to instances in which specific goals and timetables have been established. Under these conditions, the judge who handed down the order or the Office of Federal Contract Compliance Programs (OFCCP) will review figures on hirings and promotions by race and sex.

Regular monitoring by enforcement agencies has been infrequent in recent years in voter registration, higher education, and fair housing. However, implementation of these policies and the others covered in this book have frequently been analyzed by the U.S. Commission on Civil Rights. The Commission points out implementation failures and recommends corrective steps. More often than not, these reports are ignored by enforcement agencies and their superiors.

While regular monitoring of school desegregation seems to have promoted that policy objective during the late 1960s, there is no pattern that would indicate that monitoring is critical to the implementation of civil rights policy. There were substantial increases in black registration despite little monitoring, and in the area of second-generation discrimination conditions have deteriorated despite regular data collection.

Enforcement Agency

The importance of the variable concerning agencies charged with enforcement cannot be adequately tested in the course of this book. As table 7-1 reports, one or more federal agencies are involved in implementing each policy. It is not feasible, therefore, to make cross-policy comparisons of the extent to which implementation occurs when there *is* an enforcement agency and the extent to which it occurs when no such agency exists.

We may gain some insights into the importance of this variable by comparing conditions within a single policy before and after an enforcement agency was created. Other variables, however, may make longitudinal comparisons difficult. In school desegregation, active federal involvement preceded the creation of OCR, which had primary responsibility for desegregating Southern schools. The pace of desegregation accelerated following the establishment of OCR, but this agency's creation coincided with heightened monitoring and the evolution of more precise standards for determining what constituted acceptable compliance. It is unclear what role establishment of an enforcement agency played, although one would certainly not suggest that it was detrimental.

In employment, creation of enforcement agencies preceded the heightened federal activism made possible by 1972 legislation. One of these agencies, EEOC, was soon bogged down in handling thousands of complaints and for years had only a modest impact on the achievement of equal employment objectives. From the available evidence concerning civil rights, it appears that the presence of an enforcement agency alone is insufficient to produce extensive implementation.

Agency Commitment

Determining the degree of commitment of an enforcement agency's personnel is not easy because of the subjective nature of such assessments. One factor that may be related to a strong commitment is the priority assigned by an agency to promoting civil rights. Another is the creation of a new bureaucratic unit to handle a new responsibility.

Looking first at priorities, we find that bilingual education, fair housing, and higher education desegregation have never enjoyed high priority with the agencies charged with implementing them. Voting rights, public school desegregation, and checking second-generation discrimination have, in earlier times, been high-priority objectives of the enforcing agencies. Equal employment has been the only responsibility of EEOC and OFCCP. When the federal Civil Service Commission was charged with overseeing this program among federal agencies,[3] it was not a top priority of the Commission. The Reagan administration has not assigned high priority to any civil rights programs.

Turning to the three policy areas which once had top priority with the agencies entrusted with enforcing them, we find that none are as prominent today as they once were. The Office for Civil Rights began turning its attention from desegregation and toward second-generation discrimination in the early 1970s. A few years later, second-generation discrimination was supplanted by other, more pressing concerns. Neither the Education nor the Justice Department actively seeks to promote additional desegregation today. Increasingly, the Department of Justice sides with local school officials who are defendants in suits filed by private plaintiffs claiming that illegal segregation exists. Civil rights groups are also critical of the Department's flagging commitment to guaranteeing equal access to political influence. It appears that the emphasis in recent years has been more on voluntary compliance than enforcement. Voluntarism has frequently characterized equal employment opportunity enforcement and appears to be the approach preferred by the Reagan administration. Also, federal authorities often have left the achievement of higher education and fair housing objectives to voluntary compliance.

There are three policy areas in which enforcement was assigned to a newly created agency. The potential value of placing implementation responsibility with a new agency is pointed out by Orfield (1969), who found that the Office of Education was too set in its ways to effectively carry out school desegregation when it was given that responsibility in 1964. When enforcement is assigned to a new agency, the agency may initially be staffed by a number of employees who have a missionary zeal for implementing the program. Within a few years, however, many of these deeply committed souls will have left the agency or will have experienced a cooling of their ardor (Downs, 1967; Bullock and Stewart, forthcoming; Sabatier and Mazmanian, 1980). Nonetheless, during its initial years the new agency may make great strides.

Voting rights was the responsibility of the Civil Rights Division of the Department of Justice when it was first organized, and school desegregation was the first task assigned to the Office for Civil Rights in what was then HEW. The EEOC and OFCCP were created to promote equal employment opportunities. For the first two policies, the enthusiasm and commitment characteristic of a new agency probably contributed to the changes that came about. In employment, however, the new agencies (particularly EEOC) seemed to be ineffective implementers. During its first decade, EEOC foundered (Bullock, 1975), and it was not until Eleanor Norton was named by President Carter to lead the Commission that it began to handle efficiently the tasks for which it was responsible.

The overall assessment of agency commitment is that there is some evidence that it plays a role in implementation. When an objective has fallen in an agency's priority ranking, implementation has suffered. There are, however, some instances in which implementation has gone forward haltingly even though conditions usually associated with a high level of agency commitment existed, as in the early days of EEOC.

Support from Superiors

The superiors of the agencies entrusted with carrying out civil rights policy are the president, Congress, and the courts. The degrees to which these units support the enforcement activities of the bureaucracy have varied depending upon the policy, the time, and the identity of the superior. Generally, Republican presidents have been less favorably disposed toward civil rights programs than Democratic presidents. Since the 1960s, the courts have been more supportive of efforts to implement civil rights than have other branches of government, although the Burger Court has been far more conservative than the Warren Court. At some point in the past, all three branches shared an interest in seeing the objectives of each policy achieved. Had the president and Congress not been supportive, legislation assigning enforcement responsibility to an agency would never have been enacted.

The three policies for which implementation has been least realized seem never to have had great support from any branch. Congress enacted the 1968 Fair Housing Act only after Martin Luther King had been murdered. Prior to Reverend King's assassination this legislation had been rejected by the legislature. Federal involvement in higher education desegregation is derived from the provision in Title VI of the 1964 Civil Rights Act which denies federal funds to institutions that practice segregation. Public schools, and not colleges and universities, were the primary concerns of legislators who endorsed this legislation, with administrative efforts directed at higher education coming years later.

Congress ensured that the Emergency School Aid Act had some teeth that could be used in fighting second-generation discrimination (Orfield, 1975). The inclusion of specific standards was forced on President Nixon, who preferred that ESAA be nothing more than an aid program for desegregating schools. Congress subsequently showed little interest in enforcement of ESAA standards and apparently came around to Nixon's position of viewing this as simply another categoric aid program which supplied dollars to appreciative constituents.

In the past, support from superiors was greatest for those programs in which implementation has been most complete. During the latter half of the Johnson administration, all three branches actively supported efforts of Southern blacks to register to vote and to attend desegregated schools. This interlude of high support coincided with the greatest advances toward these goals.

President Nixon and, a few years later, Congress disavowed the use of busing to achieve school desegregation. Presidents Nixon, Ford, and

Reagan have given tepid support to extensions of the Voting Rights Act and have endorsed proposals which civil rights activists claim would limit the effectiveness of the legislation. During this latter period there has been little additional desegregation or black voter registration.

The implementation of equal employment and bilingual education programs has not had high priority among the enforcers' superiors. Except for President Nixon's endorsement of "hometown plans" for expanding the job opportunities of minorities on federal construction projects, there has been little presidential fervor for affirmative action, although Democrats have generally been more supportive than Republicans. Bilingual education received an essential impetus from the Supreme Court in 1974 (*Lau* v. *Nichols*) but has received little backing from other quarters. In 1981, the Reagan administration signaled a change from the benign neglect which had characterized earlier administrations' responses to this program when it acted to block the implementation of regulations that would have guided schools toward a more comprehensive approach.

Support from superiors seems to be a useful variable in understanding what promotes implementation. Greatest implementation occurred when support was most widespread, while implementation has been least when the enforcers' superiors have demonstrated little interest in seeing goals achieved.

Program Beneficiaries

As would be expected, those who would benefit from civil rights policies have generally supported their implementation. Exceptions to this general statement have been most frequent in bilingual education, where ethnic leaders disagree on the relative emphasis to be placed on the alternatives of quick socialization into the American mainstream and the maintenance of cultural identities. A partial exception is the unwillingness of black parents to support busing programs which do not take their children to schools that are substantially different in quality or racial composition from those in the neighborhoods in which they live. Also, many black politicians oppose housing desegregation and especially opening the suburbs for minorities, since a black exodus would threaten their political power base.

A fourth exception holds for higher education. Here many blacks would prefer to see the maintenance of traditionally black institutions rather than have all state-supported colleges and universities become biracial. Continuation of predominantly black campuses is justified by supporters in terms of a greater sensitivity to black interests, needs, and traditions than is provided to the minority of blacks on white campuses run by white administrators and staffed by white faculty members. These attitudes are particularly strong among black educators and graduates of black colleges. The policy preferences among blacks are for the survival of black schools but with black students who prefer to attend white campuses being able to do so free of discrimination.

When there is a split in the ranks of the beneficiaries, the pressures on policy implementers and on those who are being regulated may be reduced. However, the policies on which there is disagreement among the beneficiaries are not invariably the ones that have been least implemented, so it is uncertain how important this factor is.

Despite these exceptions, the common practice has been for beneficiaries to promote implementation by demanding compliance from state and local officials and, when these demands have been rejected, by filing complaints with the federal enforcement agency and bringing private suits in court. Private plaintiffs have been particularly active in school desegregation where they instituted the suits that: (1) overturned the separate but equal approach; (2) required the elimination of dual school systems; (3) called for immediate desegregation and an end to foot-dragging; (4) established ratios for faculty desegregation; (5) approved the use of busing as a remedy; and (6) found instances of unconstitutional segregation outside of the South and border states. While private plaintiffs were critical in exploring the frontiers of constitutional requirements for school desegregation, it does not appear that the activities of beneficiaries had much independent influence on implementation at the local level (Rodgers and Bullock, 1976).

Complaint filing has been most frequent in employment and second-generation discrimination. EEOC has concentrated primarily on complaint resolution, but has been so overwhelmed by the task that it once had more than 100,000 complaints awaiting investigation. Conditions have improved in recent years.

In second-generation discrimination, although unresolved complaints never reached the mountainous proportions found at EEOC, they were not being expeditiously processed. OCR's inattention to allegations that schools were discriminating against blacks in the wake of desegregation led private plaintiffs to seek and win a court order which forced OCR to eliminate the backlog of complaints and to institute procedures for speedy resolution in the future. The elimination of the backlog of complaints undoubtedly did result in some individuals attaining their rights. Complaint processing has not, however, eliminated evidence of second-generation discrimination in the districts involved (Bullock and Stewart, 1978).

Complaints may force the implementing agency to look into specific instances of mistreatment. This may, however, be counterproductive if a greater pay-off would have been achieved by allowing the agency to deal with broader issues or undertake work which would affect a greater number of individuals (Bullock and Stewart, forthcoming).

It is unclear what effect the activity of beneficiaries has on implementation. Private litigants can be important in bringing new issues to the attention of the courts. However, they lack the resources needed for full-scale achievement of policy goals, as the experiences with voting rights and school desegregation make clear. They can also generate complaints, but that may not be the best route for achieving widespread implementation.

Administrative Coordination

While there may be conditions under which administrative coordination or its absence affects implementation, it is not critically important to civil rights. Enforcement of three policies (voting, bilingual education, and second-generation discrimination) has been assigned to a single agency. With a single agency responsible, implementation should be greater since lack of coordination would not be an obstacle. But this is not the case, since these policies are scattered across the three categories of implementation.

For three other policies, coordination has been poor, yet for one of these (equal employment) implementation has been moderately successful. In school desegregation, HEW and the Department of Justice cooperated during the 1960s and early 1970s in desegregating the South. Since then, the Departments have not worked together. Attempts by HUD to coordinate federal agencies' housing programs to promote fair housing have been unsuccessful, as Lamb explains in chapter 6.

Costs and Benefits

The best evidence that entities being regulated will behave so as to minimize costs and maximize benefits was found for public school and higher education desegregation and for voting rights. The clearest test occurred in public school desegregation, where the ante was gradually raised until Southern school officials desegregated. Districts which had few blacks, fewer economically disadvantaged residents, appointed superintendents, and school authorities who were not unalterably opposed to desegregation were likely to negotiate a desegregation agreement (Rodgers and Bullock, 1976). Districts in which these conditions were less fully satisfied might have to be threatened with a loss of federal aid. Many districts in which conditions were least like those in the districts that did negotiate plans held out after federal aid had been cut off and capitulated only when the loss of state education funds was imminent. In chapter 5 of this book, Ayres outlines four considerations that affect the perceived cost of compliance with higher education provisions. Implementation is most likely to proceed when there are few black schools in the state.

In voting rights, the outcome has in no way hinged on the manipulation of federal dollars. Nonetheless, costs do seem to be a factor in that there has been greater support for extending the right to vote than for policies designed to ensure that the vote will have an *effect* on the choice of policymakers. The consequences of black voting can be filtered through various techniques so that the impact on policy is substantially diluted.

It appears that ESAA funding coincides with less evidence of second-generation discrimination. These funds may sometimes be used as a carrot to induce greater compliance, but the effectiveness of this inducement appears to be limited since even in funded districts there is usually evidence of discrimination against black students.

Generally, few costs have been assessed against those who practice discrimination in employment and housing, while the benefits to the discriminators are often substantial. No data are available with which to evaluate the impact of this variable on the implementation of bilingual education protections. Overall there is evidence that implementation is more likely to occur as the costs for resistance are raised. The one major exception is the greater implementation in employment than would be expected based on this variable alone.

CONCLUSIONS

Of the ten variables used in this study of the implementation of civil rights policies, six are useful in distinguishing among relative amounts of implementation which have occurred across the seven policy areas. Federal involvement, or more specifically the degree of activism displayed by federal authorities in challenging discrimination, certainly affects implementation. Other conditions related to a greater extent of compliance are the presence of specific standards, commitment within the enforcing agency, support among the agency's superiors, the assessment of high costs against the noncompliant, and, to some extent, clearly stated policy goals.

It seems reasonable to say that the greater the number of conditions favoring implementation present, the more likely it is that policy goals

TABLE 7-2 Importance of Variables for Implementing Civil Rights Policy

Important	Somewhat Important	Unimportant	Unable to Evaluate
1. Federal involvement 2. Specific standards 3. Agency commitment 4. Support from superiors 5. Costs/benefits	1. Clarity of policy goals	1. Monitoring 2. Policy beneficiaries 3. Administrative coordination	1. Enforcement agency

will be achieved. This is only a supposition, however. Another factor to be recognized, although it too is beyond the scope of this study, is the possibility that some of the variables work in combination to influence the degree of implementation (Edwards, 1980). For example, a committed agency which is applying specific standards may be much more successful than we would find with either factor operating alone.

Yet another consideration to keep in mind is that some of the relationships evident here might prove to be spurious in a more sophisticated analysis. For instance, it is possible that support from superiors affects agency commitment. If so, then agency commitment alone would not be an important variable for influencing implementation; instead, the importance of support for the agency's mission from Congress and/or the president would be even greater than it appears to be in the analysis reported.

Another possibility not addressed in this study is that compliance may be affected by a variable which has only an indirect linkage to implementation. Suppose that the attitudes of an enforcement agency's superiors are determined by what they perceive to be public preferences. Such a link would not be surprising especially during periods when civil rights issues have high salience among the public. On controversial or emotional issues, legislators are more likely to act in accord with what they believe to be their constituents' preferences (Miller and Stokes, 1963).

Of course, some variables that play a major role in program implementation may have not been considered in this analysis. A variable for which comparative information is unavailable or difficult to measure, or a factor that researchers have not yet discovered, may have a considerable impact. Acknowledging that there may be other explanations than those offered here for implementation success, we nonetheless can suggest conditions under which implementation is more likely to proceed in civil rights, and situations in which minorities and women are likely to enjoy greater freedom and opportunities. First, for the policies studied here, it has been essential that the federal government be actively involved in helping beneficiaries obtain equal treatment. Until the federal government became involved with these policy goals, in some sections of the country people who were denied their rights had no recourse. Reliance on state or local authorities to protect the rights of women and minorities was wholly inadequate.

While recognition by the federal government that a right existed was an important step, it alone provided but a slight nudge toward attainment of the right. More active enforcement, as can occur through the filing of numerous suits by federal attorneys or aiming enforcement efforts at those who appear to be guilty of serious noncompliance, is critical to extending civil rights. As part of active federal involvement, an agency will need to be given enforcement responsibility.

The mere presence of an enforcement agency is not, however, sufficient to ensure that implementation will proceed, as the failures in fair housing demonstrate. What is critical here is the degree to which the agency is committed to achieving the policy goals. Commitment is helpful, if not essential, in overcoming obstinacy. But commitment has a greater impact if agency personnel have precise standards to use when judging the adequacy of the behavior of those being regulated. The more precise the standard for judging what constitutes minimal compliance, the easier it will be to determine where enforcement efforts are needed. Although a lack of clarity need not prevent some degree of achievement of objectives, clearly stated policy goals may be necessary to achieve high levels of implementation.

Enforcement efforts are facilitated if the implementing agency is authorized to manipulate resources valued by those whose behavior is to be regulated. If it is perceived that there is little economic cost associated with acknowledging a right, such as the vote, a committed agency working with specific definitions of what constitutes noncompliance can have a great impact. Alternatively, an enforcer that can act to raise the costs of noncompliance, as was done with Southern school desegregation by threatening to cut off first federal and then state funds, can ultimately secure compliance.

Whether the enforcing agency has inducements it can manipulate and whether its personnel is sufficiently committed to pursue the objectives of the policy may depend on the attitudes of the agency's superiors. Widespread opposition in Congress or in the upper reaches of the White House, as occurred in school desegregation under Nixon (Panetta and Gall, 1971), provides those who are resisting implementation with powerful allies, making enforcement more difficult.

The execution of public policy is rarely an easy task. Numerous obstacles, many unforeseen by those who launch the policy, lurk just out of sight, always threatening to impede the way. Nonetheless, there are conditions which increase the likelihood that policy objectives can be achieved. The notable changes in civil rights, especially in voting rights and Southern school desegregation, are impressive monuments to the ability of a democratic system to attain objectives in the face of harsh opposition.

NOTES

1. In a majority black school system, if all schools had the same proportion black, then all the systems' blacks would attend majority black schools. Therefore in majority black schools, the more evenly students are spread across schools, the larger the number of blacks who would be defined as racially isolated.
2. The *Mobile* and *Dayton* decisions were subsequently overturned.
3. This responsibility has now been given to the EEOC.

REFERENCES

Bullock, Charles S. III (1975). "Expanding Black Economic Rights." In Harrell R. Rodgers, Jr. (ed.), *Racism and Inequality: The Policy Alternatives.* San Francisco: W. H. Freeman, pp. 75–123.

Bullock, Charles S. III, and Joseph Stewart, Jr. (1978). "Complaint Processing as a Strategy for Combatting Second Generation Discrimination." Presented at the annual meeting of Southern Political Science Association, Atlanta, Ga.

Bullock, Charles S. III, and Joseph Stewart, Jr. (forthcoming). "New Programs in 'Old' Agencies: Lessons in Organizational Change from the Office for Civil Rights," *Administration and Society.*

Dayton Board of Education v. *Brinkman*, 433 U.S. 406 (1977).

Downs, Anthony (1967). *Inside Bureaucracy.* Boston: Little, Brown.

Edwards, George C. III (1980). *Implementing Public Policy.* Washington, D.C.: Congressional Quarterly.

Green v. *New Kent County School Board*, 391 U.S. 430 (1968).

Lau v. *Nichols*, 414 U.S. 563 (1974).

Miller, Warren E., and Donald E. Stokes (1963). "Constituency Influence in Congress," *American Political Science Review* 57: 45–57.

Mobile v. *Bolden*, 446 U.S. 55 (1980).

Murray, Richard, and Arnold Vedletz (1977). "Race, Socioeconomic Status, and Voting Participation in Large Southern Cities." *Journal of Politics* 39: 1064–1072.

Orfield, Gary (1969). *The Reconstruction of Southern Education.* New York: Wiley.

Orfield, Gary (1975). *Congressional Power.* New York: Harcourt Brace Jovanovich.

Panetta, Leon E., and Peter Gall (1971). *Bring Us Together.* Philadelphia: Lippincott.

Rodgers, Harrell R., Jr., and Charles S. Bullock III (1976). *Coercion to Compliance.* Lexington, Mass.: Lexington Books.

Sabatier, Paul, and Daniel Mazmanian (1980). "The Implementation of Public Policy: A Framework of Analysis." *Policy Studies Journal* 8: 538–560.

Singleton v. *Jackson Municipal Separate School District*, 419 F.2d 1211 (1969).

Swann v. *Charlotte-Mecklenburg Board of Education*, 402 U.S. 1 (1971).

United Steelworkers of America v. *Weber*, 443 U.S. 193 (1979).

Van Horn, Carl, and Donald Van Meter (1976). "The Implementation of Intergovernmental Policy." In Charles O. Jones and Robert Thomas (eds.), *Public Policy Making in The Federal System*, vol. III of Sage Yearbook in Politics and Public Policy. Beverly Hills, Calif.: Sage.

Verba, Sidney, and Norman H. Nie (1972). *Participation in America.* New York: Harper and Row.

Washington v. *Davis*, 426 U.S. 229 (1976).

Name Index

Aaron, Henry, 160
Anderson, James E., 2, 5, 7, 14, 18
Ashmore, Henry L., 145
Ayres, Q. Whitfield, 118, 203

Ball, Howard, 35, 36, 52, 179
Bartley, Numan V., 7, 18
Basgall, Monte, 119, 146
Bianchi, Suzanne, 152, 180
Binion, Gayle, 37, 38, 52
Black, Earl, 46, 52
Bracey, John H., 148, 149, 179
Brown, Don W., 8, 14, 18, 56, 57, 58, 61, 66, 69, 75, 90
Brown, Tony, 131, 145
Bryson, Louis, 134, 136, 145
Bullock, Charles S., III, 1, 3, 4, 5, 7, 11, 12, 14, 15, 17, 18, 19, 22, 23, 24, 46, 47, 52, 53, 55, 56, 67, 73, 75, 76, 78, 79, 80, 81, 82, 83, 84, 85, 86, 90, 91, 92, 94, 96, 97, 116, 148, 165, 176, 179, 181, 184, 199, 202, 203, 207
Bulmer, Charles, 116, 181
Burger, Warren E., 3, 156, 157, 200
Burstein, Alan N., 180
Burton, Doris-Jean, 10, 18
Bush, George, 112
Button, James, 20, 46, 53

Campbell, David, 43, 46, 53
Carmichael, John C., 116, 181
Carter, Jimmy, 33, 49, 60, 64, 110, 111, 115, 164, 172, 176, 177, 199
Chambers, Julius, 130, 145
Christenson, Rob, 141, 145
Clark, Jim, 25
Clark, Thomas A., 148, 180
Cleghorn, Reese, 22, 32, 54
Clement, Dorothy C., 72, 90
Cohen, Richard E., 34, 36, 53
Colasanto, Diane, 152, 180
Connally, John, 1
Crain, Robert L., 82, 84, 91

Danielson, Michael N., 2, 12, 18, 148, 150, 152, 159, 160, 171, 173, 180
Derryck, Dennis, 96, 116
Dodds, Dewey, 140, 145
Dolbeare, Kenneth M., 2, 7, 17, 18
Donovan, Raymond, 111, 112
Downs, Anthony, 79, 90, 91, 148, 160, 180, 199, 207
Dye, Thomas R., 83, 84, 91

Eastland, James, 31
Edwards, George C., III, 2, 18, 205, 207
Eisenhart, Margaret, 72, 90
Eisenhower, Dwight D., 23, 57
Ericksen, Eugene P., 180

Falk, David, 159, 180
Farley, Reynolds, 83, 84, 91, 152, 180
Feagin, Joe R., 43, 46, 53
Fitzgerald, Micheal R., 83, 84, 85, 86, 91
Flory, Daisy, 145
Ford, Gerald R., 49, 111, 115, 164, 171, 172, 173, 176, 200
Forman, Robert E., 150, 178, 180
Franklin, Herbert M., 159, 180
Friedlein, Kenneth, 121, 130, 145

Gall, Peter, 12, 19, 80, 91, 132, 137, 146, 206, 207
Garfinkel, Irving, 107, 116
Garrity, Arthur, 197
Garrow, David J., 21, 22, 24, 25, 31, 53
Gerry, Martin, 136, 145
Giles, Michael W., 75, 79, 83, 84, 91
Goldman, Sheldon, 6, 18
Goldwater, Barry, 24
Greenberg, Stephanie, 180
Greenstein, Fred I., 148, 185
Groomes, Fred, 141, 145
Guthrie, Claire, 132, 145

Hall, Clyde S., 145
Hamilton, Charles V., 3, 4, 15, 18, 148, 176, 180

Name Index

Hamilton, Howard D., 148, 180
Hammond, Philip E., 2, 7, 17, 18
Hardy, Richard J., 2, 19, 104, 116, 178, 181
Harrington, Michael, 148, 180
Hartman, Chester W., 179, 180
Hatch, Orrin G., 113
Hatchett, Shirley, 180
Hauser, Philip M., 149, 150, 180
Haveman, Robert H., 107, 116
Helper, Rose, 150, 180
Hershberg, Theodore, 149, 180
Hill, Richard Child, 148, 180
Holland, Robert G., 137, 142, 145
Hollingsworth, Leslie J., Jr., 152, 154, 182
Holmes, Peter, 121, 136, 144, 145, 146
Hope, John, II, 13, 18
Huntington, Samuel P., 10, 18

Jackson, Jesse, 119
Jackson, Maynard, 119
Jahnige, Thomas P., 6, 18
Johnson, Lyndon B., 20, 25, 26, 27, 49, 50, 57, 80, 81, 94, 95, 110, 111, 115, 144, 171, 176, 200
Johnson, Sherry, 119, 146
Jones, Charles O., 2, 18, 207

Kain, John F., 152, 180
Karnig, Albert K., 46, 54
Katzenbach, Nicholas, 31
Keith, Nathaniel S., 179, 180
Kennedy, John F., 22, 57, 94, 95, 110, 111, 115, 157
Key, V. O., Jr., 22, 53, 59, 75
King, Martin Luther, 25, 119, 200
Kirby, David, 82, 91
Kluger, Richard, 56, 91
Kohn, M., 129, 146
Krane, Dale, 35, 36, 52, 179
Kurtz, Howard, 173, 176, 177, 180

Ladd, William M., 150, 180
Lake, Robert W., 148, 181
Lamb, Charles M., 1, 2, 3, 9, 12, 13, 14, 18, 99, 100, 112, 116, 148, 150, 151, 156, 157, 158, 162, 163, 171, 172, 174, 176, 178, 179, 181, 203
Laurenti, Luigi, 150, 181
Lauth, Thomas P., 35, 36, 52, 179
Lawson, Steven F., 20, 23, 25, 31, 32, 53
Lee, Blair, III, 136, 146
Lepper, Mary, 134, 146
Liebman, Lance, 182
Lustig, Mitchell S., 3, 18, 156, 181

Mandel, Marvin, 141, 146
Manski, C., 129, 146
Marshall, Thurgood, 119

Masters, Stanley H., 107, 116
Matthews, Donald R., 40, 53
Mazmanian, Daniel, 5, 17, 19, 82, 91, 189, 199, 207
McCrone, Donald J., 2, 19, 104, 116, 178, 181
Mercer, Jane R., 72, 91
Middleton, Lorenzo, 119, 146
Miller, Warren E., 205, 207
Mills, Roger, 80, 91
Mitchell, Robert E., 158, 159, 161, 162, 179, 181
Morgan, David R., 83, 84, 85, 86, 91
Mundel, D., 129, 146
Murray, Richard, 187, 207

Nakamura, Robert K., 2, 4, 6, 19
Nie, Norman H., 44, 54, 187, 207
Nixon, Richard M., 12, 13, 27, 28, 33, 49, 50, 59, 80, 81, 111, 115, 131, 132, 133, 135, 171, 172, 173, 176, 200, 201, 206
Norton, Eleanor Holmes, 199

Orfield, Gary, 10, 19, 69, 72, 80, 81, 91, 144, 146, 148, 158, 159, 161, 174, 176, 179, 181, 199, 200, 207

Panetta, Leon E., 12, 19, 79, 80, 91, 121, 132, 137, 146, 207
Peirce, Neal R., 27, 53
Peltason, J. W., 3, 4, 19
Pratt, John, 133
Pressman, Jeffrey, 2, 19, 144, 146
Prothro, James W., 40, 53

Quigley, John M., 152, 180

Rabkin, Jeremy, 144, 146
Reagan, Ronald, 29, 60, 61, 64, 76, 81, 109, 110, 111, 113, 115, 116, 133, 137, 172, 173, 176, 177, 181, 196, 198, 199, 201
Reynolds, William, 112
Robinson, Richard, 145, 146
Rodgers, Harrell R., Jr., 3, 4, 5, 7, 14, 15, 17, 18, 19, 22, 23, 24, 47, 53, 56, 67, 75, 82, 83, 84, 85, 90, 91, 93, 94, 116, 148, 165, 176, 179, 181, 202, 203, 207
Romney, George, 171
Roof, Wade Clark, 149, 182
Roosevelt, Franklin D., 94, 95, 110, 111
Rosenbloom, David H., 100, 103, 116
Rosenstone, Steven J., 44, 54
Rosenthal, Albert J., 97, 116
Rosenthal, Donald B., 179, 182
Rossell, Christine H., 82, 84, 91
Rubinowitz, Leonard S., 159, 167, 173, 182
Russell, Richard, 31

Name Index

Sabatier, Paul, 5, 17, 19, 82, 91, 189, 199, 207
Salamon, Lester M., 22, 53
Sanders, John L., 142, 145, 146
Sanders, M. Elizabeth, 46, 53
Scammon, Richard M., 27, 53
Scheingold, Stuart A., 57, 92
Scher, Richard, 20, 46, 53
Schuman, Howard, 180
Sheatsley, Paul B., 51, 53
Sherrill, Robert, 66, 92
Sloane, Glenda G., 148
Smallwood, Frank, 2, 4, 6, 19
Smith, Richard A., 158, 159, 161, 162, 179, 181
Smith, William French, 172
Sorenson, Annemette, 152, 154, 182
Starr, Roger, 160, 182
Stern, Mark, 46, 54
Stewart, Joseph, Jr., 73, 78, 79, 80, 82, 85, 90, 92, 199, 202, 207
Stith, Pat, 119, 147
Stokes, Donald E., 205, 207
Stover, Robert V., 8, 14, 18, 90

Taeuber, Alma F., 148, 149, 182
Taeuber, Karl E., 148, 149, 152, 154, 158, 159, 180, 182
Taggart, Robert, III, 179, 182
Taylor, William L., 36, 54
Thernstrom, Abigail M., 54
Thomas, Robert, 207
Thompson, Cleon, 145, 147
Thompson, Joel A., 43, 54

Thurmond, Strom, 29, 135
Tower, John, 135
Trosman, Elizabeth, 167, 182
Truman, Harry S., 94, 95, 110

Van Evera, Steven, 22, 53
Vanfossen, Beth, 83, 92
Van Horn, Carl, 5, 8, 17, 19, 189, 207
Van Meter, Donald, 5, 8, 17, 19, 189, 207
Vedletz, Arnold, 187, 207
Verba, Sidney, 44, 54, 187, 207
Vines, Kenneth N., 3, 19
Vose, Clement E., 148, 182

Walker, Thomas G., 83, 91
Wallace, George C., 66
Warren, Earl, 4, 26, 27, 33, 200
Wasby, Stephen L., 148
Wattenberg, Ben J., 27, 53
Watters, Pat, 22, 32, 54
Weaver, Robert C., 152, 159, 183
Welch, Susan, 46, 54
Wildavsky, Aaron, 2, 19, 144, 146
Wilson, James Q., 146, 179, 183
Wines, Michael, 172, 183
Wirt, Frederick M., 5, 17, 19, 82, 92
Wolfinger, Raymond E., 44, 54, 148, 183
Wood, Jack E., 149, 183
Wood, John, 72, 90

Yancy, William L., 180
Young, Andrew, 119

Case Index

Adams v. *Richardson*, 356 F. Supp. 92 (1973), 132, 133, 134, 137, 138, 145
Alexander v. *Holmes County Board of Education*, 396 U.S. 19 (1969), 11, 12, 18, 58, 90
Allen v. *State Board of Elections*, 393 U.S. 544 (1969), 37, 52

Beer v. *United States*, 425 U.S. 130 (1976), 38, 52
Brown v. *Board of Education*, 347 U.S. 483 (1954), 3, 4, 7, 18, 56, 57, 58, 61, 62, 64, 66, 69, 75, 90, 120, 184
Brown v. *Board of Education*, 349 U.S. 294 (1955), 7, 18, 61
Buchanan v. *Warley*, 245 U.S. 60 (1917), 155, 156, 179

City of Eastlake v. *Forest City Enterprises*, 426 U.S. 668 (1976), 156, 179
Columbus Board of Education v. *Penick*, 443 U.S. 449 (1979), 59, 91

Dayton Board of Education v. *Brinkman*, 433 U.S. 406 (1977), 61, 75, 91, 196, 206, 207
Dayton Board of Education v. *Brinkman*, 443 U.S. 526 (1979), 75, 91

East Carroll Parish School Board v. *Marshall*, 424 U.S. 636 (1976), 38, 53
Evans v. *Buchanan*, 447 F. Supp. 982 (1978), 61, 91

Fullilove v. *Klutznick*, 448 U.S. 448 (1980), 95, 99, 116

Geier v. *Blanton*, 427 F. Supp. 644 (1977), 120, 132, 145
Geier v. *Dunn*, 337 F. Supp. 573 (1972), 134, 145
Georgia v. *United States*, 351 F. Supp. 444 (1973), 37, 53

Green v. *New Kent County School Board*, 391 U.S. 430 (1968), 58, 61, 91, 194, 207
Griggs v. *Duke Power Company*, 401 U.S. 424 (1971), 97, 116

Hills v. *Gautreaux*, 425 U.S. 284 (1976), 155, 157, 161, 180

James v. *Valtierra*, 402 U.S. 137 (1971), 156, 180
Jones v. *Alfred H. Mayer Company*, 392 U.S. 409 (1968), 155, 156, 170, 176, 180

Keyes v. *School District No. 1 of Denver*, 413 U.S. 189 (1973), 59, 61, 75, 91

Lau v. *Nichols*, 414 U.S. 563 (1974), 61, 63, 64, 74, 79, 88, 91, 191, 201, 207

Mandel v. *United States Department of Health, Education, and Welfare*, 411 F. Supp. 542 (1976), 141, 145, 146
Milliken v. *Bradley*, 418 U.S. 717 (1974), 61, 91
Mobile v. *Bolden*, 446 U.S. 55 (1980), 29, 38, 53, 196, 206, 207
Moses v. *Washington Parish School Board*, 330 F. Supp. 1340 (1971), 63, 91

Norris v. *State Council of Higher Education*, 327 F. Supp. 1368 (1971), 120, 146

Pasadena Board of Education v. *Spangler*, 427 U.S. 424 (1976), 60, 91
Perkins v. *Matthews*, 139 U.S. App. D.C. 179 (1971), 37, 53
Plessy v. *Ferguson*, 163 U.S. 537 (1896), 56, 91

Regents of the University of California v. *Bakke*, 438 U.S. 265 (1978), 95, 98, 116
Richmond, Va. v. *United States*, 422 U.S. 358 (1975), 38, 53

Rogers v. *Paul*, 382 U.S. 198 (1965), 63, 91

Sanders v. *Ellington*, 288 F. Supp. 937 (1968), 120, 146

Shapiro v. *Thompson*, 394 U.S. 618 (1969), 4, 18

Shelley v. *Kraemer*, 334 U.S. 1 (1948), 4, 18, 155, 156, 167, 182

Singleton v. *Jackson Municipal Separate School District*, 419 F. 2d 1211 (1969), 63, 92, 195, 207

Smith v. *Allwright*, 321 U.S. 649 (1944), 21, 22, 53

South Carolina v. *Katzenbach*, 383 U.S. 301 (1966), 21, 26, 33, 53

Swann v. *Charlotte-Mecklenburg Board of Education*, 402 U.S. 1 (1971), 58, 61, 92, 195, 207

United States v. *Local 189, United Paperworkers*, 397 U.S. 919 (1970), 97, 116

United States v. *Mitchell*, 335 F. Supp. 1004 (1971), 157, 182

United States v. *Real Estate One, Inc.*, 433 F. Supp. 1140 (1977), 178, 182

United Steel Workers v. *Weber*, 443 U.S. 193 (1979), 95, 98–99, 108, 109, 116, 196, 207

Village of Arlington Heights v. *Metropolitan Housing Development Corp.*, 429 U.S. 252 (1977), 156, 182

Washington v. *Davis*, 426 U.S. 229 (1976), 196, 207

Zuch v. *Hussey*, 394 F. Supp. 1028 (1975), 157, 183

Subject Index

Administrative coordination:
  bilingual education, 83, 193, 203
  equal education, 82–83, 192, 203
  equal employment, 93, 113, 192, 203
  equal housing, 13–14, 174–175, 177, 193
  higher education, 134, 135, 143, 193
  second-generation discrimination, 83, 193, 203
  voting rights, 50–51, 192, 203
Affirmative action:
  equal education, 63
  equal employment, 63, 94, 97, 98, 99, 100, 109, 111, 112, 113, 144, 186, 201
  equal housing, 166, 169
  higher education, 122
Alabama, 21, 24, 25, 31, 33, 34, 37, 42, 45, 49, 53, 54, 65, 66, 71, 119, 123, 125, 132, 134, 135, 153, 154
Alaskan language minorities, 29, 168, 178
Arizona, 25, 28, 34, 39
Arkansas, 24, 41, 42, 45, 65, 118, 123, 125, 126, 132, 133, 137, 138, 146, 153, 154, 184
Asian Americans, 29, 63, 64, 82, 168, 178, 194, 201
Atlanta, 44, 67, 68, 71, 153, 154

Baltimore, 68, 70, 153, 154
Beneficiaries:
  bilingual education, 82, 87, 193, 201
  equal education, 13, 81–82, 87, 192, 201, 203
  equal employment, 113–114, 192
  equal housing, 173–174, 193, 201
  higher education, 130–131, 133, 193, 201, 202
  second-generation discrimination, 82, 87, 193, 202
  voting rights, 50, 192, 203
Bilingual education:
  administrative coordination, 83, 192, 203
  beneficiaries, 82, 87, 192, 201
  clarity of policy, 76, 87, 191, 194

Bilingual education (continued)
  commitment of enforcers, 80, 192, 198
  commitment of superiors, 81, 87, 192, 200, 201
  cost–benefit analysis, 85, 87, 192, 204
  DOE, 64, 81, 83, 195, 196
  effectiveness, 74–75
  equal education, 13, 61, 63–64, 70–71, 74–75, 79, 80, 81, 82, 85, 86, 88, 89, 184, 186, 187
  extensiveness, 64, 70–71, 74
  federal involvement, 86, 87, 191
  HEW, 63–64, 74, 78
  major approaches, 64
  monitoring, 74, 88, 191, 196, 197
  presence of enforcement agencies, 78, 191
  specificity of standards, 78, 191, 195
  voting rights, 21, 29, 30, 34, 38–41, 51, 184, 185, 194
Blacks:
  affirmative action, 63, 94, 97, 98, 99, 100, 109, 111, 112, 122, 144, 169, 186, 201
  black culture, 119, 130
  economic status, 46, 93, 101–108, 113, 114, 115, 150, 151, 152, 178
  employment, 94, 95, 101–103
  EMR, 55, 62, 79, 82, 89
  equal education, 11, 55, 56, 57, 58, 59, 62, 63, 64–71, 81, 82, 83, 84, 85, 87, 88, 89, 184, 200, 201, 202, 203, 204, 206
  equal employment, 93, 94, 95, 97, 101–108, 184
  equal housing, 149, 150, 151, 152, 153, 154, 155, 156, 157, 159, 161, 168, 172, 184, 185, 201
  higher education, 118, 119, 120, 121, 122, 123, 124, 125, 126, 127, 128, 129, 130, 131, 133
  holding political office, 43–46, 47, 149, 177, 184, 187, 201
  improving black colleges, 121, 122, 123, 126, 139

214

Subject Index 215

Blacks *(continued)*
 job skills, 95, 101, 103–108
 job training, 98, 101
 median family income, 104–107, 178
 migration, 149–150, 178
 occupations, 101–103
 teachers and administrators, 55, 62, 82, 119
 teenage unemployment, 104, 107
 two-spouse incomes, 104–106, 115
 unemployment, 103–104, 115
 voting rights, 4, 11, 15, 20, 21, 22, 23, 24, 25, 26, 28, 30, 31, 32, 33, 34, 35, 37, 38, 39, 40, 41, 42, 43, 44, 45, 46, 47, 184, 200, 204
Blockbusting, 151, 157, 158, 178
Boston, 60, 68, 71, 81, 84, 184
Burger Court, *see* Supreme Court
Busing, 58, 60, 61, 80, 81, 84, 85, 89, 200, 201, 202

California, 28, 34, 39, 53, 68, 70, 139, 144, 153, 154
Charlotte, 58, 67, 68, 71, 153, 154
Chicago, 70, 153, 154, 157
Civil Rights Act of 1866, 155–156
Civil Rights Act of 1957, 21, 23, 41
Civil Rights Act of 1960, 21, 23, 24, 41
Civil Rights Act of 1964:
 equal education, 57, 60, 61, 67, 76, 79, 80, 81
 equal employment, 95, 96, 97, 98
 equal housing, 14, 155, 156, 158, 162, 164–165, 175, 177
 extension in 1972, 95
 higher education, 120, 121, 131, 132, 133, 200
 limitations, 5–6, 24, 158, 162
 termination of federal funds, 57, 60, 61, 80, 133, 140, 142, 162, 165, 169, 175
 Title IV, 57
 Title VI, 14, 57, 80, 98, 99, 120, 121, 131, 132, 133, 136, 137, 155, 200
 Title VII, 96, 99
 Title IX, 57
 voting rights, 23, 25, 26, 48
Civil Rights Act of 1968, *see* Fair Housing Act of 1968
Civil rights impact, 2, 5, 22, 28, 30, 34, 38, 44–46, 67, 93, 98, 104, 148–153, 157, 158, 159, 162, 165, 184, 201, 204
Civil rights lawyers, 38, 157, 172
Civil rights leaders, 24, 25, 27, 32, 33, 85, 119, 133, 136, 173, 186, 199, 200, 201
Civil Service Commission, U.S., 26, 32
Clarity of policy:
 bilingual education, 76, 87, 191, 194

Clarity of policy *(continued)*
 equal education, 6, 75–76, 87, 190
 equal employment, 108–109, 190, 194
 equal housing, 162–163, 191, 194, 206
 higher education, 135–136, 191, 194
 second-generation discrimination, 76, 191, 194
 voting rights, 47–48, 190, 194
Commission on Civil Rights, U.S., 13, 28, 95, 112, 162, 167, 171, 172, 175, 197
Commitment of enforcers:
 bilingual education, 80, 192, 198
 equal education, 10, 11, 79–80, 87, 88, 90, 192, 198, 199
 equal employment, 111, 192, 198
 equal housing, 9, 170–171, 177, 193, 198, 206
 higher education, 134, 193, 198
 second-generation discrimination, 80, 193, 198, 199
 voting rights, 9, 48–49, 192, 198, 199
Commitment of enforcer's superiors:
 bilingual education, 81, 87, 192, 200, 201
 equal education, 11–12, 80–81, 87, 192, 200, 206
 equal employment, 111–113, 192, 200, 201
 equal housing, 171–173, 176, 177, 193
 higher education, 127, 131, 132, 133, 135, 143, 193, 200
 second-generation discrimination, 81, 87, 193, 200
 voting rights, 20, 49–50, 192, 200, 201
Compensation for past discrimination, 60, 97, 98, 99, 100, 108, 121, 126, 139
Compliance (*see also* Monitoring; Noncompliance):
 affirmative action, 63, 94, 97, 98, 99, 100, 109, 111, 112, 113, 144, 186, 201
 cost–benefit analysis, 83–85, 87, 88, 114, 138–140, 204
 equal education, 8, 11, 64–69, 83, 84, 85, 88, 184, 185, 186, 198, 199, 202, 204
 equal employment, 94, 95, 96, 97, 99, 109, 186
 equal housing, 148–177, 186, 199
 evasion, 24, 63, 66, 67, 96, 114, 130, 131, 140, 148, 149, 150, 151, 152, 153, 154, 155, 156, 157, 202
 forcing, 4, 7, 15, 27, 37, 51, 67, 80, 114, 155, 156 157, 163, 202
 goals, 95, 98, 99, 109, 113
 higher education, 120–130, 137–141
 incentives, 14–15, 36, 51, 114, 176
 negotiations, 58, 60, 67, 81, 82, 83, 97, 109, 124, 137, 138, 163, 164, 165
 quotas, 95, 98, 99, 109, 113
 state autonomy, 140–142, 143

216   Subject Index

Compliance *(continued)*
  terminating federal funds, 10, 14, 15, 57, 60, 61, 67, 80, 85, 114, 133, 140, 142, 162, 165, 169, 175, 203, 206
  terminating state funds, 85, 203, 206
  timetables, 95, 109, 196
  voluntary, 7, 8–9, 26, 31, 43, 48, 64, 66, 95, 97, 99, 109, 169, 176, 192, 199
  voting rights, 47–48, 186
Congress, U.S.:
  equal education, 57, 58, 59, 60, 67, 80, 81, 88
  equal employment, 97, 99, 108, 111, 112–113
  equal housing, 156, 157, 158, 160, 163, 165, 169, 171, 172, 176, 187
  higher education, 120, 132, 200
  second–generation discrimination, 200
  voting rights, 20, 21, 24, 25, 26, 28, 29
Constitution, U.S.:
  Fifteenth Amendment, 21, 23, 30, 184
  Fifth Amendment, 157
  Fourteenth Amendment, 56, 98, 120, 121, 155–157
  Twenty-Fourth Amendment, 21
Co-optation, 9–10, 49, 79
Cost–benefit analysis:
  bilingual education, 85, 87, 193, 204
  equal education, 14–15, 83–85, 87, 192, 203
  equal employment, 114, 192, 204
  equal housing, 15, 148, 175–176, 177, 193, 204
  higher education, 137–142, 143, 145, 193, 203
  second-generation discrimination, 85, 87, 193, 204
  voting rights, 51–52, 192, 203, 204
Courts, *see* Supreme Court; Lower federal courts
Cross-sectional analysis, 17, 185, 188–204

De facto segregation, 59, 84
De jure segregation, 58, 61, 118, 119, 121, 190, 195
Delaware, 40, 61, 64, 65, 66, 123, 125, 129, 132, 134, 153, 154
Department of Education (*see also* Office of Civil Rights):
  bilingual education, 64, 76, 78, 196
  equal education, 60, 76, 83
  higher education, 121, 123, 124, 125, 126, 128, 130, 132, 133, 187
Department of Health, Education, and Welfare (*see also* Office of Civil Rights):
  bilingual education, 63–64, 88
  equal education, 10, 12, 57, 58, 59, 60, 61, 76, 77, 79, 82, 84, 89, 197, 199, 203

Department of Health, Education, and Welfare *(continued)*
  ESSA, 62, 73, 79, 80, 86, 88, 89
  higher education, 121, 122, 123, 124, 125, 126, 128, 130, 131, 132, 133, 134, 135, 136, 138, 139, 140
  second-generation discrimination, 62–63, 78, 83
Department of Housing and Urban Development:
  authority, 162–166, 191
  compliance reviews, 162, 165, 166, 169
  implementation weaknesses, 157, 162–166, 169, 171–172
  regulations, 166, 171–172, 179
Department of Justice:
  Civil Rights Division, 35–36, 49, 50, 51, 112, 190, 199
  equal education, 11, 12, 57, 58, 59, 60, 61, 67, 80, 81, 82, 83, 84, 190, 197, 199, 203
  equal employment, 97, 99, 112, 114
  equal housing, 163, 169, 172, 173, 174, 175, 176, 177, 179, 191
  higher education, 132, 137
  voting rights, 13, 20, 27, 31, 32, 34, 35, 36, 37, 39, 44, 48, 49, 50, 51, 52, 190, 191, 192, 195, 199

Economic inequality:
  education, 93, 115, 186
  employment discrimination, 93, 97, 101, 107, 108, 113, 115
  equal housing, 149, 160, 161, 186
  job skills, 93, 95, 101, 103–108
  national economic conditions, 93, 108, 114, 115
  racial income disparities, 46, 93, 101–108, 115, 161, 186, 187
  tax policies, 159–160
Educable mentally retarded programs, 55, 69–74, 76, 79, 82, 86, 88, 89
Effects test, 38, 156, 195, 196
Emergency School Aid Act of 1973, 62, 73, 76, 77, 79, 80, 81, 83, 86, 88, 89, 200, 204
Enforcement agencies, presence of:
  bilingual education, 78, 191
  equal education, 8, 78–79, 87, 190
  equal employment, 111, 190, 198
  equal housing, 166–170, 191, 206
  second-generation discrimination, 78, 191
  voting rights, 48–49, 190
Equal education opportunity (*see also* Bilingual education; Second-generation discrimination):
  administrative coordination, 82–83, 89, 192, 203

Subject Index 217

Equal education opportunity *(continued)*
  beneficiaries, 82, 87, 193
  black school administrators, 68, 69, 73, 76, 86, 88
  busing, 58, 60, 61, 80, 81, 84, 85, 89, 200, 201, 202
  clarity of policy, 6, 75–76, 87, 190
  commitment of enforcers, 10, 11, 79–80, 87, 88, 90, 192, 198, 199
  commitment of superiors, 11–12, 80–81, 87, 192, 206
  cost–benefit analysis, 14–15, 83–85, 87, 192, 203, 206
  DOJ, 11, 12, 57, 58, 59, 60, 61, 67, 80, 81, 82, 83, 84
  educable mentally retarded, 55, 69–74, 76, 79, 82, 86, 88, 89
  elementary and secondary, 3, 4, 6, 7, 8, 10, 11, 12, 13, 14, 15, 29, 55–62, 64–69, 75, 76, 77, 78, 79, 80, 81, 82, 83, 86, 87, 88, 184, 185, 186, 187, 189, 194
  ESSA, 62, 79, 80, 81, 88
  federal involvement, 15, 85–86, 87, 190
  housing patterns, 59, 60, 84
  lawsuits, 60, 66, 67, 78, 82, 83, 192, 202
  monitoring, 7, 62, 79, 83, 86, 88, 89, 190, 198
  negotiations, 58, 60, 67, 81, 83, 203
  North, 6, 11, 58, 59, 68–72, 75, 76, 77, 80, 83, 84, 85, 86, 88, 190, 202
  OCR, 9, 10, 11, 56, 59, 64, 69, 76, 78, 79, 81, 83, 86, 88, 89, 190, 198, 199
  presence of enforcement agencies, 8, 78–79, 87, 190, 198
  progress in the South, 46, 55, 65, 67–69, 75, 86, 184, 187, 189
  redrawing attendance zones, 59, 185
  rural districts, 66, 80, 81
  specificity of standards, 6, 77–78, 190, 198
  Supreme Court, 56, 57, 58, 59, 60, 61, 75, 76, 80, 81, 195
  terminating federal funds, 10, 14, 15, 57, 60, 67, 85, 203, 206
  terminating state funds, 85, 203, 206
  Title VI, 57, 60, 61, 67, 76, 79
Equal employment opportunity *(see also* Economic inequality; EEOC; OFCC):
  administrative coordination, 93, 113, 192, 203
  affirmative action, 63, 94, 97, 98, 99, 100, 109, 111, 112, 113, 144, 186, 201
  beneficiaries, 113–114, 192
  black teachers, 62–63, 73, 77, 86, 101, 188
  clarity of policy, 108–109, 190, 194
  commitment of enforcers, 111, 192, 198

Equal employment opportunity *(continued)*
  commitment of superiors, 111–113, 192, 200, 201
  compliance timetables, 95, 109, 196
  cost–benefit analysis, 114, 192, 204
  DOL, 94, 99, 111, 144
  FEPC, 99, 111
  federal contractors, 94, 95, 96, 99, 109, 112, 114, 201
  federal involvement, 110–111, 190
  hiring goals, 15, 94, 95, 97, 98, 100, 109, 113, 114, 115, 196, 197
  job training, 93, 95, 101–103
  labor unions, 94, 96, 97, 98, 109
  lawsuits, 95, 97, 112, 114
  monitoring, 94–97, 100, 109–110, 190, 197
  OFCC, 94–96, 99, 110, 111, 112, 198
  OPM, 99, 100, 110, 111, 114, 115
  penalties, 94, 95, 96, 112, 114
  presence of enforcement agencies, 111, 190, 198
  progress achieved, 101–108, 115, 184
  private employers, 94, 95, 96, 97, 98, 99, 109, 200
  public employers, 15, 94, 95, 96, 97, 99
  quotas, 98, 99, 109, 113
  specificity of standards, 109, 190, 196
  state and local governments, 97, 99
  Supreme Court, 95, 98, 99, 108, 109
  timetables, 94, 95, 113, 197
  training, 95, 98, 100
Equal Employment Opportunity Commission:
  active role, 97, 99, 100, 109, 110, 111, 112
  complaint backlogs, 96, 99, 100, 110, 198
  complaint processing, 96, 97, 99, 202
  creation, 95, 96, 199
  enforcement powers, 97, 110
  filing lawsuits, 95, 97, 100, 112, 190
  impact, 96, 97, 100, 109, 110
  implementation weaknesses, 96, 110, 111, 112, 199
  large businesses, 97, 109, 110
  negotiations, 97, 109, 190, 202
  passive role, 96, 110, 111, 113
  reorganization of 1978, 95, 99–100, 110, 111
  small businesses, 99, 100
  staff, 96, 110, 190
Equal housing opportunity *(see also* Department of Housing and Urban Development):
  active enforcement, 172, 176, 177
  administrative coordination, 13–14, 174–175, 177, 193
  beneficiaries, 173–174, 193, 201

218 Subject Index

Equal housing opportunity *(continued)*
  blockbusting, 151, 157, 158, 178
  cities, 148, 150, 160, 165, 172, 173, 176, 177, 193
  clarity of policy, 162–163, 191, 194, 206
  commitment of enforcers, 9, 170–171, 177, 193, 198, 206
  commitment of superiors, 171–173, 176, 177, 193
  complaints, 163–165, 169
  Comptroller of the Currency, 167, 168, 169, 171, 174
  constitutional protections, 153, 155, 158, 177
  cost–benefit analysis, 15, 148, 175–176, 177, 193, 204
  data, 165, 166, 169, 171, 174, 175
  economic status, 149, 160, 161, 168, 171, 177, 178, 186, 187
  effect, 150, 151, 162, 167, 177
  exclusionary zoning, 3, 150, 156, 163, 171, 177
  Federal Deposit Insurance Corporation, 167, 168, 169, 171, 174
  Federal Home Loan Bank Board, 167, 168, 169, 171, 174
  Federal Housing Administration, 159, 167, 171, 193
  federal involvement, 176–177, 188, 191, 206
  Federal Reserve System, 167, 168, 169, 171, 172, 174
  ghettos, 148, 149, 150, 152, 156
  highways, 159, 160
  implementation process, 162–177
  intent, 150, 151, 167
  lawsuits, 4, 151, 155–157, 163, 167, 169, 172, 173
  lending institutions, 9, 150, 158, 159, 161, 162, 165, 171, 174, 177, 179, 193
  locating federal jobs, 159, 160, 174
  locating public housing, 159, 161, 177
  lower federal courts, 4, 151, 155, 157, 163, 177, 187
  minority dispersal, 148, 149, 150, 151, 152, 153, 154, 155, 156, 157, 159, 161, 172, 173, 176, 177, 201
  passive enforcement, 148, 155–171
  political obstacles, 148, 149, 150, 152, 156, 157, 158–162, 171–173, 176, 177, 201, 206
  property values, 150, 151
  proposals of 1979–1980, 158, 165, 172, 176
  public transportation, 161, 173
  redlining, 151, 163, 172, 187
  regulations, 153, 159, 160 163, 166, 167, 168, 177
  specificity of standards, 163, 191, 195, 206

Equal housing opportunity *(continued)*
  statutory protections, 153, 155, 158, 177
  steering, 150, 151, 152, 157, 158, 177, 178, 185, 187
  suburbs, 148, 152, 155, 156, 158, 159, 160, 161, 165, 172, 176, 177, 193, 201
  Supreme Court, 4, 153, 155–157, 161, 167, 168, 177
  taxes, 150, 159–160, 175
  terminating federal funds, 162, 165, 169, 175, 206
  Title VI noncompliance, 14, 162, 164–165, 175, 177
  Title VIII noncompliance, 164–165, 175, 177
  urban renewal, 157, 159, 161, 178
  Veterans Administration, 159, 167, 168, 170–171, 193
  white attitudes, 148, 153, 176, 177
  white flight, 69, 152, 153, 159, 160, 185
  white homeowners, 150, 153, 159, 160, 168, 170, 172, 173, 176, 177, 193
Exclusionary zoning, 3, 150, 156, 163, 171, 175, 177
Executive Orders:
  E.O. 8802, 94, 95, 110
  E.O. 9980, 94, 95, 110
  E.O. 11063, 155, 157, 158, 166
  E.O. 11114, 94, 95, 110
  E.O. 11246, 94, 95, 110, 144

Fair employment, *see* Equal employment opportunity
Fair housing, *see* Equal housing opportunity
Fair Housing Act of 1968 (*see also* Equal housing opportunity):
  affirmatively promoting, 163, 166, 169
  clarity of policy, 162–163
  exemptions, 162, 163
  proposals of 1979-1980, 158, 165, 172, 176
Federal involvement:
  active role, 15, 20, 21z, 27, 30, 57, 62, 67, 79, 81, 85, 88, 97, 98, 110, 111, 126, 127, 128, 131, 133, 134, 172, 176, 177
  bilingual education, 86, 87, 191
  equal education, 15, 85–86, 87, 190
  equal employment, 110–111, 190
  higher education, 127–129, 188, 191
  passive role, 14, 15, 26, 27, 44, 62, 80, 82, 86, 88, 96, 110, 111, 126, 128, 131, 133, 148, 155–162, 163, 164, 165, 166, 167, 168, 169, 170, 171, 175, 176, 177
  second-generation discrimination, 86, 87, 191
  voting rights, 15, 20, 25, 26, 30, 31, 43, 47, 49, 190

Subject Index

Florida, 24, 41, 42, 45, 48, 65, 69, 70, 71, 123, 124, 125, 126, 132, 133, 135, 137, 138, 141, 145, 147, 153, 154
Freedom of choice, 57–58, 118, 194

Georgia, 24, 25, 31, 33, 34, 42, 45, 65, 71, 85, 123, 125, 126, 132, 133, 145, 153, 154

Higher education desegregation:
  administrative coordination, 134, 135, 143, 193
  beneficiaries, 130–131, 133, 193, 201
  black disagreement, 118, 130, 131, 136, 142, 201
  Civil Rights Act of 1964, 120, 121, 131, 133, 200
  clarity of policy, 135–136, 191, 194
  commitment of enforcers, 134, 193, 198
  commitment of superiors, 127, 131, 132, 133, 135, 143, 193, 200
  cost–benefit analysis, 137–142, 143, 145, 193, 203
  desegregation plans, 132, 133, 140, 142
  versus elementary-secondary, 118, 129–131, 142–144, 201
  education quality, 119, 126, 129, 138–139, 140, 141, 143
  elite attitudes, 137, 142, 143
  experience, 133, 134, 143
  explaining implementation inconsistencies, 134–135
  federal involvement, 127–129, 191
  improving black colleges, 121, 122, 123, 126, 139
  lawsuits, 118, 120, 122, 124, 132, 133, 134, 136, 137, 138, 142
  level of federal activity, 127, 128, 129, 131, 133, 134, 135, 136, 137
  monitoring, 132, 137, 141, 143, 191, 197
  OCR, 121, 122, 123, 124, 125, 126, 128, 130, 131, 132, 133, 134, 135, 136, 137, 138, 139, 140, 143
  policy goals and means, 121–122, 141
  policy success, 122–127, 143
  presence of enforcement agencies, 134, 191
  racial identifiability, 118, 121, 122, 123, 124, 125, 126, 128, 129, 130, 131, 134, 135, 136, 137, 138, 139, 140, 143, 144
  research universities, 139, 140, 142
  selected colleges and universities, 118, 119, 120, 124, 131, 135, 138, 139, 140, 141, 145, 147
  specificity of standards, 123–124, 191
  state autonomy, 140–142, 143
  state budgets, 138, 140, 141, 142
  state response, 127, 128, 129, 135–142, 143, 203

Higher education desegregation *(continued)*
  students' choice, 128, 129, 130, 143
  terminating federal funds, 133, 140, 142
Hispanics:
  bilingual education, 13, 61, 63–64, 70–71, 74–75, 79, 80, 81, 82, 85, 86, 88, 89, 184, 186, 187, 194, 201
  conflict among, 13, 201
  discrimination complaints, 9
  economic status, 178
  equal housing, 149, 168, 184
  holding political office, 44, 46
  migrants, 4
  occupations, 103, 187
  racial hostility, 185
  voting rights, 26, 28, 29, 38, 39, 40, 44, 47, 49, 184, 185

Implementation success:
  active enforcement, 15, 20, 21, 27, 30, 57, 62, 67, 79, 81, 85, 88, 97, 98, 110, 111, 126, 127, 128, 129, 131, 133, 134, 172, 176, 177, 189, 205
  administrative coordination, 203, 204
  beneficiaries, 201–203, 204, 205
  clarity of policy, 194, 204
  commitment of enforcers, 198–200, 204, 205, 206
  commitment of superiors, 200–201, 204, 205, 206
  conclusions, 185–206
  cost–benefit analysis, 203–204, 206
  explaining variations, 189–206
  federal involvement, 188–189, 204
  greatest implementation, 188, 190, 192
  least implementation, 188, 191, 193
  moderate implementation, 188, 190, 191, 192
  monitoring, 196–197, 204
  passive enforcement, 14, 15, 26, 27, 44, 62, 80, 82, 86, 88, 96, 110, 111, 126, 128, 131, 133, 148, 155–162, 163, 164, 165, 166, 167, 168, 169, 170, 171, 175, 176, 177
  presence of enforcement agencies, 198, 204, 206
  problems measuring, 185–186, 205
  specificity of standards, 195–196, 204, 205
  variables, 4–17, 185–206
Indians, Native American, 28, 29, 39, 168, 178
Intent of civil rights laws, 6, 9, 28, 115, 200
Intent test, 38, 59, 156, 195, 196
Intent to discriminate, 29, 38, 73, 77, 156, 195
Interest groups, 13, 20, 28, 29, 32, 43, 49, 50, 66, 72, 113, 114, 120, 130, 133, 163, 167, 172, 174

Subject Index

Kentucky, 40, 65, 70, 123, 125, 126, 132, 134

Lau remedies, 61, 74, 91
Legal Defense and Education Fund, 130, 133, 136
Litigation in civil rights:
  federal, 4, 8, 15, 57, 58, 60, 67, 78, 82, 83, 95, 97, 112, 114, 132, 133, 151, 155–157, 169, 172, 173, 175, 176, 179, 190, 196, 199, 205
  private, 14, 15, 60, 66, 67, 81, 82, 98, 114, 133, 167, 173, 174, 176, 199, 202
  state, 98, 120, 122, 132
Los Angeles, 10, 81, 153, 154
Louisiana, 24, 25, 31, 33, 34, 37, 42, 45, 48, 49, 65, 71, 98, 123, 125, 132, 133, 137, 138
Lower federal courts:
  equal education, 57, 60, 61, 62, 63, 67, 83, 88, 197, 202
  equal employment, 97, 98, 100, 196
  equal housing, 151, 155, 157, 163, 172, 173, 187
  higher education, 118, 120, 122, 124, 132, 133, 134, 136, 137, 138
  voting rights, 23, 24, 26, 27, 28, 37–38

Maryland, 40, 64, 65, 70, 71, 123, 125, 132, 133, 136, 137, 138, 140, 141, 144, 153, 154, 160
Mississippi, 11, 12, 24, 25, 31, 33, 34, 42, 45, 49, 58, 65, 66, 88, 119, 123, 125, 132, 133, 137, 138
Missouri, 65, 118, 123, 124, 125, 132, 134, 135, 153, 154
Monitoring (*see also* Compliance; Noncompliance):
  ambiguity of standards, 63, 108–109, 162, 163
  bilingual education, 74, 79, 88, 191, 195, 196
  by beneficiaries, 12–13, 48, 72, 114
  budgets, 12, 35, 51, 169–170
  data, 7, 8, 14, 29, 31, 36, 48, 79, 83, 95, 97, 165, 166, 169, 171, 174, 175, 197
  equal education, 7, 62, 79, 83, 89, 190, 197
  equal employment, 94–97, 100, 109–109–110, 190, 197
  equal housing, 163–166, 191, 197
  higher education, 132, 137, 141, 143, 191
  on-site inspections, 8, 31, 48, 74, 79, 96, 132
  second-generation discrimination, 79, 191, 197
  staff size, 36, 49, 51, 79, 90, 96
  staff training, 7, 8, 14, 32, 96, 110
  voting rights, 31, 48, 52, 190, 197

NAACP, 32, 66, 68, 130, 133, 136, 172, 174
Nashville, 71, 122, 134, 153, 154
National Committee Against Discrimination in Housing, 167, 174
New Orleans, 44, 57, 67, 70, 184
New York, 28, 34, 153, 154
New York City, 28, 41, 43, 70
Nixon's Southern strategy, 27, 49, 50, 137
Noncompliance (*see also* Compliance; Monitoring):
  penalties for, 9, 14, 15, 36, 37, 51, 57, 80, 95, 96, 98, 99, 114, 120, 121, 131, 132, 133, 136, 137, 155, 157, 162, 165, 169, 175, 200
  reasons for, 12, 35, 36, 66, 114, 148, 149, 150, 151, 152, 153, 156, 157, 159, 161–164, 175–176, 202, 205
North Carolina, 24, 25, 41, 43, 45, 48, 65, 67, 71, 119, 123, 124, 126, 129, 132, 133, 136, 137, 139, 140, 141, 145, 147, 153, 154

Office of Civil Rights (HEW and DOE), 9, 10, 11, 56, 59, 64, 69, 76, 78, 79, 81, 83, 86, 88, 89, 121, 122, 123, 124, 125, 126, 128, 130, 131, 132, 133, 134, 135, 136, 137, 138, 139, 140, 141, 142, 190, 198, 199
Office of Federal Contract Compliance:
  authority, 94, 95, 99, 111
  compliance reviews, 95, 197
  compliance timetables, 95, 197
  creation, 94, 199
  disbarments, 95, 96
  failures, 95, 110, 111, 112
  federal contractors, 94, 95, 112
  guidelines, 94, 95, 112
  hiring goals, 95, 109, 197
  lawsuits, 95, 96
  monitoring, 95, 96, 109, 114, 197
Office of Personnel Managment, 99, 100, 110, 111, 114, 115
Ohio, 70, 71, 118, 119, 123, 125, 126, 132, 134, 153, 154
Oklahoma, 40, 64, 65, 71, 75, 123, 125, 126, 132, 133, 137, 138, 153, 154

Pennsylvania, 118, 123, 125, 132, 133, 153, 154
Philadelphia, 70, 95, 153, 154
Political parties:
  Democrats, 28, 49, 144, 192, 200, 201
  Republicans, 28, 49, 109, 115, 135, 144, 176, 192, 200, 201
Postdesegregation discrimination, *see* Second-generation discrimination
Poverty, 1, 2, 43, 50, 107, 108, 115, 152, 173, 178

Subject Index 221

Precision of standards, *see* Specificity of standards
Presidents:
  Carter, Jimmy, 33, 49, 60, 64, 110, 111, 115, 164, 172, 176, 177, 179, 199
  Eisenhower, Dwight D., 23, 57
  Ford, Gerald R., 49, 111, 115, 164, 171, 172, 173, 176, 200
  Johnson, Lyndon B., 20, 25, 26, 27, 49, 50, 57, 80, 81, 94, 95, 110, 111, 115, 144, 171, 176, 200
  Kennedy, John F., 22, 57, 94, 95, 110, 111
  Nixon, Richard M., 12, 13, 27, 28, 33, 49, 50, 59, 80, 81, 111, 115, 131, 132, 133, 135, 171, 172, 173, 176, 200
  Reagan, Ronald, 29, 60, 61, 64, 76, 81, 109, 110, 111, 113, 115, 116, 133, 137, 172, 173, 176, 177, 181, 196, 198, 199, 201
  Roosevelt, Franklin D., 94, 95, 110, 111
  Truman, Harry S., 94, 95, 110
Public opinion, 11, 20, 24, 25, 173, 205

Quotas, 95, 98, 99, 109, 113

Redlining, 151, 163, 172, 187

San Francisco, 63, 68, 71, 153, 154
School desegregation, *see* Equal education opportunity
Seattle, 68, 71, 153, 154
Second-generation discrimination (*see also* Educable mentally retarded programs):
  administrative coordination, 83, 193, 203
  beneficiaries, 82, 87, 193, 202
  clarity of policy, 76, 191, 194
  commitment of enforcers, 80, 193, 198, 199
  commitment of superiors, 81, 87, 193, 200
  cost–benefit analysis, 85, 87, 193
  ESSA funds, 62, 73, 88, 191, 197, 204
  faculty or staff, 63, 82, 188
  federal involvement, 86, 87, 188, 191
  OCR actions, 62–63, 78, 82, 83, 202
  presence of enforcement agencies, 78, 191
  specificity of standards, 62, 63, 77, 191, 195
Separate but equal, 56, 64, 161, 201
Sex discrimination, 9, 10, 93, 95, 97, 100, 101, 107, 111, 112, 113, 115, 149, 155, 162, 168, 171, 187, 196, 205
South:
  border states, 24, 56, 64, 65, 66, 68, 69, 74, 187
  civil rights progress, 46, 55, 65, 67–69, 75

South (*continued*)
  Deep South: 21, 24, 26, 31, 66, 67
  equal education, 3, 4, 7, 11, 12, 14, 15, 55, 56, 57, 58, 59, 64–69, 75, 77, 78, 80, 83, 86, 87, 88, 129, 184, 189, 190, 194, 197, 198, 200, 203
  equal housing, 150, 153, 154
  ex-Confederate states, 21, 40, 41, 56, 66
  political officials, 22, 23, 24, 31, 32, 35, 36, 39, 43, 44, 47, 48, 51
  second-generation discrimination, 73
  voting rights, 9, 11, 15, 20–21, 22, 23, 24, 25, 32, 35, 37, 40–44, 49, 50, 51, 186, 192, 194, 200
South Carolina, 24, 25, 33, 34, 42, 45, 48, 65, 123, 124, 125, 132, 134, 135
Southern Christian Leadership Conference, 32, 174
Spanish-speaking Americans, *see* Hispanics
Specificity of standards:
  bilingual education, 78, 191, 195
  equal education, 6, 77–78, 190, 195
  equal employment, 109, 190, 196
  equal housing, 163, 191, 195, 206
  higher education, 123–124, 191, 195, 198
  second-generation discrimination, 77, 191, 195
  voting rights, 190, 195
Steering, 150, 151, 152, 157, 158, 177, 178, 185, 187
St. Louis, 71, 75, 153, 154
Supreme Court, U.S.:
  equal education, 3, 4, 7, 8, 11, 12, 18, 38, 53, 56, 57, 58, 59, 60, 61, 63, 64, 66, 69, 74, 76, 79, 80, 81, 88, 90, 91, 95, 98, 120, 184, 191, 194, 195, 196, 201, 206, 207
  equal employment, 4, 95, 97, 98, 99, 108, 109, 116, 196, 207
  equal housing, 4, 151, 155–157, 161, 167, 170, 176, 179, 180, 182
  under Earl Warren, 4, 26, 27, 33, 56, 57, 58, 80, 155, 156, 168, 200
  under Warren E. Burger, 3, 38, 50, 58, 59, 60, 81, 97, 98, 99, 155–157, 161, 195, 200
  voting rights, 21, 22, 26, 29, 33, 37–38, 49, 50, 52, 53, 196

Tennessee, 24, 41, 42, 45, 65, 70, 120, 123, 124, 125, 132, 133, 134, 135, 153, 154
Texas, 9, 24, 33, 34, 39, 41, 42, 44, 45, 65, 68, 70, 71, 123, 125, 132, 134, 135, 153, 154, 186
Title VI, *see* Civil Rights Act of 1964
Title VIII, *see* Fair Housing Act of 1968

222 Subject Index

Virginia, 24, 25, 34, 42, 45, 65, 70, 120, 123, 125, 126, 129, 132, 133, 137, 139, 142, 143, 145, 153, 154, 160
Voting rights (*see also* Voting Rights Act of 1965):
  administrative coordination, 51, 52, 192, 203
  annexations, 22, 34, 37, 38, 50, 195
  at-large elections, 22, 34, 37, 50
  Attorney General, 23, 26, 27, 28, 29, 30, 31, 32, 33, 34, 35, 36, 37, 38, 44, 48, 52
  beneficiaries, 50, 192
  bilingual requirements, 21, 29, 30, 34, 37, 38–41, 47, 49, 51, 184, 185, 186, 187
  blacks, 4, 11, 15, 20, 21, 22, 23, 24, 25, 26, 28, 30, 31, 32, 33, 34, 35, 37, 38, 39, 40, 41, 42, 43, 44, 45, 46, 47, 184, 192, 200
  character references, 22, 25
  Civil Rights Act of 1964, 23, 25, 26, 48
  clarity of policy, 47–48, 190, 194
  commitment of enforcers, 9, 48–49, 192, 198, 199
  commitment of superiors, 20, 49–50, 192, 200, 201
  cost–benefit analysis, 51–52, 192, 203, 206
  counting ballots, 32, 34, 37
  data collection, 29, 31, 36, 48, 51
  diluting minority voting power, 22, 34, 35, 38, 47, 50, 195, 204
  DOJ, 13, 20, 27, 31, 32, 34, 35, 36, 37, 39, 44, 48, 49, 50, 51, 52, 190, 192, 199
  effectiveness of minority votes, 30, 47, 50, 52, 184, 203
  election law changes, 21, 34, 35, 36, 37, 38, 48
  Enforcement Acts of 1870 and 1871, 21, 23
  enforcement agency presence, 48–49, 190
  Federal District Court in Washington, D.C., 26, 27, 28, 29, 33, 34, 35
  federal examiners, 15, 26, 27, 29, 30–33, 41, 43, 44, 48, 49, 50, 51, 195
  federal involvement, 15, 20, 25, 26, 30, 31, 43, 47, 49, 190
  federal observers, 26, 27, 29, 30, 31, 32, 35, 44, 48, 50, 195
  gerrymandering, 22, 34
  Hispanics, 26, 28, 29, 38, 39, 40, 44, 47, 49, 184, 185
  illiterates, 29, 32, 37, 38, 44
  impact of black voting, 22, 34, 44–46, 184
  increased black voting, 24, 40–44, 47, 184, 186

Voting rights (*continued*)
  increase in black elected officials, 44–46, 184
  intimidation and harassment, 21, 22, 23, 24, 32, 34, 37, 39, 41, 43, 48
  lawsuits, 23, 24, 27, 28, 33, 35, 37, 38, 47, 194
  literacy tests, 21, 22, 23, 25, 26, 27, 28, 30, 43, 194
  local election officials, 4, 15, 22, 23, 24, 31, 32, 35, 36, 39, 43, 44, 48, 51, 194
  local Southern judges, 9, 22, 24
  location of polls, 34, 37
  lower federal courts, 23, 24, 26, 27, 28, 37–38
  monitoring, 31, 48, 52, 190, 197
  news media attention, 24, 25
  on-site inspections, 31, 48, 190
  poll taxes, 21, 22
  poor whites, 21, 30
  public opinion, 20, 24, 25, 51
  racial harassment and violence, 21, 22, 23, 24, 25, 27, 28, 31, 32, 34, 37, 39, 41, 48, 184, 185
  redistricting, 34, 37, 38, 47, 50
  registration, 2, 4, 15, 20, 21, 22, 23, 24, 25, 27, 28, 29, 31, 32, 34, 35, 37, 40–43, 47, 48, 49, 51, 186, 189, 194, 197, 200
  socioeconomic differences in voters, 43, 44, 47, 49, 50, 52, 53, 196
  Supreme Court, 21, 22, 26, 29, 33, 37–38, 49, 50, 52, 53, 196
  specificity of standards, 190, 195
  supplanting local or state authority, 4, 15, 47, 176
  weak enforcement, 13, 24, 33, 35–36, 39, 48, 49, 50, 52, 185
  white primaries, 21, 22
  white voting rates, 40, 42, 47
Voting Rights Act of 1965 (*see also* Voting rights):
  impact, 27, 30, 39, 41–46
  implementation, 30–41
  legality, 26, 37–38, 47, 49
  original act of 1965, 25–27
  renewal of 1970, 21, 27–28, 49, 51
  renewal of 1975, 21, 28–29, 38–39, 49, 51
  renewal of 1982, 21, 29–30, 196, 201
  Section 4 "trigger formula," 25, 26, 28, 30, 190, 195
  Section 5 preclearance, 26, 27, 28, 29, 30, 33–37, 38, 47, 48, 50, 190, 195
  weaknesses, 24, 51

Warren Court *see* Supreme Court
Washington, D.C., 13, 27, 28, 33, 34, 35, 40, 56, 64, 65, 68, 70, 160

West Virginia, 40, 64, 65, 123, 124, 125, 126, 132, 134, 135, 143
Whites:
  equal education, 84, 185
  equal housing, 69, 148, 149, 151, 152, 153, 154, 155, 156, 157, 159, 160, 161, 168, 170, 171, 186

Whites *(continued)*
  income levels, 101, 103, 104, 105, 106, 107, 178, 186
  racial hostility, 57, 67, 184, 185
  voting, 21, 30, 40, 42, 47
  white flight, 69, 152, 153, 159, 160, 185

266378
c.2